Leaving

How I Set Myself Free
from an Abusive Marriage

KANCHAN BHASKAR

SHE WRITES PRESS

Published 2023
Printed in the United States of America
Print ISBN: 978-1-64742-475-6
E-ISBN: 978-1-64742-476-3
Library of Congress Control Number: 2022918856

For information, address:
She Writes Press
1569 Solano Ave #546
Berkeley, CA 94707

Interior Design by Tabitha Lahr

She Writes Press is a division of SparkPoint Studio, LLC.

All company and/or product names may be trade names, logos, trademarks, and/or registered trademarks and are the property of their respective owners.

Names and identifying characteristics have been changed to protect the privacy of certain individuals.

Disclaimer

This book is written to the best of my memory. Some of the dates may be off, but this is how I remember the events. In the interest of keeping the past in the past, some specifics have been altered to maintain anonymity. At her request, most details of my daughter's life have been kept out of this story. I have also refrained from naming my guru.

My story of transcendence from a survivor of domestic violence to an advocate and a coach.
Forming a true relationship with my inner self.
Now living a life of joy and purpose.

All on my own terms and in Alignment.

To my sweethearts, my reason for who I am today:

My parents, Om and Shashi, smiling down at me from up there.
My lifelines: Nina, Kabir, and Kuber.

To all those who rise and fall and rise again with the
rough tides of living with an abusive partner.

And to my guru, my compass in this vast turbulent ocean,
which points the needle toward the Still, the Source.

Contents

Preface

I grew up in New Delhi, India, and my dreams were built on the romance and jubilation in which I was brought up. I imagined my married life to be as blissful and tender as that of my parents, who truly cherished and treasured each other and nurtured their four offspring with love and warmth. They lived more as partners than as a traditional Indian husband and wife.

Having been raised in this progressive environment, I acquired a unique perception of life—a woman was an equal partner in a marriage, one to be honored and valued. Marriage meant love, companionship, and caring. I couldn't fathom it being any other way. Violence of any kind in marriage was unthinkable. A woman was to be respected—period.

My future husband would not share these perceptions. I found myself in an arranged marriage to a bright and deceptively-charming man, who revealed his true nature only after our wedding. The first time he hit me, my world spun upside down. When it righted, I had gotten myself stuck in a tumultuous, abusive relationship with a narcissistic alcoholic, in whose captivity I was trapped for more than twenty years.

The desperate mother of three innocent children who were casualties of these circumstances, I had to get away, but my escape had to be carefully planned with no room for error. If I divorced, I'd lose one or all of my children to the man I needed to escape from, which was not an option.

There had to be a way out.

I searched until I found it.

This story narrates how I built a ramp to climb out of the abyss, little by little, using a myriad of tools to bring me closer to freedom. Although I was alone in my fight for survival, I had deep faith in the higher power which presented me with collaborators in the form of angels and mentors to light my way.

My work was slow but steady. The ramp collapsed a few times and had to be rebuilt stronger. I shaped myself into a resilient woman, a tigress who could fend for her cubs. It wasn't easy, and each day was a struggle, yet I remained determined in my single mission to protect my children and provide them with the best, as I had been provided with. This focus gave me the courage and spirit to keep forging ahead relentlessly.

Belief in self and belief in the Universe became my weapons of ultimate escape, the foundation for my liberation and re-earned dignity.

The story doesn't stop with gaining my freedom but describes my continuing journey on the path of spirituality. In this book, I share my dawning realizations and the period of self-resurgence, which resulted in a triumphant, purpose-driven life.

Belief in spirituality provided the foundation and a new beginning on the path toward the emancipation of mind and soul.

Today a free woman, I'm happily settled in Chicago, living life on my own terms. I walk with my head high and chin up. The first flowers of spring in their divine colors make me smile. I can laugh again at a joke, find stillness in trees, and plan without fear, making up for the lost time.

I'm reminded of my favorite lines, my motto, from Robert Frost's "Stopping by Woods on a Snowy Evening":

The woods are lovely, dark and deep,
But I have promises to keep,
And miles to go before I sleep,
And miles to go before I sleep.

A Message from My Daughter

Domestic violence touches everyone involved. Children living in an environment where one parent is abused must learn to deal with violence. We grow up faster than other children, feeling the need to become the protector of the abused. But we cannot protect them, making us feel helpless, frustrated, guilt-ridden, and failures. Growing up witnessing domestic violence undermines our foundations and affects our mental health. We have traumatic childhoods with which we may never come to terms. It also affects our relationships, since the only model we have is our parents.

Children learn from their parents. If they see violence, mental or physical, their map for building loving relationships becomes skewed. It takes a lot out of children to see their loved ones hurt and helpless. And that helplessness changes the way we think, the way we understand the world. We may distrust the world in general and become shy and withdrawn, prone to addiction, violence, and even criminal activity. The children of domestic violence constantly subvert their needs and desires to those of everyone around them. In our effort to please others, we lose ourselves.

I'm lucky to have a tigress of a mother.

She was strong for us through the turmoil. She stood between the ugly world—my father—and us. A survivor, she never portrayed herself as a victim, which in turn showed us that the children of domestic violence could be positive, good human beings and contributors to society. They could maintain healthy relationships and advocate for survivors of—or those still caught up in—domestic violence. She instilled great values in us to become people who are satisfied in their lives.

We were lucky to have such a distinguished role model to look up to, who inculcated important values such as kindness, humility, gratitude, humanity, honesty, and spirituality. Despite everything, we're thankful to God for having been given such a great mother. She could have earned her own gratification by remarrying and not worrying about our adoption or custody issues, but she made us her life's mission. Society shamed her, the law did not protect her, and her own husband held her hostage, but she did not deter and kept working toward her single focus of making us good human beings, which shaped us into the kind of parents we will be—loving, thoughtful, kind, and firm—and not victims or abusers ourselves.

If abusers aren't willing to invest in the children they brought into this world, they will receive no sympathy or empathy from me. If they are grappling with anger issues, alcoholism, or mental illness, they must seek help to remain part of their children's lives and stop the pattern of abuse. If abusers are willing to change and put in hard work, they deserve a second or even a third chance. My stance may seem harsh, but after witnessing my mother give my father chance after chance, it is my biggest disappointment that he wasn't willing to change for us kids.

We weren't important enough for him to make an effort.

Thankfully, we were—and are—important enough to our mother, who left him for the sanity of us all.

Chapter 1

The Beginning

1980–1981

I was a new bride, standing at the rundown, ramshackle Old Delhi railway station on a cold, dark winter night. I was draped in a pastel-pink sari, my head covered with the far end. I was continuously pushing it back from falling on my forehead, trying to tame my hair going wild from my errant sari. The uncaring wind blowing through the open station in the cold December was not helping, either. Handling the sari had been a constant struggle.

I was surrounded by my new family, that of my husband, which I inherited as a result of an arranged marriage. My interactions with them in the ten days since our wedding had been brief and few. They were still strangers to me. Vijay, whom I had met merely twice before our wedding, and with whom I had exchanged a handful of letters during our six-month courtship, seemed less of a stranger, yet he still lacked the familiarity of a husband. Was that enough to really know him?

However, I was filled with hope that the new path set for me was full of wonder, thrill, and whirlwind romance, confirming my dreams since adolescence.

My father-in-law Dev, older sister-in-law, and two brothers-in-law had gathered at the station to see us off, their newly wed son and daughter-in-law. It was time to say our goodbyes as we waited for the overnight train Vijay and I would board to Nandoli, my new home.

A married woman covering her head was a way to show respect toward older men, an archaic tradition accepted by the majority of the patriarchal society, where men were considered superior to women. However, my own brothers' wives weren't required to follow this tradition, owing to my parents' progressiveness, so, in practice, this observance was somewhat new to me.

My sari was a fifteen-foot-long by six-foot-wide piece of silk cloth wrapped around my petite body. The wide portion of the cloth tucked into my petticoat, a long underskirt tied tightly around my belly, suffocated my normal breathing. This reminded me of learning in high school about the Egyptian mummies wrapped compactly in cloth before being buried. I was expected to not only breathe but also walk gracefully, just as my mom had done in this very elegant garment. Discomfort aside, I was nervous about catching the hem of the sari with my heels and tripping. It would be a shame if I were to topple and fall in front of my in-laws. After all, this was all about forming the right first impressions.

I focused intently on holding the sari high with one hand and keeping it from touching the filth on the grubby floors of the Old Delhi railway station. My other hand was constantly engaged in tugging the sari covering my head so the silk material would not slip off. Every time it did, leaving my head uncovered, Shiela, my sister-in-law, would skewer me with a daunting long stare or nudge me hard on my shoulder. I managed to take it in stride, respecting their values and traditions.

Dev tried to make small talk, perhaps in an attempt to break the silence, which required me just to nod or shake my head. Dev looked elegant, a tall, lanky man in his well-fitted, deep-brown, checkered jacket and brown slacks. The golden-framed eyeglasses went well with his fair skin and sat firmly on his high-bridged nose. His eyes brightened when he smiled, which he did most of the time. His erect, military-like walk complemented his authoritative tone. Being the eldest among his four siblings, a sister, and three brothers, he was used to being in charge. He was a sensitive person but good at hiding his emotions. Perhaps the early death of his middle-aged wife three years before had left him embittered and scarred.

I was not supposed to open up with him, even if I wanted to. It was too forward in the family's eyes. Small talk was the only form of accepted communication between the two of us.

Sanjay, two years younger than Vijay at thirty-one, and Ajay, three years younger, kept smiling warmly when my gaze met theirs without saying a word. Perhaps we had yet to break that ice. My sister-in-law Shiela was two years older than Vijay and ten years older than me. She kept a stiff front, not giving her lips a chance to widen in a smile unless necessary. I gave her the benefit of the doubt. It couldn't be easy mothering three adult brothers and a widowed father at the age of thirty-three. Her father, I understood, had not been able to find a suitable match for her, and since all the siblings were only a couple of years apart, he decided to marry off the next one in line, my husband, already past the marriageable age. Being a woman, I understood what Shiela's feelings might be about my engagement with her brother at twenty-two and marriage at twenty-three.

On the surface, it appeared like a close-knit family, but something was awry in the bonding of siblings. They didn't joke, tease, or share with each other. Everyone kept to themselves. Perhaps a common thread, which bound them together, was amiss. Maybe it was the mother who had kept them together, as that's what mothers did.

The father was more affectionate toward the younger two sons. Shiela, his firstborn and only daughter, with the burden of running the household, was more like a confidante and a partner in crime, helping him make decisions. He seemed to have pride in Vijay but not the same affection, as if Vijay had broken his trust somewhere down the line.

Since college eight years earlier, Vijay had worked and lived in Nandoli, a small, remote town 435 miles southwest of New Delhi. He was an industrial engineer working at the MGM tire factory on the outskirts of Nandoli in Rajasthan, the largest state of northern India, known for its arid desert lands, beautiful green Aravali hills, and colorful handicrafts. Nandoli was situated forty-four miles from the state capital, Udaipur, also known as the City of Lakes or the "Venice of the East," a popular tourist destination famous for its magnificent eighteenth-century palaces on an island in the middle of Rajsamand Lake. Though I'd never heard of Nandoli before, I'd seen Udaipur on a map of India in my high school geography class, so I was extremely excited about living near Udaipur with my life partner.

I was leaving my in-laws behind. I didn't know them enough to feel sad. It was my parents and siblings I was going to miss dearly. However, my joy about going to my future home and a new life outweighed my sorrow.

The long, shrieking whistle of the Udaipur train announced its entry into the railway junction. Smoke diffused from the oncoming engine and filled the air, stuffing my nostrils with the sharp smell of burning coal. I was overcome with nostalgia for my summer vacation trips to my grandma's house in Punjab each year. Those were my favorite vacations, full of childhood fun: playing I Spy You in sugar cane and corn farms with neighborhood kids, or picking fresh vegetables from the gardens, or bathing under the thick stream of water coming from a tube well run by big buffaloes or oxen going in circles around the well.

The Udaipur Express approached the platform. Its brakes screeched and squealed, followed by a loud thud as it stopped in front of us. Its arrival brought with it a tornado of men, women, and children running in all directions as they pushed, pulled, and shouted with no consideration for anyone, as if getting into the train was their only mission in life.

My eyes burned from coal exhaust, and my body jostled, bruised by passengers ripping through the crowds, yelling "Coolie, coolie!" and waving to the scrambling porters to help with their bags. I inched closer to Vijay.

"There is no need for you to rush," Dev said. "The train stops here for a good twenty minutes."

Ajay ran ahead to look for our compartment, and Dev followed him. Sanjay hurried off to buy some water bottles for our journey. Shiela took out a polyethylene bag and handed it to me.

"This is for your journey," she said, not making eye contact. "I made stuffed *aloo paratha* [mashed-potato-stuffed, shallow-fried flatbread] and some spicy mango pickles. I put in mild red chilies and packed some extra pickles. I noticed you like them."

I took the bag and gave her a hug.

A sliver of a smile came to her stiff lips, confirming she did have a heart. The two of us walked quietly in Dev and Ajay's direction. Vijay stayed behind, waiting for the porter to come back and help with the luggage.

Since it was my first time at this station, I wasn't expecting it to be so grimy and unhygienic. The air smelled of desiccated garbage and unbathed bodies.

People of all ages, colors, creeds, and races—Hindu, Muslim, Sikh—dressed, for the most part, poorly and shabbily, wearing oversized, mutilated sweaters or shirts with gaping holes, having not washed for weeks, trying to protect themselves from cold. It was the most humbling sight.

Noise was at its peak. It was not only the crowd who hollered and roared, but the vendors shouted incessantly. Tea sellers screeched, "chai, chai, chai," carrying oversized tea dispensers in one hand and stacked earthen throwaway cups in the other.

"Chaat, samosa, tikki!" bellowed the purveyors of snacks, carrying huge, round cane baskets overflowing with homemade, deep-fried, spiced goodies on their dangling heads, balanced by their typical gait.

"Boot polish, boot polish, boot polish," called the shoe-shine juveniles.

People slept or merely laid down haphazardly on the floor. Some were tired, some were bored of waiting for late or canceled trains, and others were homeless. Bundles of baggage and huge delivery packages blocked the walkways.

The poverty was appalling. I had been sheltered from this side of the country, and seeing these conditions wrenched my heart. Up ahead, Dev leaned out the window of one of the train cars, waving at us. He had found our seats. I looked for Vijay, still waiting for a coolie to help him.

The lanky coolies—some old, others malnourished—piled and kept one customer's luggage by the train and then were off to find another customer. The more people they serviced, the more money they would make. Simple logic. The sheer weight and volume they balanced on their heads and hung from their shoulders was astounding. Even a donkey would refuse to carry such a burden. But their poverty, their worry about feeding their large families— their fleet of children, their elderly dependent parents—fueled their drive and gave them the strength to keep going.

Getting closer to our car, Shiela and I approached the tracks. The stink was horrendous. The latrines on the trains didn't have receptacles to hold the waste, so it landed directly on the tracks. I felt like throwing up. I had a strong urge to cover my nostrils with my sari but avoided it since Shiela did not. *It's okay*, I told myself. *I can bear it.*

At our car, I stopped, hesitant to put my foot on the knee-high first stair. If I slipped, I'd fall into the gap between the train and the platform onto the track. My rebellious sari wasn't making this any easier. But I grabbed the railing and jumped to the first step. *I made it!* Juggling between hiking my sari hem and grasping the railing with one hand, I pulled myself into the train, pressing my sari to my head with the other, desperate to avoid another of Shiela's glares. She seemed much more strident about covering my head than her brothers were. Would Dev be as offended by my exposed head?

What was I doing with such an old-fashioned family? The thought appeared for a flicker of a moment and was soon replaced by thoughts of my new love, my lifelong partner, which was all that mattered. A smile of victory came to my lips. I peeked out the window, looking for Vijay. I saw the coolie running with our bags. He jumped onto the train, with Vijay close behind.

When the coolie had stowed away our luggage, Vijay, a little breathless after following the porter hustling through the crowd, paid him the dues. I handed Vijay a bottle of water. I wanted to stand closer to him and dab the perspiration from his forehead but abstained from showing my open affection in front of Dev and Shiela. There would be ample time later. The train whistle shrieked, announcing it was about to leave the platform.

My in-laws prepared to disembark. In parting, I bent to touch my father-in-law's feet, another norm of showing respect observed by traditional families.

Knowing he was marrying a modern, fashionable girl, Vijay should have warned me about the conservative ways of his family to avoid any surprises and prejudices against their traditions and rituals. Still, I didn't take his lack of forewarning to heart. We'd get to understand each other's ways. I desisted from hugging my brothers-in-law since I was unsure if Dev would approve, and I could guarantee Shiela wouldn't. Dev took out a five-rupee note and handed it to me. Giving money as a parting gift was customary, though I did secretly judge my father-in-law's miserliness.

My in-laws now stood on the platform beneath our window. The train gave a sharp jerk before rolling away. My new family waved goodbye as the train gained momentum, taking us to our destination. My husband and I continued waving out of the open window until his family grew smaller and smaller.

I sighed deeply once we newlyweds were left to ourselves for the first time since our wedding. Time for us to settle. We looked at each other and smiled. *He has a charming smile*, I thought, and not for the first time. We had two sleeper seats, one above the other. Vijay unrolled the bedding we brought, making up both bunks. We were exhausted from the last few days of ceremonies and dinners at the homes of friends and relatives. We sat together, hand in hand, oblivious of attracting the attention of all eyes in the car, my red sparkly bangles on my wrists in both arms, and a red dot—*bindi*—on my forehead, a typical sign that I was a newlywed. We were both sleepy, so Vijay helped me up to the top bunk.

As I laid down, my thoughts drifted toward the last few days at my father-in-law's house. How did that dwelling compare to Vijay's, where we would now live?

His father's house in Delhi was simple, with the bare minimum of basic necessities and no decoration or homey touches. Yet, everything was kept clean and tidy. The house was unusually packed with relatives from all over, gathered under one roof. The women would huddle in the kitchen all day to wash and cut vegetables, cook three meals, clean, and gossip in hushed tones so their voices would not reach the men sitting outside. The women covered their mouths with the ends of their saris or their *dupattas* (shawl-like scarves) to suppress their laughter.

Because she was the daughter of the house, Shiela had left her head uncovered, her long black hair parted on the side and neatly braided. And because she ran the household, when she entered the kitchen, the other women—even those older than she was—would stop joking and laughing. They seemed to fear her. Were they simply showing their respect to her and the position she held as the eldest child of the eldest brother? Or was it part of their culture to fawn over the woman who ran the household? Or maybe Shiela was truly the dictator in the family.

The men would sit on the veranda outside the kitchen to chat freely, joke, laugh loudly, and sip cups of masala chai, oblivious to any of the household responsibilities. The eldest men in the clan smoked the hookah, passing the mouthpiece among them, each deeply drawing in the tobacco smoke. They held their breath and made loud gurgling sounds produced by vibrations due to rumbling smoke. It left an atmosphere of lingering tobacco and made them relaxed and laid back.

The younger men weren't supposed to smoke in front of the elders. Instead, they sneaked out to smoke cigarettes, eating a green cardamom pod afterward to camouflage the smell. The older men pretended they didn't know what the younger men were doing.

The movement of the train finally rocked me to sleep. And then I heard Vijay yelling. He shook me to wake up. Having barely slept, I opened my eyes, startled.

"Coolie, coolie!" Vijay shouted. He shook me again. "Get up and climb down! We overslept. We'll miss the local Nandoli train."

I was dumbfounded. I heard the urgency and desperation in his voice. I jumped from the bunk, ignoring the ladder. Vijay dashed from one compartment to the next in search of a porter, yelling, "Coolie, coolie!" as he battled through the narrow corridor of the train still in motion.

I was disoriented and confused. When we'd discussed the trip, Vijay hadn't mentioned we had to change trains. I shook my head out of the daze, quickly rolled the bedding, and made sure everything was packed. I had no time to retie my loosened sari or brush my tousled hair. Vijay sprinted back, breathing heavily, with a porter behind him.

"Pick up all the luggage quickly." He signaled at all the luggage pieces and then, with nervous looks, instructed me to head for the door. The train squealed to a sudden halt, giving a jerk. Our car hadn't stopped at the platform but a little past it. The terrain was rough, and the steps of the car were higher off the ground.

"Jump!" Vijay shouted from behind me. "Jump, or we'll miss the train on the Nandoli line."

Panicked, I blindly jumped on my heels, without thinking of the consequences of damaging my ankle or the sari catching as I leaped from the train. I was mechanically doing what was asked of me. Vijay jumped down after me, followed by the porter balancing our two big suitcases on his head and two bundles of bedding, hanging one on each shoulder. We raced for our train through the middle of the train yard, three tracks to the right of us, and two to the left.

Vijay ran past me, one of the bags hanging from his shoulder, and I heedlessly followed, toward the local line, eight hundred yards away. The porter kept pace. I kept looking back to see if he was okay, running with all the heavy luggage, and then realized it was his profession and he would do fine.

"Run faster!" Vijay yelled over his shoulder.

I kept running, unnerved and flustered. But surely Vijay knew what he was doing. Then abruptly, Vijay stopped, yanked his bag off his shoulder, and tossed it on the track. I continued running until I was next to him, then stopped, following his gaze to the train farthest away as it pulled away from the station.

"*Bhanchod, madarchod!*" Vijay screamed. "Sister f-er, mother f-er!"

His string of curses was the most vulgar swearing anyone could say. And he shouted it in front of a woman—his wife! He wouldn't look at me. I didn't have the courage to ask him at that moment what we were going to do next. His startled movements were rough and angry. He searched in his pants pockets, took out his Wills Gold cigarette packet and a matchbox, and struck the match anxiously at least five times before it ignited. He lit his cigarette and took three long drags, pulling the smoke deep down into his lungs.

"*Bhanchod,*" he said, spitting on the tracks and launching into another string of cursing.

I was not only shocked but embarrassed—my husband, an educated man, spattering out curses. But this was not the time to express my disapproval. Instead, I gave Vijay the presumption of candor, blaming the situation as an excuse for his swearing and abusing. I grasped his free hand.

"It's all right, we can take the next train," I said as we headed across the tracks toward the tiny local station.

Vijay dropped my hand almost immediately. I sensed a moment of rejection but kept walking. Once we were across the tracks, I stopped to catch my breath and remove my heels to give my feet a brief reprieve. My ankles throbbed.

"The next train isn't until this evening," he snapped, sounding defeated, inhaling the nicotine, and releasing a cloud of smoke into the air. He took another drag and peered into a void, perhaps thinking deeply.

What does he see? What is he thinking about?

As he inhaled and exhaled quickly, nonstop, and smoke billowed, his widened eyes came back to normal, although from his thick glasses they looked smaller than they were. His lips stopped quivering, his breathing smoothened, his nerves seemed to calm, and his confidence returned.

He threw the cigarette butt onto the tracks. "Follow me," he said.

Vijay moved fast. The porter ran behind him. I squeezed my feet into my heels once again and followed the porter. After about ten minutes, we arrived at an area where several trucks were haphazardly parked, a chaos of red-, green-, and yellow-colored huge metal bodies decorated with strings of fake marigolds hanging from the tops. Young boys, lean-bodied, their clothes scruffy and unkempt, carried buckets and rags, eager to clean trucks for pennies. These were cargo trucks, their freight covered in tarpaulins, carrying commercial merchandise to Nandoli and Udaipur. The drivers, big burly men in large turbans and bushy mustaches, announcing their chauvinism, lounged on cots and smoked hookahs.

Vijay approached one of the drivers. I asked the porter to rest. After some back and forth between Vijay and the driver, my husband came toward us.

"Grab the luggage," he instructed the porter, then signaled me to follow him.

I objected to his body language and authoritarian tone, but given the circumstances, I let it go. He walked up to a massive truck with a giant driver and opened the passenger door, waving at me to get in. I pulled myself up, then poised on the step. I looked at him with questioning eyes.

"Are you serious?"

"Unless you want to stay in the isolated station for twelve hours, this is the only solution," he said.

I nodded and quickly accepted it as part of the adventure of starting my new life. I asked him to sit in the middle, and I would take the window. He nodded and slid past me. I moved close to him until we touched. I felt comfortable and safe with my man next to me. I took his hand, and this time he didn't drop it . . . he gripped it. My body tingled. I held it tighter, and he nudged closer. How very comforting and romantic. All my stress and doubts vanished as I melted into his body, while the driver focused on the road ahead.

By the time we reached Nandoli, four hours later, Vijay and the driver were deep in conversation. I stared out of the open window at dry land and bare trees. *Am I to live in the desert?* Vijay hadn't mentioned it to me. He had spoken only of Udaipur, the City of Lakes, and that he lived nearby.

Lean trunks of leafless branches were thirsty, desperate for water in the scorching sun. The barren, dry land was sketched with haphazard designs like amoebas, and plenty of dried ditches with cows and buffaloes seeking refuge, shooing flies with their tails. Stray dogs, shown as skeletons, barked at each vehicle with a hope for some compassion from a passerby to throw food at them.

We are in a desert.

Maybe not as barren as the miles of sand dunes shown in *Reshma Aur Shera*, the Sunil Dutt movie starring Waheeda Rehman, where they shot interiors of Rajasthan—the hills made of just sand, not a drop of water for miles, where it rained sand and only utter poverty existed. A new bride was expected to bring barrels full of water in their trousseaus instead of jewels, as that was the only demand from groom's family.

This landscape looked better than that. I shook my head at my ignorance. What was I expecting to see in the largest desert state of India? Lush green hills?

None of his family had prepared me for this kind of environment. Normally, a hard-core Delhiite wouldn't want to spend time in a remote village like this. It was a blessing for Vijay that, although I was raised a city girl, I was down-to-earth and free-spirited, with an open mind. My dad called me *gaggri* (gypsy girl), owing to my unconventional ways and love of colors and traditional costume jewelry, which I had worn plenty during my college days.

True, I would have loved to have been in a cosmopolitan city like New Delhi, advanced and modern, or a big city like Mumbai. But I was open to this new experience I had only seen in movies.

This small town of fewer than twenty-five thousand people looked like a series of tiny villages with thatched huts and houses made of stone, old and parochial.

All women we passed were dressed ethnically in a *ghagra* (a long, gathered skirt) and a sexy-looking backless *choli* (a blouse tied with strings at the back). The garments were dyed in every color: purple, mustard, burgundy, blue, and orange with a patch-work of a contrasting color. The women wore *chunris* (stoles) like ornate veils draped over their heads, their arms full of thick ivory bangles, made from elephant tusks, reaching up to their shoulders.

Later, I found out they covered their arms to protect their skin from the scorching heat of the sun. Also, because of the scarcity of water to bathe in, they covered their arms so sand and dust wouldn't settle on their skin. They wore large, oxidized silver earrings. Their noses were studded with oversized silver nose pins. Their features were chiseled, and their bodies were taut. They were true Aryan beauties.

The men mostly wore white frock-like tops with loose pants tapering around the calves and wide Rajasthan-style turbans. All men sported thick, long mustaches curled upward at the ends, showing off their machismo.

Both men and women were adorned in heavily inked tattoos—on their arms, hands, faces, necks, and any exposed skin—often the names of their loved ones or symbols of their deities. They wore thick lines of kohl around their eyes, which was supposed to ward off evil.

Finally, the truck stopped, and Vijay nudged me to get down. "From here, we'll take a bicycle rickshaw a quick twenty minutes," he said.

As we stepped down from the truck, a bicycle rickshaw came by, the rickshaw-wallah asking if we needed a ride. Vijay talked to him in broken Mewari, which he'd picked up from the locals. I grabbed the rickshaw frame with both hands and tried climbing on, first leading with my right foot, then trying my left, but with the rickshaw's slanting seat, I kept slipping off.

Vijay didn't notice. He puffed on a cigarette, lost in his own thoughts. The rickshaw puller extended his arm to me so I could get seated. Vijay climbed in after me, and the rickshaw- wallah adjusted our luggage before he started peddling.

We passed through narrow lanes paved with stones of all kinds and sizes, heaps of garbage visible around the small houses. Children played in the streets, barefooted. Cows, buffaloes, were tied outside in the courtyard of some houses. I presumed the varying numbers of cattle were reflective of the economic situation of the household. Women were making round pancake-like things from cow feces to use as fuel. A few stray dogs ran alongside the rickshaw.

I had arrived in a tiny village, not a small town as Vijay had suggested. It was already noon, and I was hungry, frazzled, and exhausted. I thought of the stuffed paratha Shiela had packed for us, waiting to be eaten.

Vijay instructed the rickshaw-wallah to stop in front of a two-storied concrete house.

"We're here," he said.

I got a boost looking at the concrete building, followed by two more in that lane. I climbed down and found a slim, petite, middle-aged woman, draped in a jazzy sari, holding a platter with marigold garlands, waiting to welcome us inside the gate. She looked at Vijay. "You didn't tell me your train time. The Udaipur Express has long gone. I was worried."

"This is Chanda Bai," Vijay said.

Chanda Bai welcomed us by putting marigold garlands around our necks and a red powder mark in the center of our foreheads, as per the norm. After Chanda Bai went into the house, Vijay told me she was the household help. She did the cooking and cleaning.

"Oh, I thought she was a neighbor." Or if not a neighbor, at least more than a servant, given the way she was dressed in a nice sari with a matching blouse, big earrings, a dozen bangles on both arms, and how she questioned Vijay with the authority of a relative. *This could be part of the culture here*, I said to myself.

"Let's go in," Vijay said.

I followed him up the four steps from the ground level onto a large, tiled platform. It contained three units with a small common veranda. We stood in front of the three doors.

Vijay pointed at the one on the right. "This is Sharma's," he said. "The middle door is Venkateshwara's."

The black-painted door on the left was ajar. Vijay gestured toward the entrance, then stepped in. I followed him, placing my hand on my heart before entering my new heaven. This is where my dreams of our future would unfold, although, judging by the neighborhood and the small village, they were not quite playing out as I'd thought. I pushed the thought down and entered into a rectangular room. It was big enough, maybe thirteen by eighteen feet. By the front door sat a black-painted, worn wooden sofa with brown cushions and two black wooden chairs around a rectangular black wooden table. A niche in the wall contained neatly stacked books.

There was a full-sized black wooden bed on the other end of the room, made up with clean white sheets and white pillows. I spotted a door to the left of the bed and opened it, thinking it must be our master bedroom. It didn't occur to me that the area surrounding the black bed was our bedroom. I found myself in a long, narrow bathroom. Vijay followed inside. The bathroom was equipped with one plastic bucket, a plastic mug, and a brass tap. I indicated the open window on the far wall of the bathroom. "What's on the other side of the window?" "It's the kitchen," he said.

We left the bathroom, stepping back into the rectangular room, the main room of the studio apartment.

"This is it," he said, spreading his arms wide. "I bought all this furniture, including the bed, in a sale for four hundred rupees," he said with a big, wide smile, which appeared wider because of his thick, black, trimmed but broad mustache covering the space between his nose and upper lip. His eyes shone with pride.

My heart skipped a beat.

The household was unassumingly basic, just like his father's. It was not what I expected. I was trying my best to hide my dumbfounded expression, though I was not sure how well I was able to. My face had always been an open book.

"But where's the door to the kitchen?" I asked.

"It's not attached to the house. One goes outside and down four steps and then, on the right, there is a long corridor to the kitchen door at the end."

I quickly walked out of the door to avoid meeting his eyes and followed the directions, to find Chanda Bai at the door to a long, narrow room, the entrance full of boxes and clutter. At the far end of the room, a four-by-four-feet space was the kitchen. A rectangular wooden table, three-by-four feet, held the kerosene pressure stove. I had always feared pressure stoves, which were known for combusting from over-pumping. I preferred kerosene wick stoves, which were much safer. A portion of the table was reserved for cutting vegetables and making roti (a round, grilled flatbread made from whole-grain flour kneaded with water).

Shelves lined the wall above the table, holding bottles of spices, condiments, lentils, and other staples. Near the rectangular table sat another table, small and round, with a battered cane chair next to it. Was this Vijay's dining table? I didn't see a second chair for me, yet! The kitchen appeared more like a makeshift cooking space set up in a big room. It was somewhat disheartening, but I was okay with it all. This was probably how bachelor pads were supposed to be.

Now that I'd come into Vijay's life, I'd make this a home. My focus was to start my married life and bond with my husband. The rest could come later.

Beginnings could be rough. I thought of my parents, how they struggled and built their own lives from nothing. I wouldn't let my dreams and fantasies of a happy married life be eclipsed by material concerns.

When I returned to the main room, I found Vijay in the bathroom, the door closed. I settled down on the couch, and Chanda Bai brought us tea and cookies on a tray. I searched for the stuffed paratha in our bag and handing the packet to Chanda Bai, asked her to warm them up and bring them. I was famished and thought Vijay must be, too.

Chanda Bai appeared to be a nice woman, a wide smile adorning her long, triangular face. She was older than I initially thought. At first glance, her white dentures had made her look younger to me. She addressed me as Bhabhi Ji, which is how a brother's wife is addressed, although I noticed later that every younger woman was addressed as Bhabhi Ji and every older woman as Bai Ji.

After the tea and a little siesta, Vijay brought me to the wide front window. He showed me a well across the street under a huge banyan tree where a local woman was bathing. It was a common practice in the villages. I'd seen farm laborers bathing at the well in my grandma's little town in Punjab. Instead of carrying a bucket or two of water home, they bathed at the well. Men took off their clothes, except for their underwear. Women kept their blouses and skirts on to preserve their modesty, to the extent they could in wet clothes.

This woman who Vijay insisted I watch, had a heavy bosom and a thin, bare waist. Her wet clothes stuck to her petite, well-shaped body. As she poured water on herself, her clothes became almost transparent. It was like the scene from the movie *Satyam Shivam Sundaram*, where the gorgeous, tall, curvaceous, and very sexy-looking Zeenat Aman stood under the waterfall in one piece of white muslin cloth covering her bare body, taking a shower. Men in the movie halls hooted and whistled at the scene.

With mischief in his eyes, Vijay gave me his charming smile, his tone teasing. "Sometimes my friends and I stand here to watch these women."

I smiled back, but I felt uneasy. I didn't know what to make of it.

After we left the window, he pulled a small old suitcase from under the bed and took out a few books he'd hidden away—I wasn't sure from whom, as he lived by himself. He brought one wrapped in an ancient newspaper turned brown and sat beside me. Carefully, he unwrapped the thin book and opened it. The yellowed pages, half of them loose and falling out, were filled with Kama Sutra poses. "Kama" the name of erotic Hindu God and "Sutra" being the teachings of love, desire, and sex. The poses showing the art of lovemaking were well-depicted in the form of semi-naked or naked figures carved in stones in famous ancient Hindu temples. Khajurao, Madhya Pradesh, which was the nation's UNESCO world heritage site; Sun temple in Konark-Orrisa; Jain temples Ranakpur, Rajasthan, and many more. The book looked well-used, perhaps passed around among his friends. I was getting anxious about the way the evening was going. But, I was quite open to it.

Although we had lain together in a bed for the last ten days after our marriage and held each other, we hadn't gone beyond that, as Vijay was conscious of his widowed father and unmarried sister sleeping next door. I'd been modest about it, too. Now I was excited for a romantic evening and the beginning of a new loving life with my husband.

As the night approached, my anxiety increased with the fear of the unknown. My breathing was shallow, and the insides of my hands perspired. At the same time, I was looking forward to being in an embrace with him without any hesitation, just the two of us in the room. I could see Vijay equally excited, as his pace of walking and talking had amplified, so had his coy and charming smiles at me.

It was my first time. Sex before marriage was a taboo and not talked about, even among friends. I didn't know what to expect but was eager to make love to my husband, which, per my limited knowledge, meant we'd lie down, hold hands, kiss, and embrace each other. No one, not even Leena, my married, older sister, had shared any details with me before. Vijay had lived by himself for eight years now, and I hoped this was his first time, too.

After dinner, we prepared to go to bed by the bathroom door. I asked Vijay to turn off the lights. I was too shy for him to see my bare body. He softly argued but then switched them off. I was comfortable now. He was gentle with me, making sure I was fine, being careful not to force himself on me. Since we had a space of our own, away from his family, we could open up and explore this part of marriage further.

The first morning I woke up in my new home, I found Vijay sitting at the table in the far corner, already sipping his first cup of morning tea—black tea with a few lemon drops—and reading the newspaper. He had his cigarette to his lips. He looked at me with a mischievous smile, and I shied away with the thought that I had surrendered my whole body to him, which I had kept covered so far, to a stranger the night before. He downed two more cups of tea and snuggled the paper under his arm, holding his *lungi*, made of cotton cloth wrapped around the waist like a towel, which some men wore at home, like his father did.

He paced toward the bathroom to get ready for work. The window between the bathroom and the kitchen was open, which didn't feel hygienic to me. I noticed Chanda Bai standing by the window, looking into the bathroom. Vijay closed the bathroom door, and all I heard was water running from the tap into the bucket.

The bathroom door opened again, and Chanda Bai again appeared at the window. She had probably just migrated to the window at the sound of the door opening, I told myself. Perhaps that's how she and Vijay might communicate if he needed something from the kitchen.

The days of our new life were wonderful—love, romance, sharing, and handholding. How lucky I was! Vijay left for work in the morning, came for lunch, and returned at the end of day around 5:30 p.m. Before he came home, I dressed up and sat on the steps, where I could watch him arrive from a distance. Chanda Bai visited three times a day to cook all three meals and clean the house.

Five days passed. Vijay and I were in the kitchen, sitting down to lunch, just as we had done every day. He sat on the cane chair and I on a three-legged stool, which had been added to the kitchen table for me. We had barely seated ourselves and started a conversation, when a plate whizzed by my face, shattering to pieces on the floor. A cold chill filled me. My breath stuck in my throat. I held it there. What had just happened?

Everything seemed to be moving in slow motion. Nothing registered. I stared at the smashed china plate, the spicy flat poppadum that had been sitting on it scattered in pieces among the shards.

Vijay, his face red with fury, snarled, "Why is this here on the table?"

I was petrified, not sure whether he was yelling at Chanda Bai or me.

"Don't you know poppadum is served *after* the lunch, a last course?" he shouted.

He was yelling at me. I was the one who had asked Chanda Bai to serve poppadum with the meal, as we did in northern India. I hadn't known it was customary in this part of India to serve the fried paper-thin bread after the meal. Why hadn't she told me?

I was silent, holding my breath. My hands had gone cold, and my eyes wide and stuck in horror. I didn't know where to look.

Vijay stared at me, his nostrils flared and his eyes red. "Let's eat."

Just like that, it was as though his raging had never occurred. He was back to normal.

I was not. My breathing had not yet normalized, and my hands were still cold. I could barely force any food down my throat, unlike Vijay, who quickly finished his lunch and walked out the kitchen door to go back to work.

The ruined plate, wasted food, shouting, and his red, furious face stayed with me the rest of the day.

Yet, come evening, I sat on the front steps. But this time, I sat as part of my routine rather than waiting to greet my husband. I was still trying to understand his rage. He came back from work his usual self, making small talk. So, I did, too.

Three days later, I sat on the common veranda with Mrs. Sharma, the next-door neighbor. We were sipping a cup of tea when she set down her cup, hesitated a moment, and then asked, "Did your parents ever run a background check on your husband?" Her voice held a tone of concern.

I was perplexed by her question but ignored it, quickly changing the subject. The truth was, my dad hadn't verified Vijay's background. He trusted the words of Mr. Behl, who had acted as the mediator between the two families and spoke on behalf of Vijay's family.

Mrs. Sharma's words kept echoing in my ears. How could Dad trust Mr. Behl's words when we didn't even know him well? Had we been too hasty? Is that what she'd implied? I kept brushing her words away, not wishing to plant seeds of doubt. But why would Mrs. Sharma ask me that question?

As the days passed, I found Vijay to be a chain smoker. At first, he indulged in only a few cigarettes in the evening. Maybe he had been holding back because of me but not anymore. The small house was hazy with his smoke. The couch and bedding stank. But I didn't say a word.

I hoped he was not hiding his drinking as well. So far, I hadn't seen him drink, although he'd told me he indulged occasionally.

In Delhi, social drinking among men was normal, so when he told me he drank socially, I understood. But now he'd begun to brag about his drinking buddies and how they competed and played games, betting on bottles of local whiskey. It was not something to brag about. His friends seemed to be extreme.

"How about you?" I asked him one night after dinner. "Do you play those games, too?"

"I drink only rarely, just to keep them company. After all, there's not much for a bachelor to do in this small town. Instead, I smoke." This, at least, was true. He accepted being a chain smoker. There was no hiding it. His constant smoker's cough was a proof.

I had no reason not to believe what he'd told me about his drinking.

After all, a married couple's relationship was built upon love and trust.

Chapter 2

The End of the Beginning

1981

I had been in Nandoli for two weeks now, attuning to the days in this small so-called town to an entirely new life and life-style. There wasn't much to do in this one room since Chanda Bai cleaned and cooked. But surprisingly, I wasn't bored. Neither was I missing city life. I took things easy, moving at a slow pace. The nights and early mornings were very cold, 20°–30° F. The days then became warm due to the sandy desert. With no air conditioning or fans, I adjusted to the changing weather by wearing layers of clothes. The local language was different but explicable. When I had to speak to anyone, I used my sign language skills. Amazingly, no one locked their houses when they stepped out. They seemed simple, less materialistic, and trustworthy.

I'd found two novels on the bookshelf: *The Razor's Edge* by William Somerset Maugham, which I'd started to read, and *To Kill a Mockingbird* by Harper Lee, which I planned on reading next. I was fascinated that fiction could be an interest Vijay and I could share, although he hadn't yet mentioned if he enjoyed reading novels and short stories. *I know him so little.*

During the day, I took pleasure in sipping a cup of tea with my next-door neighbors, Mrs. Sharma and Mrs. Venkateshwara, while sitting on the veranda. Mrs. Sheri, who lived across the street, joined us sometimes. In her midforties with three children, she was very affectionate and treated me as an older sister would. Her husband and his nephew worked at the MGM tire plant and were good friends with Vijay. Although I was growing accustomed to my new life, I missed my parents and my siblings, and wrote to them often.

It was New Year's Eve.

"Be ready in the evening," Vijay hollered before he left for work. "We're invited to the celebrations with people from my office in the banquet hall not far from here."

"Oh, good."

I was a little surprised he hadn't mentioned it before, but I was excited about going out, meeting his colleagues, and celebrating the New Year. I had enjoyed the celebrations with my college friends when several of us gathered in the central shopping hub of New Delhi's Connaught Place. A modern-day, happening place, especially for the younger crowd, known for its restaurants and nightlife. Last year, my friends and I had gone down the stairs next to the Regal Theater to experience the newly-opened discotheque, Cellars, a new wave in New Delhi, a sensation for all of us college kids.

Since it was my first appearance with the MGM crowd, I needed to dress up and look my best. I'd brought only a few saris with me, so choosing one wasn't difficult. I picked my favorite: an elegant magenta and purple Patola silk sari with gold flowers and a gold embroidered Zari border. I wore a matching magenta silk blouse and my golden stiletto heels, bought in the up and coming, glamorous underground-chic Palika Bazaar, in the center of Connaught Place. I wore silver anklets and toe rings on my feet, which I loved. Instead of wearing gold jewelry, which was customary for a new Indian bride, I wore matching costume jewelry.

I was so fond of the sleek, heirloom, south Indian jewelry my mom had passed on to me, but Shiela forbade me to take any gold jewelry with me because it "wouldn't be safe." My sister-in-law sat with me when I had started to pack for Nandoli. She picked the dresses I could carry with me from the trousseau given to me by my parents. I watched silently as she separated jewelry and clothing into separate piles—one to stay with her for safekeeping and one to go with me. Her, making the choices made me morose, as if I were a little girl who could not decide on her own. I'd spent months choosing my trousseau and had pictured myself wearing all my new dresses after my wedding. Vijay supported his sister on this, and although I went along with her picks, I was not all right with her selecting what I could and could not wear. I was afraid she would make a scene if I said something, since I was still an outsider among my new in-laws. I accepted the situation and remained a silent observer.

Shiela also insisted I leave behind my red velvet bangle box, my favorite wedding gift. I would safely keep my colorful, delicate glass bangles in it. Every time I put it in the suitcase, she took it out. I had hoped to set it on my dresser in Nandoli. However, in Nandoli, there was no dresser. There was not even a full-length mirror—just a small hand mirror Vijay used when he shaved. I managed with it, although looking into a full-length mirror head to toe before stepping out had its own charm and satisfaction.

I braided my silky black, hip-length hair neatly and left it loose on my neck, which looked nice next to my face. My makeup was simple. I had hardly applied any during college. No one did. But now I lined my eyes with kohl, then rubbed a smudge of lipstick on my cheeks and finally applied the same stick on my lips. I was ready!

Vijay arrived from work, looked at me, and nodded with approval. Then he went into the bathroom to freshen up and change for the party.

Everything in the small town of Nandoli was within walking distance. The banquet hall was a mile away, a bit far but still walkable, though walking in heels on the uneven, pebbled street did not make it easier.

Men and women stood in small groups in the banquet hall, laughing, snacking, and drinking. I was eager to meet the crowd.

Vijay introduced me to a few couples and then left me with the Oberois to see his other friends. It was an uncomfortable situation, being left alone at a work party with strangers, but I managed pretty well. I reminded myself, after all, I was a New Delhi girl, to boost my ego. I walked up to a younger couple—Sudhir, a senior vice president with the company, and Sharleen, his wife—whom I talked to for a bit. They seemed to be my kind of people. Sudhir was from New Delhi and Sharleen from the hills in the north near Delhi, so we had things in common to talk about.

They introduced me to another couple. As I chatted, my eyes searched for Vijay. I wanted to spend time with him on our first New Year's Eve, but I didn't see him. Finally, about an hour later, I spotted him, watching me from a corner, a whiskey glass in his hand. I smiled and waved at him, but he just stared back. I caught glimpses of him, smoking a cigarette, whiskey in hand, watching me from the far corners of the room, his expression inscrutable. When I tried to approach, he strangely disappeared into the crowd. Near the end of the party, when all the couples had left or were leaving, he stood by the bar. He walked toward me, his gait unsteady, smiling sheepishly.

"Let's leave," I said.

He gulped the rest of his drink. "Wait here," he said, and staggered toward the exit.

He could barely walk. I hadn't witnessed anyone drunk except in movies, where it was usually portrayed humorously. There was no drinking in my parents' house or any social drinking in the larger society in which I was raised.

Loud voices came from outside the hall. Baffled, I walked out into the dark night. I spotted Vijay and stopped, terrified. He and another man were at each other's throats, pulling shirts and cursing at each other, vulgar and loud. My stomach dropped. I did not know what to do.

Luckily, Sudhir and Sharleen had not yet left. Sudhir grabbed Vijay's arm and dragged him away from the other man toward me. I took my husband's arm, and without creating any fuss, walked toward home, pulling him along. In the middle of the night, the one-mile walk seemed never-ending, and my heels were hurting me. I was frightened of the dark, but my energy was focused on reaching home. I was not even getting scared of the stray dogs following us, steadily increasing in numbers. Occasionally, I turned sideways to look at Vijay. His head wobbled back and forth as he weaved his way down the road. I kept pulling him onward. He blathered incoherently the entire way home.

When we arrived, Vijay slipped off his shirt and pants and then, wearing only his underclothes, frantically searched the room. He rifled through drawers, reaching behind the curtain, and pulled out that small suitcase from under the bed. He yanked it open, staggering, falling, picking himself up, and then staggering some more. I watched him in silence, my heart   beating rapidly.

Vijay finally found what he was looking for. From behind the books on the shelf, he pulled out a bottle of whiskey.

"Aha!" he said, handing me the bottle. "Make me a peg."

I did not want him to get angry in this state. I took the bottle and asked, "How much whiskey?"

"Patiala peg," he said, squatting on the sofa. It meant a large peg, but I didn't understand, so I poured some whiskey in a glass, handed it to him, and went to the bathroom to change.

"Where are you going?" he called after me.

When I came out, he was sitting on the floor. After finishing off one more Patiala peg, he ordered me to sit next to him. I perched on the edge of the sofa. He reeked of alcohol. It was nearly impossible to sit next to him. My fear had increased. Since I'd never seen him drunk, I didn't know what to expect of him.

"You think you people are very smart," he said. He got up, pushed me, and sat next to me.

By "you people," I assumed he meant my family.

He grabbed my chin hard and lifted it. "Look at me. You think you people are smarter than me."

I tried pulling his hand away, but it was of no use. I tried turning my face away. His fingers dug into my jaw as he yanked my head back to face me. I turned away. He tugged once again. Back and forth we went. I was extremely frightened. I urged myself to close my eyes and ears and assume nothing was happening. I wanted to get up and shut myself in the bathroom but sat still, controlling my breathing, my hands cold.

He dug his fingers deep into my cheeks, then pushed my tousled hair from my forehead and tucked the strands behind my ears. I tried to pull back my face from him, but he smiled viciously, staring into my eyes. He looked different.

"He thinks he's very smart," he said. "I have dealt with that lot for half my life." Then he started cursing my dad.

"Don't drag my dad into this," I said, pleadingly.

Vijay sprang up, his eyes red. He grabbed my hair and pulled me up and toward him. I looked him in the eye.

He shouted, "Eyes down!" pointing his fingers right into my eyes and repeated it until I looked down away from him.

"My dad has done nothing wrong to you," I whispered.

Then I saw his open palm coming toward me. His eyes bulged out, his teeth were clenched, puffing his breath at me, and he slapped my face with all his strength.

I staggered, my hair fell on my face, the room spun. I was in shock. *What just happened?* Then it registered what he had done. I kept my hand on my burning, bruised cheek.

"You bitch!" he screamed. "You will take your dad's side over me! Who am I to you? Do not dare take your dad's side! I am your husband, your Shrinath, your god."

My heart pounded. Was he going to hit me again?

I sat on the sofa, shocked into silence, unable to stand because of his tight grip on my upper arm, his fingers digging in, hurting me. He sat down, continuing to curse my dad. He put his face right into my face. The smell of liquor coming off him made me want to gag. He lit his cigarette, letting go of my arm to do so. I tried standing, but he grabbed my arm and hauled me back down. I sat there trapped, trembling. Was he going to slap me again? I didn't know what he would do. I didn't know this man. I couldn't be alone in a room with this man I didn't know. A stranger. All I wanted to do was cry aloud and set myself free. All I wanted was my mom and dad to come and take me away from this hell to their safe haven.

"Please, let me go to bed." I pleaded with him.

I hadn't done anything wrong, so how could he slap me? How could my very own husband slap me? He was not the man he appeared to be. He couldn't be normal.

He finally released my arm, perhaps sensing that should be enough for a first dose. He had me under his control.

I ran to the bed, pulled the sheet over me, and sobbed silently without making a sound. If he heard me crying, he would surely drag me out and hit me again. Finally, all cried out, I didn't know when I fell asleep.

When I opened my eyes in the morning, I saw Chanda Bai serving him breakfast. I closed my eyes, holding absolutely still. I didn't want to see his face. He had betrayed my trust and snatched away my love for him. I hated him.

As soon as Vijay left for work, I pulled myself from under the covers and walked into the bathroom. I didn't feel like taking a shower or changing. I was terrified of what would happen when he came home. I burst into tears and then wiped my eyes. *Is this the man I married? How can he raise his hand to me? How could he?* All day, I lay in bed, my eyes open. I couldn't think clearly. When I shut my eyes, I saw my husband's face contorted with rage, his open hand swinging toward me. I was sad, deep in my heart. I felt I should talk to someone but didn't know who. All the neighbors were his colleagues at work. My parents were more than four hundred miles away, with no phone lines in this remote area.

While growing up, I had heard women adjusted in their marriages and didn't complain. I didn't know the magnitude of that adjustment. Was being slapped and living with it considered "an adjustment"?

Vijay did not come home for lunch, and I was not hungry. He returned in the evening. He took off his work clothes and, wearing only his underpants, sat down on the sofa, trying to gauge my mood.

"How was your day?" he asked me, as Chanda Bai brought him a glass of water.

I remained quiet.

Seeing him sitting in his underwear brought last night crashing back. He kept talking to me, and I didn't respond. He then slid from the sofa and sat on the floor at my feet, held my hands tight, and asked me to forgive him.

When I tried to free my hands, he started to cry. "I swear to you that this will not happen again."

I was uneasy and felt awkward with him sitting at my feet. His tears and pleas for forgiveness made me uncomfortable.

Then he got up and quickly walked into the bathroom, calling Chanda Bai through the window. He asked her to get him something, but I couldn't hear what.

He came out of the bathroom as quickly as he had gone. "I have demons in me. Chanda Bai knows what to do."

Surely, he did not literally mean that demons possessed him. He was trying to make a fool of me.

Chanda Bai entered, carrying a heavy brass pot, the smoke from the boiling hot oil diffusing from its brim, filling the room with the pungent odor of mustard oil and red chili pods. She made me nervous, holding the smoking pot right next to me. What if it spilled on me?

Vijay sat on the sofa, placing one hand flat on his head, as Chanda Bai circled the smoking pot around his upper body, chanting words I couldn't make out. What was going on? My heart pounded. I feared for my safety. Yet, clearly, this wasn't the first time he and Chanda Bai had performed this ritual.

After Chanda Bai finished, Vijay moved to the bed and lay quietly on his back, perhaps waiting for the second part of the ritual. Chanda Bai picked up the small bottle of head balm, Amrutanjan, which he kept in front of the books on the shelf. I had noticed the bottle when we arrived but didn't think much about it. Chanda Bai applied the balm to Vijay's forehead while he lay on his back, bare-chested, in his underpants. I couldn't watch. It felt wrong that Chanda Bai was sitting so close to him, and he was allowing it. It felt wrong he wore only his underpants with her in the room. It felt just as wrong she was performing such an intimate ritual. How could an educated engineer from a premier institute in New Delhi be so ancient in his ways? Filled with anguish and sick to my stomach, I looked away.

When Chanda Bai left the room with the pot, Vijay got up and sat on the floor next to my chair. He held my hand tightly, again pleading with me to say I forgive him. He started crying again and constantly wiped his running nose.

"Okay," I said out of frustration to end that. But I could never be the same with him again. I was left with no respect for him.

Two days later, the shock of the incident hadn't yet left me completely, but I was somewhat relieved Vijay admitted his mistake. Maybe he had gotten a little too drunk and he wasn't used to being intoxicated. I convinced myself this was the first time he'd done anything like this. He couldn't be a wife beater. His family seemed courteous, and a bright, educated person couldn't beat his wife. I assured myself, he was out of his senses from drinking.

However, the clearing-the-demons ritual never left me. It wasn't the only time I witnessed the ritual of casting away evil. Chanda Bai and Vijay repeated it almost weekly. Each time, she came into the room in the evening and looked into Vijay's eyes, as if checking them.

"I can see the evil again," she would say.

She would either perform the same ritual or bring a glass filled with water, wave it around his face, pour some into the cupped palm of her hand, and sprinkle it on him.

I soon learned Chanda Bai was in her midforties and married to a much older man, almost ninety now. She had two stepsons and one son she had given birth to. They all worked at the tire company. She was energetic and giggly and dressed in colorful saris, matching bangles, and decorative bindis, which were round red dots worn in the middle of the forehead. She also wore a long line of red powder, known as a *sindoor*, along the center part in her long, black hair.

I'd often noticed Chanda Bai and Vijay glance at each other with coquettish smiles. Then there was the strange issue of her coming to the bathroom window. The matter of the unhygienic conditions in the kitchen, with all the clutter and dirty clothes hidden in boxes, was unacceptable, so I fired her, not once but a few times. And every time, the next morning, she came to stand in front of the window by the sofa. My husband would go outside, they would talk, and she was rehired. Obviously, I disliked Vijay not respecting my word and that they had both settled her rehiring without me present.

Life started to normalize over the next two months. Vijay took me to the famous Shrinathji Temple and Kumbhalgarh, one of the hill forts of Rajasthan, perhaps trying to make up. However, my love and respect for him were not the same as on the day we got married.

Holi festival fell on March 17, announcing the arrival of spring. Holi signified the triumph of good over evil. It was a time to forget any animosities and embrace one another. Men and women of all castes and religions got together to rub colorful powders on each other. Children filled balloons with colored water to throw at people. It brought together people, society, and ethnicities. I'd been married for three months. The first Holi after marriage held a great deal of significance and hope that the vibrant festival would bring color and goodness into our lives.

The celebrations included playing *dhols* (drums) in the streets and drinking *bhang* (a cannabis leaf paste mixed with milk and green cardamoms prepared in large earthen pots, customarily served only to men).

Holi had been my favorite fun festival. This year, I made a silent prayer to the higher power, beseeching Him to create peace and harmony in my marriage.

We had finished our breakfast when a group from MGM tire came to the front gate, calling us out. We joined them. After a couple of hours in the neighborhood, I was covered in red, green, and magenta powder. I was also wet from colored water but not drenched like some others. Men, women, and children were having fun. Everyone talked loudly and made jokes. The men were busy drinking bhang, though I had noticed Vijay holding a glass of whiskey. It was hot and humid. Suddenly, I felt tired and dizzy and then nausea set in. I caught hold of Vijay, and I told him I needed to go home.

When we arrived, I threw up a couple of times. Feeling extremely weak, I lay down, unable to keep my eyes open, shaking, and cold. Vijay ran out to call Mrs. Sheri.

After hearing my symptoms, she smiled.

"Kanchan is pregnant," she said. "She should go for a checkup in the morning. I'll stop by to take her."

I felt nothing at first. *Pregnant?* "Oh God."

After a few seconds, it registered. I was going to be a mother. Suddenly, I felt the rush of hormones in my body. I would be a mother! I turned toward Vijay. He didn't meet my gaze and didn't say a word. He was as quiet as dead wood.

Maybe he was in shock. Maybe he was not ready. Maybe it was too early for him to get excited. I thought about how in movies, when a husband heard his wife was pregnant, he got ecstatic, jumped out of joy, picked up his wife, and hugged her. I shook away the thought. I didn't have the energy or will to be disappointed. I just wanted to sleep.

I woke up late that evening and found the room filled with the smoke of cigarettes and the smell of booze. I opened my eyes to see Vijay sitting on the floor in the corner, the back of his head resting on the wall and his legs spread, quite drunk. As soon as he heard me get up, he got up from the floor and gave me a smirk smile. I expected something good to come from him after the news.

He grabbed my arm, pulled me out of bed, smiled brutishly, and dragged me onto the floor with more strength than I expected from a man his size. He made me sit opposite him while he blathered incoherently. I tried to get up, but he grabbed me by the wrist, hard, until it felt as though my bone might snap. I quietly sat there, shocked and frightened. As he continued his rant, I couldn't make out a single word. I suspected something dreadful was coming. It was horrific. I trembled out of fear, pressing my lips. *Not again!*

I wanted to get up and go back to bed, but there was no furniture nearby to pull myself up from the floor, and I was too weak to stand on my own. Helpless, I started to cry.

He grabbed both my legs and dragged me on the floor toward him. Once he'd dragged me opposite him, he kicked me in the belly, hard. I lost my breath and voice and screeched in pain. With my face aghast, I looked at him traumatized. *Why is he doing this to me? What is he punishing me for?* And he kicked again and yet again. I cried out aloud and begged him not to kick me.

"What's wrong with you?" Fractured, I placed both hands on my belly and kept them there to protect my fetus. Vijay kicked on my hands till they were bruised.

"Stop it, will you!" I screamed. He leaned forward to cover my mouth tight, gagging me. And then he released his hand.

His blathering continued. I could hear him now.

"I do not want this child. I do not want this child." He was continuously moving his head.

"Why are you saying this? What do you want? What have I done to you?"

He drooled and coughed. He smelled horrible, like some ruffian off the street. His hold on me loosened, and I jumped up and ran to the bathroom to hide. I shook, sobbing, trying to catch my breath. *Will he kill me tonight? I have to get away, but where?*

I kept myself locked in the bathroom, howling and crying. If I went to my parents with this news, what would it do them? My dad's heart would give out. He'd die of shock with the knowledge that he'd failed in choosing this man for me. He'd never forgive himself. If he didn't die of shock, the guilt would do him in. He couldn't know. My mind continued to make these arguments, and I sobbed at my fate, the fate in which I never believed.

When I emerged from the bathroom after almost an hour, Vijay was in a stupor. He sat on floor, leaning against the wall. I tiptoed to the bed and pulled the covers over my head. By the middle of the night, I couldn't hold my bladder any longer and slowly made my way to the bathroom. When I pulled down my pajama pants, I saw blood on the fabric and more dripping down my legs. Perhaps my womb was emptied, which seemed like an abortion. I climbed back into the bed, numb and devastated.

The next morning, I waited in bed until Vijay left for the office. When Mrs. Sheri stopped by to confirm the visit to the doctor, I told her about the blood but not the incident. She was still hopeful about the fetus being intact. She called a rickshaw, and we headed to the hospital.

The rickshaw bumped all over the uneven road I named Abortion Road. We reached the hospital, an old, dilapidated building with bricks showing through the whitewash.

Inside, the walls were covered in the red spit of betel or tobacco leaves, which people chewed. The corridor didn't smell pungent and musty with disinfectant, like hospitals do.

Is it sterilized and hygienic?

Dr. Agarwal was a short, heavyset woman with facial hair and a drooping face who looked as though she'd given up on life. She didn't even wear a doctor's coat.

"Lie down here," she said, curtly.

I am a patient, so have some compassion, I thought to myself. The bed was wobbly and covered in dirty linen. I stared at it with apprehension.

"Quick, I have a line of patients waiting outside," Dr. Agarwal said assertively.

I lay down, hesitantly. She was very crude in her checkup. She took hold of an injection and gave me a shot, without a word or an expression on her face. She was cold and mechanical. Perhaps this environment had made her uncouth.

I asked her delicately, "What was the shot you gave me?"

She was noncommittal. "To hold the fetus and prevent further loss of blood. You will need two more shots the following days."

I gathered myself, thanked her, and came out. Mrs. Sheri was already waiting in the rickshaw, and we came back home on the same Abortion Road.

Mrs. Sheri came with me into the house and volunteered to check on me when I used the bathroom. I was expelling more blood clots, so she sent her nephew to get Dr. Agarwal. I was given a couple more shots, an extra shot of Proluton to retain the fertilized egg, and another shot of a sedative to put me to sleep. She advised bed rest with my legs raised on pillows for the next few days. She was a different person in the home setting. I could see the human side of her. I empathized with her. She was probably frustrated in that dilapidated hospital environment.

When Vijay came home, I lay quietly. He tried to talk, but I didn't say a word. Mrs. Sheri again came in the night and informed Vijay about our visit and doctor's visit.

That evening, he asked Chanda Bai to stay over. I was drowsy and drifted in and out of sleep. Sometime during the night, I turned over to discover Vijay wasn't in bed. I looked around and saw two makeshift beds on the floor, one close to the foot of the bed and the other a little apart. And then I saw them, Chanda Bai and Vijay, leaning toward each other, their faces ready to touch. They heard me move and quickly separated. I was not sure if Vijay knew I'd seen him. I didn't want him to know. At the same time, oddly, I didn't care if he did. I just wanted to get away.

The next morning, after Vijay went to work, my thoughts were fixed on being able to save my fetus and going away from this place. *But how? How can I travel?* Vijay handled all the finances. I didn't even get an allowance. I had no idea how to navigate the roads, where to locate a rickshaw stand, or the distance to the railway station. Running away might sound easy and like the only option available, but I was frightened to ask anyone, worried my inquiry would get back to Vijay. And what if he caught me at the bus stop? Or what if the neighbors saw me and told him? What would he do to me?

I desperately wanted to be with my parents and my siblings. I craved their hugs.

Mrs. Sheri came the next morning. She was the only person I knew a little better than anyone else, but I didn't know if her husband was close friends with Vijay and if they'd believe me.

"I want to go home," I told her and started to cry.

"What happened? Why are you crying? Everything will be fine."

"No," I sobbed. "Nothing will be fine. It's all over."

"You are hiding something from me. Are you missing your parents?"

And then I blurted out what Vijay had done to me.

She was shocked. She had no knowledge of his anger issues. No one had. Everyone around knew about his boozing with friends but not the extent. I made her swear not to tell anyone, including her husband.

Mrs. Sheri hugged me tight, wiped my tears, and sat there sobbing herself.

"How can he do this to you?"

Then she went home and brought lunch for me. She advised me with all her compassion not to travel for the next three or four days. Once I was stabilized, I would be able to leave. In the evening, she came by again and told Vijay it would be best if I went to the city so that if something happened, I could get better medical care. When I told him I wanted to go to Delhi, to my surprise, he agreed instantly.

Five days later, Vijay saw me off at the bus station on the condition that I would first go to my in-laws' house. On the way to Delhi, I decided I would never let my parents know this part of my tragic life. My dad had a couple of minor strokes and suffered from angina pains. I could never bear it and forgive myself if something happened to him.

So, this was the man I married. He was far away from the man of my dreams. I didn't want to see him ever again. I couldn't go back to him. I would not go back to him.

This was the end of the beginning of my new life.

Chapter 3

A Love Story

1957–1978

My life before marriage was unusually cheerful and gratifying, my childhood filled with enthusiasm, warmth, hugs, and lessons about good values and fairness. This built a strong foundation for a delightful and self-assured young woman.

My dad, Om, married his beloved Shashi, my mom, on July 12, 1947. He was nineteen and Shashi was sixteen, a marriageable age in the 1940s. Om would say it was love at first sight, and he would tell us again and again the story of how my mother's simplicity and charm mesmerized him.

My siblings and I would sit around them to hear the story, usually some late evening after dinner. Dad would do the talking while Mom shied away, blushing, even twenty years later, and pressing Dad's hand to stop, while we listened keenly. He was a talented storyteller, engaging us with all the twists and turns of their story. We hung on his every word, as if we were hearing their tale for the first time.

Dad was taken away by his father to live with him in Iran in 1941 at the age of thirteen. Although his years in American-influenced

Iran were spent in privilege, it was his stepmother's imposing presence that was ill accommodating. At fourteen, he decided to live a life of his own free will.

Soon, however, he would learn the world was about survival of the fittest.

And survive he did!

My father came back to India to visit his family in Gujranwala, now a part of Pakistan, in June of 1947, two months before the British left India and the country was divided into present-day India and Pakistan.

The day after his arrival in his town, he saw my mother walking with her friends to school. He was immediately attracted to her sheer beauty. She noticed the handsome new face in town, asked her mother about the new face in the town.

Dad would say, "Every day for the next ten days, I stood by the corner of her street to get a glimpse of her." He wanted to make this petite, pure beauty his life partner.

But then the unthinkable happened. Before he could talk to Shashi's mother, the black clouds of riots moved in like wildfire, reaching Gujranwala. They brought large-scale violence, rapes, murders, and an overwhelming refugee crisis. The continent was divided into two countries: Hindustan, now called India, for Hindus and Sikhs, and Pakistan, for Muslims.

My Hindu parents in the soon-to-be Muslim state separately made the decision to flee before they too, became victims of this mutual genocide. My mom, her mother, and her grandmother were particularly vulnerable due to their gender. My father helped them flee to the Indian refugee camps in army trucks. It was at this refugee camp that my father asked for my mother's hand in marriage.

Two days later, they got married around the Holy Fire, called *pheras*, the Hindu ritual of taking vows by the to-be couple tied together by a stole or dupatta walking in circles seven times around the firepit supposed to be sacred and sanctified amid Sanskrit shlokas or mantras chanted by a Hindu priest the Pundit outside the refugee camp, taking pledges never to be apart.

Like millions, both had been forced by circumstances to migrate, penniless, from Pakistan. But the circumstances would not rob them of their courage and determination. They struggled, hand in hand, collaborating with each other as partners starting life from scratch. They were blessed with a premature son, Ravi, and two years later a daughter, Leena.

I was born six years after Leena, in September of 1957. Within two years, my younger brother, Neel, arrived. My mother was twenty-six and my father, twenty-nine. True to his progressive ways, my father decided to get a vasectomy.

I was five in 1962 when my dad's new job moved us to the Institute of Technology (IT) in the posh area of South Delhi. This was a significant transition for all of us. We were moving from the small town of Delhi to the heart of New Delhi's sprawling IT campus, a one-of-a-kind premier institute run in collaboration with funding by the British royalty. The foundation was laid by Prince Philip, Duke of Edinburgh. It was an institute of eminence, surrounded by historical monuments such as Qutub Minar, Red Fort, and Humayun's Tomb.

The architecture of the gated residential campus was unique from other modern office buildings and residential blocks. The residential blocks were four-storied, with an exterior of red bricks. These housed faculty and administration staff. Well-manicured green lawns and maintained roads marked the campus. It was a city within a city, with amenities that included a shopping center, a school, a hospital, its own water supply, and a backup electricity supply. It was a model community, nowhere else in India.

The people in the community were well educated: a mix of professors, doctors, civil engineers, researchers, and administrative staff. The campus was a popular place in South Delhi, nestled amid upscale supermarkets, fashion boutiques, and exclusive uptown areas built by big names in the real estate industry. Dad and Mom, with their relentless efforts, had landed managerial jobs, and Mom took over the position of a school principal.

Whenever I have heard the story of their partnership, arduous work, and humble beginnings, I have felt their pain and admired their persistent struggle and pure intentions to give their children the best. Dad was my absolute hero. Dignified, he always smelled good and dressed impeccably, his hair combed neatly. He never gave up his playfulness.

Mom and Dad created a home filled with love and harmony. We had strong family values based on caring, respect, trust, and, most importantly, gender equity.

"Daughters and sons get equal treatment in the Bhaskar household," Dad and Mom would say with conviction.

Their progressive thinking was inconsistent with the societal norms of that time. Our lives in the tight-knit community were simple yet fulfilled. There was safety, regard, and warmness. People were honest and humble.

Dad, at a young age, had hypertension and angina, which didn't disrupt his daily life, thanks to him religiously taking his meds. We were all cognizant of his health, especially after he had a couple of mild heart attacks. I resolved to keep him stress-free and make sure he would never have to worry about me or be disappointed in me.

However, twice on separate occasions—once, when I was traveling with my school group to another state for a camp in high school, and another time when I scored poorly in mathematics—he said, "Do not ever betray me."

The word "betray" pricked my heart like an arrow. I didn't know exactly what he meant (and I still don't today), but I interpreted it to mean not to do anything to break his trust or go against the values of our family.

My undergrad education from 1973–1976 was at a prestigious British college, which attracted students from affluent, prominent families. The college was in the center of New Delhi. Education was a priority for me, but I didn't want to so deeply immerse myself in books that I missed out on experiencing the world. This was the time when my feminist thinking became stronger.

Although I never joined a particular organization, I felt passionately about women's rights and freedoms. At that time, in the midseventies, new brides were being burned alive in rural, as well as urban, areas by greedy in-laws who wanted a greater dowry in cash or gold.

I remember signing a memo to take an oath that I would not take any dowry or trousseau from my parents' hard-earned money. The number of girls and their parents falling victim to this age-old practice was on the rise. I was at the forefront when we joined hands with social workers who protested the burning of young brides on the roads of New Delhi and in front of the Parliament.

I enjoyed my college life. It was a good balance of studying and fun. I'd take the public bus to college, attend the first two classes, and then skip the other two. A group of friends would walk to the Bengali Market next door, famous for Nathu Sweets, or to Shankar Market and the Connaught Place Center in New Delhi. This was where the so-called "cool crowd" from surrounding colleges used to hang out. These were the times when male students were respectful and protective of girls. They did not push themselves on girls without mutual consent.

My friends and I would sit across from DePaul's, the famous and first-of-its-kind coffee shop, to do some "bird" watching (birds being boys). Motorbikes fascinated me, the trendiest being Yamaha and Bullet, and the boys would run them without the mufflers, performing their gigs on the road.

I took a couple of rides with campus neighbor boys I knew, to satisfy my burning desire to ride on one. But I realized I was fearful of accepting an invitation to ride alone with another boy. *What if he held my hand or kissed me? Will it lead to a proposal of marriage . . . or something else?* Keeping one's virginity prior to marriage was a big deal in that generation and dating most commonly led to marriage. And, of course, Dad's warning, "Do not betray me," was always in the back of my mind.

The first movie I saw in a theater on a 70mm screen was *Love Story*, starring Ali McGraw and Ryan O'Neal. My friend Kavya and I skipped classes and went to Chanakyapuri Theater. During the movie, when Ryan kissed Ali on the steps of the college, I whispered in Kavya's ear, "Look at both of them kissing. This is the way to kiss, passionate but pure."

She laughed and repeated what I'd said to all of her friends for days after that, even one of her cousins, who used to come to see her on his motorbike. He was quite surprised this came from me, since he had the impression I was one shy girl.

There were tons of novels available at home, since my dad used to read a lot—all famous authors of the time. There was one particular British author—Harold Robbins—whose novels he would read, and then hide before he went to work. Not from Mom, obviously. Curious, I'd steal and read them. There were a lot of steamy, cozy scenes, which were fascinating and sometimes overwhelming, the precise reason Dad hid these novels. But Harold Robbins was a one-of-a-kind storyteller. I loved his writing style. *The Betsy*, *The Carpetbaggers*, *Never Love a Stranger*, *Stiletto*, *The Pirate*, and many more. I read them all.

However, the first novel I read, when I was twelve, was Pearl S. Buck's *The Good Earth*. Very soon, I realized I liked romantic novels, so Mills & Boon and Barbara Cartland became my go-to. Their novels created the dream world I had been in since my adolescence, fantasizing like other girls about a tall, dark, and handsome (TDH) prince who would appear one day from the clouds, riding on a white stallion, and sweep me away to his magnificent palace.

After receiving my undergrad degree, I started my master's degree at the Delhi School of Social Work, Delhi University, majoring in social work. The large campus encompassed all the premier colleges of Delhi University, with students attending from all around the country.

Vrinda and Mrinal became my best friends. The three of us were called The Deadly Trio. I was nicknamed Infectious Smile by a group of classmates. I loved the attention I got, which made me yearn for a life not ordinary, my favorite line being, "Life is short, so let us live it."

While pursuing my master's degree, I became infatuated with one particular boy from the faculty of management studies who frequented my college cafeteria. He did not completely fit the TDH (tall, dark and handsome) type from a Mills & Boon story, but surely, he was suave and handsome. He always wore Ray-Bans and drove a Fiat at a time when owning a car was not common among students.

Each day I waited in the cafeteria to have a glimpse of him, but I never worked up the courage to talk to him. My infatuation was so strong, I lost my appetite and couldn't sleep. I was sick with love. I later understood love is never one-sided. One day he was accompanied by a girl, and I watched as she reached familiarly into his jacket pocket and pulled something out. He already had a girlfriend. I felt low for days, my dreams shattered.

At home, we followed spirituality rather than an organized religion. When my grandmother and great-grandmother landed in Punjab from the refugee camp after partition, they needed stability, and they looked to faith. They heard about this ashram, a sacred place headed by a guru, a spiritual teacher who was secular and didn't preach or follow any particular religion. He had many followers. The guru preached meditation and stillness to focus on the sound that connects one to the higher conscious, merging with the soul and hence to the supreme power.

This sounded very much in line with my grandmother and great-grandmother's viewpoints, so they visited the ashram in Punjab, northern India, called Dera. His daily discourse was based upon the foundations of morality, honest living, a model character, meditation, and no alcohol. Also, animals were not to be killed and eaten. The guru quoted Christ, Saint Matthew, Guru Nanak, Allah, Bulleh Shah, Kuber, Buddha, and many others in his discourses. Both women not only found solace in Dera but also a sense of security and stability. They both became disciples, and so did Mom.

Dad followed guru's teachings and attended his discourses with my mom. I never saw my parents going to discourses regularly or meditating, but everyone in the house followed the path and often prayed in the evenings. We all followed the practice of bowing to his framed photo, a big picture of him on the door of the house and taking his blessings before stepping out.

Two of guru's guidelines were written in stone in our house: no eating meat and no drinking alcohol. We never had meat, fish, poultry, eggs, or any kind of alcohol in our home and never tasted any of these items inside or outside our home.

When Dad took the vows for chanting mantra given by his guru in 1968–1969, my trust in guru grew stronger. I always valued my father's decisions. His opinions mattered.

Spirituality, to my young mind, meant that we believed in the presence of a higher power, the creator, who created us and the world all around us. That higher power resided in the sky beyond the clouds and was always watching over all of us, so it was of utmost importance for us human beings to be honest and kind to all his creations. I was convinced and clear in my fundamentals of spirituality. My belief and faith in the existence of a higher power watching over us took its roots at that tender age.

And that faith only grew.

Chapter 4

Prince Charming

1978–1980

Growing up, I watched my grandmother, mother, and older sister work hard at their teaching jobs and equally hard at home. I saw them neglecting themselves to make everyone happy and do everything right. So once the fun of college was over and my classmates applied for jobs, I didn't want to work. I wanted to have an easy, relaxed life, unlike my mother and sister. I was given the freedom to decide about my life and my career. Still, if I decided to work, I convinced my parents I had a master's in social work and specialization in personnel management, so I'd have no trouble finding employment.

What I really wanted after I earned my degrees was to marry the man of my dreams and be a full-time homemaker and mother. Therefore, my dream included a Prince Charming as the provider. I was twenty-two and understandably naive. Marriage meant romance, traveling, wearing lots of jewelry, and bringing up lots of children. In my fantasy marriage, even with four kids, I had enough time to look after myself. Although these were dreams, getting married to an educated, successful professional with good future prospects was more realistic.

My close friend Vrinda's story led me to make the paradigm shift back from my dream world to the real one. The Deadly Trio made a plan to help Vrinda elope with her childhood sweetheart, Shubodh, as he was weak and could not gather the courage to tell his parents of his choice of betrothed. Nor did he turn up at the location we had decided. He left Vrinda to marry the Bengali girl his parents had chosen. Vrinda went through her grief.

A few months later, Vrinda told us she was marrying a scientist—a nuclear physicist—a match chosen by her parents. Vrinda had liked him instantly for his honesty and transparency and was excited about her upcoming marriage. "He dressed simply," she said with a smile, "in casual, plain clothes, and flip-flops. He was honest and rather direct and did not put any icing on the cake."

He told Vrinda with no hesitation that, in addition to running the household, he needed a partner to support him in looking after his aging parents, both of whom suffered from dementia. His modesty appealed to her, and she planned to accept marriage in place of the new job she'd been offered.

I was extremely touched by what Vrinda had decided to take on. My respect for her went up exponentially, and I felt her experience matured me soon thereafter.

I wanted to get married even more after Vrinda's marriage. Since I didn't have any particular match in mind, my wedding would have to be arranged. Traditionally, marriages in India are arranged by parents or other relatives or by word of mouth among neighbors.

But for families like mine who didn't have relatives, it was common to place an ad in the matrimonial column of a popular national newspaper, which appeared every weekend. We'd receive replies from prospective candidates, sort through the letters, and reply back to suitable ones. "Boy" or "girl" was how we referred to an unmarried man or woman looking to get married, regardless of their age. The process was very much like a job interview. The best candidate would get the job.

I went through the list of parameters in my head. It was long, but it had five must-haves. I was always attracted to men in uniform—army, air force, or navy—or living abroad somewhere like the United States, but my future match had to be:

- Financially independent
- Intelligent and well educated (wearing glasses was a big "no")
- Living on his own, independent of his parents
- Brought up and living in a posh area of South Delhi
- Mature and emotionally balanced, with a modern outlook

The man of my dreams would have to meet all five criteria. And love would come with time because familiarity breeds love. Love after marriage was a given. It was the main part of the marriage equation. I had watched my parents in their seemingly perfect, loving, close relationship for twenty-two years of my life, so I couldn't fathom someone not being in love after marriage.

One night, while my mom and I were taking a walk after dinner, I asked, "So, when do you think I will be getting married? Vrinda has already gotten married. Mrinal is engaged to be married to her sweetheart."

I would be the last of The Deadly Trio to get married.

Mom didn't answer, so I continued. "I think you should start looking for a match for me. It may take a while. It had taken more than two years to match a suitable boy for Leena." Mom remained quiet and we turned toward home. When we got home, Mom shared my thoughts with Dad.

"So, tell us about your boyfriend," he said to me. "You must have one."

"No," I said, astonished.

They were both surprised. "We didn't think you would put us through the hard work of looking for a match for you the way your older sister did."

I was taken aback. They had never told me this. I wished they had, especially since the only reason I didn't have a boyfriend was to not cause them shame or embarrassment or "betray" them. I thought love marriages were still not accepted by society in general.

My classmates who could be potential marriage candidates were not yet employed and settled. And I had not even had a crush on anyone since the boy with the Fiat.

We placed an ad:

A suitable match required for a Brahmin Hindu girl, five foot two inches tall, master's in social work, a doctor or engineer preferred, no dowry, caste no bar.

Caste is a form of social stratification characterized by the lineage, social interaction, social status, and functional status. Three thousand years back Aryans, the descendants of Indians, divided the population into four categories: Brahmins, the priests; Kashatriyas, the warriors; Vaishyas, the merchants; and Shudras, the ones who served the other three classes.

Although the class system still exists, it has more or less diminished in urban society. My family never believed in the caste system. We were Brahmins, respected all other classes and never boasted of our class. For me, education, intelligence, and the values a person had been brought up with mattered most.

Mom and Dad were quite sure I'd make it tough for them to choose a befitting groom for myself, exactly the way I made a fuss choosing to buy my clothes. They knew I had a long wish list.

Several replies came that week. We sat with the file box full of letters in front of us, and my parents and I sifted through them.

One letter stood out, but not in a good way. It was written in a blue-colored inland letter, which folded into an envelope. Very few details about the boy were written, stating simply he worked outside Delhi as an industrial engineer. It listed his salary, education, and job title but no other details. I picked a few letters from potential matches and gave them to Dad to review and respond. I put the letter the industrial engineer under the box of letters we were filtering through. Not only were the details sparse, but also the postmark was unacceptable. It had been mailed from Gurmandi, which meant "jaggery market," a town from Old Delhi area located inland.

I hoped to get married in New Delhi neighborhood in which I had grown up with progressive outlook: Gulmohar Park, Niti Bagh, Vasant Vihar, Maharani Bagh, Friends Colony, or a similar neighborhood. When I read the return address, I didn't want my dad to reply.

With a few shortlisted letters in hand for replying, Dad rose from the table, but before leaving, he lifted up the box and grabbed the letter slipped underneath it.

I pulled it from his hand and put it back under the box. I said, "No, we are not replying to this letter."

"But they are Hindu Brahmins," he said.

"But you and I do not care about the caste, Dad!"

"If we can get a good Hindu Brahmin boy, why not?" Dad asked. "They are more compassionate people. In any case, this is the first round. Let me reply to them, and if you do not like the boy, we can always decline." He took the letter.

Within a week, we'd forgotten which letter was connected to which boy. The first boy came to see me by himself. He was smart, good-looking, and from a neighboring state, outside New Delhi which was already a "no" from me. I preferred someone from New Delhi, if it was to be from India, or from abroad, especially the United States. His first question was whether I liked Chinese food. I was looking for more depth in a person rather than whose first conversation rested around food.

The second boy came with his father, who was the head of the English department at Delhi University, a prestigious position. The boy was in the army and stationed as a pilot in the airfield. I loved a man in uniform, and the boy was tall, handsome, and modern-looking. I still remember his name—Captain Rajiv Sharma. We talked for an hour in the adjacent room by ourselves. It was a big okay from both sides. But my dad didn't agree. Since this boy was flying planes, chances were higher of him having an accident and dying an unnatural death.

There were two more proposals: one from Canada, and the other from the United States. Both boys were from good families, and both the Canadian and US embassies vouched for their character.

But the next morning, Dad walked up to me, hugged me, and said, "I cannot even dream of sending you so far away. I cannot lose you."

A couple of days later, Mr. and Mrs. Behl from our neighborhood within the campus knocked at our door. We had hardly any familiarity with them. They told Dad they were here at the request of one of their close friends who'd responded to the ad. "What could be better?" my parents said to me. "The Behls are vouching for the boy's family."

My parents agreed the Sharma family could visit us.

The day of the meeting, I had returned home from my summer job at Escorts Motorcycle Division, the manufacturer of famous Yamaha motorcycles. It was a long day, but I changed into a salwar suit and a dupatta. The house was set up, and my parents were waiting. Ravi and Leena were married and lived with their spouses away in other towns, and Neel, my confidant and co-conspirator, was vacationing with his friends. My mom gave the signal when they neared our house, so we all stood by the kitchen window overlooking the street, watching the Behls, and an elderly man presumably the father of the boy, followed by one woman and three younger men, approach the house.

The woman and three of the men appeared to be the same age. Two were tall and lean, and the third was shorter. I went to the bedroom when they got closer, while my parents waited in the living room. Both rooms had doors opening onto the front porch, and I had bamboo chick blinds on the bedroom door rolled up a bit so I could catch a glimpse of the boy as he entered the house. I saw only the last one to enter, the shorter one wearing glasses.

Mom immediately came into the bedroom and whispered, "The boy seems like a good match, so do not make a fuss."

For thirty minutes, I waited in the bedroom, guessing which of the three boys was for me. Mom ushered me into the over-crowded living room.

The room filled with my parents and guests was suddenly quiet. I was uncomfortable showing myself to a bunch of people, asking for their approval. But since it was customary, I had not taken any objection to it.

"Namaste," I said, greeting them with folded hands. Each eye was staring at me. Mrs. Behl introduced the boy. He was the shorter one with glasses.

"I just came from work," I said, to break the odd silence. I continued, "I travel to Faridabad Industrial area every day on a chartered bus to Escorts Motorcycle Division. I am doing a summer job in the human resources department there," moving my head around to address everyone and also have a look at the boy. They all listened and nodded or smiled, while they gazed at me. My mom, in the meantime, was serving tea and snacks.

The boy whose name was Vijay asked, "What project you are doing?" And this helped build the conversation.

Then the woman, who it turned out was the boys' sister, Shiela, said, "We should give them a chance to talk to each other." This meant the family had approved me.

I got up and went to the next room, and the boy, Vijay, followed. Obviously, the doors were kept open.

The first question he asked was, "What are your aspirations?" He kind of sold me with that one. We talked about what books we read, the university, and my summer job. We talked easily and naturally, just getting acquainted.

After about twenty-five minutes, Shiela came in. "How much will you both talk? Leave something for next time."

With that, we went back to the living room.

Before leaving, we all stood on the veranda, and I observed Vijay keenly. He had a very charming smile. He also had nicely-textured, lustrous, thick black hair, parted neatly on the side, and long side-burns with a few gray hairs, which made him look fashionable and mature. He wore a striped shirt and dark gray, nicely fitting pants. I had not realized I would be attracted to someone quite older than I was. He was close to thirty-one. And while the glasses were a big "no" on my checklist, they were black-rimmed and suited him, giving him an intellectual, professorial appearance. However, I hadn't made up my mind. There were several other matches on our list.

The next day, I had just come back from work when Dad called Mom at home, "Vijay is in my office, can you come over?" I remained inquisitive to know why Vijay was in Dad's office.

Mom came back an hour later. "Go outside quickly," she said. "He's waiting to take you out for coffee. He is leaving town tomorrow."

I had not yet changed into casuals after coming from work, so I stepped outside and down the front path to meet him. I saw him watching me walk toward him and we exchanged a smile. He later told me he was impressed by my gait. I sat on the back of his two-wheeler scooter, keeping my hand softly on his right shoulder while riding and we drove to a coffee place outside the engineering campus.

We agreed on a corner seat by the window, and I picked up the menu to let him start the conversation. I caught him looking at my hands. He said he was hungry and would like to order some snacks. So, our conversation began with our likes and dislikes over the snacks in the menu before he picked a couple and ordered. He appeared bright and smart with good command of English. He constantly looked into my eyes and kept his smile while we talked. There was something about his smile—it was addictive. He spoke in a soft tone, which carried conviction and authority on the few subjects we had time to discuss. His charm had started to work on me. His continued gaze with a demure smile suggested he already liked me. He conveyed he had no monetary responsibility of his family, only moral, being the eldest son, which meant keeping himself involved with their general well-being. On the other hand, he took no money from them, either. He was a self-made man. He'd paid his college tuition himself by teaching mathematics to students. His transparency was a big check mark.

Then he said something I would not have expected so soon. "I would really like to spend my life with you."

I shied away from his comment and tried to hide the expression of surprise on my face by just smiling. We parted with me saying, "Let's see what our parents decide." I was not decided, either. It required some thinking.

I missed my younger brother, Neel, deeply in that moment. I knew he could have helped me make this decision. Even so, my dad surely wouldn't agree to this match. Vijay lived four hundred miles away, and the only public transportation was a twelve- to fourteen-hour trip by bus. A flight from America would take less time or the same time. Why would he agree to this proposal when he had rejected earlier proposals from Canada and the United States?

A day later, Dev and Shiela arrived unannounced in the evening. They wanted to see me one more time. Vijay's father kept smiling affectionately at me, while Shiela praised her brother. She said Vijay's college friends had stopped by the day before to give them Vijay's message.

"She's the one Vijay wants," his friends told them.

My parents were then invited to visit Vijay's family at their house. They returned satisfied with their way of living, although I would learn later, Vijay's family had exaggerated their assets, and my parents took them at face value.

Since no eyeglasses was a major part of my parameter list, although petty, I was in a quandary about Vijay wearing them. Indra, my close friend's husband who was a CPA, wore glasses, too. I called to ask if glasses got in the way. If I was in the mood to kiss and my husband said, "Wait, I have to remove my glasses," it might ruin the mood.

She laughed and said, "No, the glasses don't get in the way."

She mentioned this to her husband, and he teased me. "Wow, what a question to ask!"

My parents and I didn't believe in horoscopes or numerology, but the in-laws asked for mine to match the compatibility points. Later, my sister-in-law told me that thirty-two out of thirty-six points matched. Even though I didn't know how it worked, I knew I'd passed, and the engagement was set for June 23, 1980. It was now official.

The engagement party, which was ritually arranged by the girl's side, was a big affair: colorful tents, decorations, caterers, high tea with snacks, and a variety of desserts and drinks arranged in the lawns of our house. Many relatives and friends came from

Vijay's side. The ceremony started with a *pundit* (priest) chanting in Sanskrit, giving blessings to Vijay and me. Vijay slid a ring onto my finger, my hand shaking, a bit shy to be in front of so many strangers. As part of the ceremony, my parents gifted Vijay's family boxes of sweets and fruit baskets, as was customary. I heard my dad saying to his dad, "From today, my daughter is yours and your son is mine."

I couldn't hear his dad's response.

The marriage date was firmed up for December 6, 1980.

My friends came around to look at the ring. I liked the ring but later that night, I noticed one small diamond on one side missing. It was the very first night, and I had lost a diamond out of the engagement ring! I felt terrible and had trouble falling asleep. I hoped it was not a bad omen!

After the engagement, shopping for the wedding began. My dad, mom, and I went to the choicest shops and exhibitions to buy my saris, bags, and heels. I'd come home and parade my new outfits in front of my parents. They said they wouldn't be able to see me wearing them since I'd be living so far away, so I had better show them then. The shopping for kitchen utensils, cutlery, and crystal came next, then furniture for living room, and bedroom stuff, all a part of the trousseau.

Vijay paid a visit two months after the engagement. He called Dad to say he was in town and wanted to see me. I went with him for coffee. He touched my hand a couple of times when we were seated. It felt warm, cozy, and assuring.

Vijay said he'd taken ten vacation days for the wedding, but the last five days he would be busy with his first cousin's wedding, which would be held immediately after ours. He looked into my eyes and said softly there would be no time for a honeymoon and finances would be short. To make him feel less embarrassed, I said, "In any case, we're going to be by ourselves after ten days of staying in your father's house, so it's all right if there's no honeymoon."

We were exchanging letters. I wrote almost every other day, offering the details of my day and asking him about his. Typically, he replied twice a week. I used to sit on the patio for the mail to arrive, and if the postman had a letter, he would hold it up on his bicycle from a distance and wave his hand—by then, even he got familiar with me waiting on the patio. I soon developed feelings for Vijay, and he did for me. I even started to keep his picture under my pillow, filled with a possessive warmth.

Then came a disturbing letter, which seemed to be written with malice. I read it a few times and couldn't make out what it meant.

"You do not love me enough," he'd written. "You write about yourself. What about me? I expect you to love me more."

My dad sensed my despair.

He smiled and said, "He needs you to write some love language, so do it."

I had shared with Vijay in my letters about my signing of the no-dowry memorandum in college as a statement against the practice. When we were buying my trousseau stuff, I asked him if my parents should buy furniture since we wouldn't be living in Delhi.

"The furniture will go to my family," he wrote.

I did not feel good about this, especially since I'd shared with him my beliefs. I kept thinking I'd write back to him to ask him about his response, but never did.

Weddings were typically a four- or five-day affair, a tradition from when travel took longer, and relatives came from afar. Mine was three days long. During this time, far relatives and close friends filled our house, and cooks were hired to prepare daily meals and sweets. The house was filled with chatter and fun.

There was one day of *sangeet*, an event to relish the joy with *dholak* (two-sided drum), folk songs, and dancing. The henna ceremony took place the next day, with henna specialists tattooing the palms of all female relatives. As the bride, I had henna tattoos with flowery designs covering my feet and hands. I had to sit with open palms for hours until the henna dried, to keep from ruining the tattoos.

On the third day, the wedding arrangements turned out beautifully. The decorations, an integral part of Indian weddings, were elegant and included the *mandap* (a stage where the bride and groom were seated), the guest seating, or the overall venue. The *pandal* (an open-sided venue) was all white, adorned with marigold and rose flowers, colorful decorations hanging from the top of the pandal, and lighted paper balloons hanging all around. It looked stunningly gorgeous. Festive Indian instrumental music, considered to be auspicious, welcomed the guests.

As the bride, I wore a red chanderi sari filled with gold thread work, gold jewelry, my mother's heirloom jewelry, and thick bangles. I had a light makeup, with my hair tied up into a bun and my head covered with the end of the sari.

The bridegroom's party, over two hundred relatives and friends known as *baraat*, entered the pandal with the groom on a horse, with Vijay's friends and cousins following. They danced to the beat of loud drums and Bollywood music.

When Vijay saw me, he complimented me, whispering, "Looking good."

I raised my head at him and smiled.

We exchanged garlands made out of marigold and rose flowers amid blessings and laughter. The sanctity of this tradition stated, "You are mine, from today on."

An elaborate dinner awaited all the guests, followed by the *pheras*. The pheras meant so much to me as they were the true promises made to each other that they will love and respect each other, look after each other and will be there for each other. I was quite emotional listening to the translations and interpretations of the Sanskrit mantras. This ceremony was quite similar to the vows at a Christian wedding.

Doli was the sad moment when I would have to leave my parents' house. It's customary for the bridegroom and his family to take the bride to their house to live with them. These were the most sentimental moments for the bride and her family, marking the end of a role as a daughter and readiness to establish herself as a wife and daughter-in-law. Most certainly, the bride and her family shed tears of separation. It was a gloomy time, unlike Western weddings, where the bride and groom leave the party in fun, smiling, and kissing.

I did shed tears, parting from my loving parents and siblings to go with strangers, not knowing when I would see them again.

My stomach wrenched even before pheras, as I knew the time for parting from my loved ones was a few hours away. My palms were cold and perspiring. The excitement of being a bride had vanished.

Early the next morning, at 5:00 a.m., Ravi, Neel, Leena, Jeej (as I called Leena's husband), Vrinda, and Mrinal walked me toward my in-laws' car. All of us were emotional, sobbing quietly, wiping our eyes and wet noses. As I came closer to the car, I searched for my mom and dad. I couldn't see them! My father-in-law and sister-in-law hurried Vijay and me along, impatient to get us into the car and to their house, not realizing I needed to say goodbye to my parents.

Finally, my mom came running from the house. She hugged me tightly before I stepped into the car. I broke down. Mom sobbed and signaled toward Dad, who stood off in a corner, wiping his eyes. He waved and came no closer. He didn't have the heart to give his darling daughter away with his own hands. I stepped away from the car, ran to him, and hugged him. He kissed my forehead, and so did Mom. It must have been the most grievous moment for them, parting with their daughter, as it was for me. Then I tore away from them and didn't look back. Neel opened the car door for me, his eyes red, and I slid inside, still sobbing. My new husband and my sister-in-law slid in from both sides and shut the car doors, and my heart sank. I had a similar weird feeling in my stomach that I always got riding on a giant Ferris wheel when it began its descent.

The reality of going away with strangers, to a house I had never been to before, hit me suddenly. I had bid farewell to my family of twenty-three years. My stomach was in knots, and I continued sobbing. Without any tissue in my hand, I used the corner of my sari to wipe my nose and tears.

Neither my sister-in-law nor my husband held my hand or wiped my tears. The car rolled while Ravi, Neel, Leena, and Jeej walked behind it, waving. I looked back, and then they all disappeared with the car gaining momentum.

I wanted to hold my husband's hand as an assurance he was there for me and would take care of me. But I refrained, as my older, unmarried sister-in-law sat on my other side. There was intense silence in the car, except for my own breathing.

When we arrived at my in-laws' house, still early in the morning, it was foggy and extremely cold as usual in the month of December in Delhi. I walked up to the second floor of what looked like a government flat. I was told to sit on a carpet on the floor, where I was surrounded by women and kids, my head and face half covered with the end of my sari. There were some more rituals and traditional ceremonies to be performed by the groom's family. I was tired, hungry, and groggy by noon, sitting in the middle of the room surrounded by women and kids.

I didn't know where the men were. Perhaps they were out on the veranda, relaxing after the long night.

I'd not had a glimpse of my husband since the car. I was eager to see him and peeked through the curtain on the door, but he was nowhere.

It was unlike a wedding scene in Hindi movies, where the bride was surrounded by giggling girls and boys. The groom would be next to her, teasing her, or they might hold hands assuring her, "Do not worry. I'm here with you. Don't feel like a stranger. You are doing well."

And the bride would blush.

By late that night, still in the same sari from the previous day, I was directed to the last room, where I found Vijay waiting.

We were staying for our first night together in a makeshift storeroom with big baskets filled with Indian sweets. On one side of the room was a full-size bed. I removed my jewelry and then lay down on the bed in my sari, and he lay down next to me. We could hear all the relatives in the next room, so we talked only in whispers.

Whenever I would move my hand, while talking and gesturing, my bangles would clatter. But these heirlooms from my mom weren't coming off my hand. So, my intelligent bridegroom found a solution. He took his socks out of his shoes and tied one on each wrist to silence the bangles, so their tinkling did not reach the adjoining room. We were in an embrace but nothing beyond it. Vijay felt too conscious with his father and sister in the next room with just a six-inch wall between us. I was not sure of the full "first night" act, as they called it, but I was relieved when Vijay refrained from anything other than holding each other.

As I was falling asleep, I heard some rattling. My eyes opened, and I saw three big fat rats of unusual size jumping between the baskets of sweets. Vijay quickly put his hand over my mouth to keep me from shrieking loudly. I hid under the covers, tucked from all sides, hugging Vijay, and fell asleep, feeling secure.

When I opened my eyes, it was already morning. Light filtered through the ventilator on top of the door. I jumped out of bed, and wearing the same sari with my head covered, came out of the room, and went to the kitchen, where all the women were crowded. Some of them were cutting veggies, some were preparing breakfast, and others were talking and giggling. They all stopped when I entered. They examined my face teasingly, asking after my first night. I smiled coyly.

They could not realize, my first night had been spent hiding in fear of giant rats.

Chapter 5

A Frog in the Well

1981–1982

Three months later, I found myself back in the same room with the big rats. However, this time, I was alone, not with my husband.

Before I had boarded the bus from Nandoli for New Delhi, Vijay had said, "I would like you to go to my father's house first and not share the incident with anyone on either side of the family."

Since I didn't know what lay ahead, I decided it was best to go to my in-laws' house first. My parents came to see me the next evening. I hadn't seen them since my wedding. Mom and Dad came to my bed side to hug me, all of us tearful, meeting after three months. Then they pulled their chairs next to the bed with concern in their eyes. The only information they had was that I'd nearly had a miscarriage. They were oblivious of the cause, and I was not going to tell them.

"Have you seen a doctor since you arrived?" my dad asked.

"No."

His eyes cringed, while his head moved sideways. Then he took a deep sigh. This meant he was going to take charge of the situation. He got up like a spring, took an extra pillow from the bed, and put it under my legs. He then asked Sanjay to get two bricks to raise the feet of my bed. Given his fascination with reading medical books, he knew what needed to be done. I could see my in-laws exchanging looks of disdain, as if to say, "Oh, so he comes and takes charge, but he does not make decisions in this house."

After the bed had been raised, my dad turned to my father-in-law.

"I would like to take my daughter home," he said. "She is unwell and would feel more comfortable with us around."

"This is not necessary," my father-in-law said. "We have doctors here, too."

Since India is a patriarchal society, the husband's family dominates and has the upper hand over the daughter-in-law's family. Their decision is taken as final and mustn't be questioned. There was nothing my father could do or say. He lowered his head and thumped himself back on the chair. His face had shrunken with signs of helplessness. I could feel his suppressed emotion through his clenched jaw. Mom pressed Dad's hand, asking him to remain calm.

The next evening, my father-in-law took me to a clinic. The male doctor advised bed rest. By the fourth day of quiet, anxiety, and fear of the unknown, I gathered the courage to ask my father-in-law if I could be sent to my parents' house.

I needed space and time to think, craving some pampering by my parents. This time, he agreed. His ego had been satisfied by declining my dad's initial request. In the absence of an elderly woman in the house, they didn't know how to take care of me. I hadn't yet visited an obstetrician, so it was more convenient for them to send me to my parents' house.

I felt pleased and incredibly light that he had agreed. When I arrived in a taxi, unannounced, my parents let out a deep sigh of relief. I was safe and cared for, under their roof. My parents were worried about my health, as well as the well-being of my child growing inside me. The next day, they took me to All India

Institute of Medical Sciences (AIIMS), the most reliable and prestigious government hospital in New Delhi.

Dr. Thakkar was the head of obstetrics and fortunately, would be my obstetrician. She walked into the examination room, dressed in a pastel sari under her doctor's white coat and with a big red dot (bindi) in the middle of her forehead, a mark of being married. She was polite, brusque, and assertive, either because of her personality or the long line of female patients she examined each day in the semi-free government-run hospital.

While the semi-free service attracted all strata of people from within, the main draw was the amount of talent available at AIIMS. All good interns aspired to practice there. She assured me all the doctors at AIIMS were experienced, handling hundreds of cases each day, and the hospital was equipped to handle any emergency and circumstance, which was a point in their favor since mine was a complicated pregnancy due to my near miscarriage.

I was impressed by Dr. Thakkar's professional demeanor. She advised complete bed rest for the remaining term and a shot of weekly Proluton injections to strengthen the uterine muscles so the fetus wouldn't be expelled. Dad arranged for a male nurse from the IT hospital to give my injections. I was to stay in my parents' house due to the need for bed rest. This was a relief and a blessing.

Once I was established in my parents' house, the beneficiary of all their comforting, I felt more at ease, both physically and mentally. Although they both went to work each day, my mom would come home earlier in the afternoon before Dad did in the evening.

I continued to have anxiety, but now it was my child's health that pushed me to remain cheery to give positive vibes.

My appetite had increased two-fold. I had a craving for *rasgulla*, and Mom bought the sweet dumplings in bulk, keeping them in the fridge for me.

The fetus was growing well. My hair looked shiny and long. My skin glowed. Some of the women in the neighborhood visited and commented I would deliver a girl from the way I looked. Their prediction made me happy. I had always wanted my first child to be a daughter, whom I could nurture and dress in cute clothes. I also wanted a girl child who would grow up to become the voice of women who were treated as the weaker sex in our society, who would stand for her own rights and fight for freedom from ancient taboos set for women.

A couple of months passed, and there was no communication from Vijay. I had not expected it, either. But one late evening, he showed up. Dad opened the door, surprised to see his son-in-law.

He welcomed him to the living room and hollered, "Look who is here!" Both he and my mom were still unaware of the truth. Mom quickly came to me to announce Vijay's arrival.

I forced a fake smile. I didn't know what to think. After a few moments, I walked into the living room, not wanting my parents to think there was anything wrong between us. However, they surely had an inkling something wasn't right since there'd been no phone calls or letters. I had refused to talk about it. I did not want to have a confrontation in front of them.

I wasn't sure if I felt any emotions or was devoid of them. Maybe a mixture of both or maybe, confusingly, nothing at all.

"Hello, what a surprise!" I said, sitting on the sofa next to Dad.

A sheepish smile tugged at Vijay's lips, mouth skewed to the right, which was typical of him when he was embarrassed or guilty. His gaze met mine. He had dark circles below his eyes, and he raked his hair with his fingers. He was trying to figure out the genuineness of my smile and my verdict. I couldn't keep my gaze at him, so I immediately turned my face.

After the formalities of serving him tea and exchanging a few words, my parents left us alone.

"What are you doing here?" I asked.

He immediately got up to sit next to me on the sofa. Leaning closer, he took my hand in his. "Did you think about me these past months?"

I pulled my hand. He repulsed me. Didn't he understand what he had done to me? Was he manipulating me now?

Then, just like that, he was on his knees. "I'm so sorry. I am ashamed. It shouldn't have happened. I'm a dumbass. I am a foolish man. But you are intelligent. You should have stopped me. Why didn't you stop me? Why did you let me do that to you? What will I do without you?" He pulled my hand to his cheek. "Slap me now. I deserve it."

I clenched my teeth, my heart beating as fast as the wings of a hummingbird. Why was he apologizing now? What had changed? What did he mean, he was an ass? Was that a way to excuse his actions? What did he mean by saying I should have stopped him? Was he putting the blame on me? Was he truly sorry?

Seeing him sitting on his knees on the floor, a man I had loved, had been intimate with, pleading in front of me and asking for forgiveness, I did not know what to do with it all. I'd never witnessed such a scene, not even in movies where the stories revolved around male chauvinism. It was only the villain who pleaded for forgiveness.

Okay, he felt bad. He was out of his senses. Did he really mean it?

I was quiet, avoiding his gaze.

He continued to assure me that there would be no more incidents of abuse. Sitting at my feet, holding my hands tight and not letting me free them, he said, "I will not let go of these hands until you forgive me."

My parents were in the next room, and I was worried they might be listening or walking in any moment. Watching him plead and beg for my forgiveness, I was clouded with a desire to let go of my resentment toward him. I was pregnant with his child. I might cling to his promise and give him a chance, relief from the chaos in my life and my unborn child's life.

My heart seemed to change. My mind told me God had put some sense into his head, so I should forgive him for what he did.

"It's okay," I said, loosening my hands from his grip, then shaking them as if to rid them of his touch. Perhaps, my mind had let go, but heart had not yet. I held him by his shoulders and asked him to sit back on the sofa. He got up and kissed my cheek with a loud smack, which embarrassed me, as my parents could certainly hear it. I wasn't sure if his exuberance was born of relief or if, because he was unsure if I'd shared the drama with my parents, he meant to deliver a message to them— "All is fine between your daughter and me."

My dad walked past the living room. From where he stood, it appeared everything was indeed fine.

I was still confused. The clarity was missing. But the stark truth that I was carrying his child inside me remained. I wanted to let go of the episode to free my mind, to feel relieved of the pain. Forgiving him was the only discernible solution to attain freedom of my mind.

Vijay started writing letters after the visit. I also made an attempt to reply, to keep the relationship alive. His were comforting letters and soon enough, I found myself becoming hopeful.

I could feel the vibes of joy seeping into the environment. I did not have to hide myself behind my fake smiles anymore. I was happy and smiled genuinely. I was delighted to be a mom soon. My child had started to move and kick inside me. That was the ultimate, blessed sentiment of becoming a mother.

My mom, after coming home from work, would sew nappies from soft white toweling material, putting pink silk piping on, per my desire. I often watched her sewing and knitting for my child, their grandchild. Although this would not be their first, their enthusiasm was not less than their previous grandchildren. Watching her knit distinct colors in different patterns in a rhythm and listening to the needles clicking was very comforting and therapeutic. I would have loved to do this with my own hands for my little baby, but since I was mainly lying down, I was unable to. However, I would fulfill my desire by helping Mom with hemming the frocks or knitting some with no patterns while I sat back with pillows propped up.

During my thirty-fourth week of pregnancy, Vijay surprised me with his second visit. Mom opened the door, and he immediately walked into the bedroom. He hugged me. I was equally excited to see him. I wondered if I missed him and hugged him back.

He pulled the chair close to the bed and sat, holding my hand. "I have great news to share. I have taken up a job in Delhi so that you can stay back in your favorite city, New Delhi, and be close to both families. I will soon look for apartments near Nehru Place, in the center of New Delhi, where we will move after your delivery," he said, all in one breath. He peered into my eyes, searching for a reaction.

"That's great news. How did it all work out?"

"I happened to talk to the consultants working for MGM tires. They hired me in their consulting group in Delhi." He shrugged his shoulders while his arms opened as he completed the sentence. His charming smile was back.

"I am truly happy," I said. "That's a good move."

❋ ❋ ❋

At the onset of my thirty-sixth week, Dr. Thakkar admitted me to the hospital due to the swelling in my feet and body. The next morning, Wednesday, November 18, Dr. Thakkar came on her early morning rounds at 7:30 a.m. and announced she was going to induce my labor for a timely delivery. I was wheeled into the prep room. Mom, Dad, Leena, and Jeej came to the hospital. Inside the labor room, after an hour of inducing, the first contraction gripped me with an unimaginably excruciating pain, which took my breath away.

With every contraction after that, I felt I'd die of a cardiac arrest. How could a heart the size of a fist bear pain the size of a mountain? Dr. Saha, the young house surgeon, heard my shrieks and came to my rescue by offering his arm for me to bear down on. With each contraction, I gripped his arm harder as the pain rose, releasing it when it subsided and gripping when it inevitably returned. During the intervals, he gave me pep talks, just like a doctor does to a toddler before giving a shot.

"What do you want, a son or a daughter?"

"A daughter," I said.

His eyes widened, and several lines appeared on his forehead when he raised his eyebrows. "Why a girl? Everyone wants a boy!" he asked, sounding a bit amused.

"I want my first child to be a girl."

And then the thought lingered in my head. Isn't it a woman who understands another woman better?

I had named her Nina, and Vijay liked it, too. I was so certain my first child would be a girl; I had picked only a girl's name.

By 4:00 p.m., the nurse had finally felt the baby's head crowning. I was wheeled to the delivery room. When I saw Dr. Thakkar, I felt so relieved, I relaxed to take a brief moment of respite. My relaxed muscles stopped my contractions.

Dr. Thakkar, in a loud, ruffled voice, very unlike her, said, "Push, push, push!"

I was trying my best. For the past eight hours, I'd been pushing. Utterly exhausted, I had no energy left.

Then she saw the head and asked for forceps to pull the child out. At 5:02 p.m., I heard a baby's shriek, and then my body went limp. After about five minutes, a nurse came holding a beautiful white and pink child wrapped in a white towel. She declared a girl had been born. She was a real beauty. My dream had come true! I took a deep breath of relief. *I did it.*

Once they'd taken her to the nursery, my father hurried off to visit her. He counted her fingers and toes and checked all her body parts to make sure, externally at least, the near miscarriage had done no damage.

Months after I gave birth, my dad told me he'd worried about me delivering a healthy, fully-formed baby from the minute I'd come to stay with them.

My dad and mom paced toward the nursery when the nurse told them they could bring Nina. Dad held my little daughter, wrapped in a pink baby blanket and wearing a pink baby suit, to my bed in the ward. She was soft like a cotton ball, her eyes dark black and her round head full of silky black hair, which had been parted neatly on the side. The forceps had left a rose-pink mark on both sides of her rosy cheeks. Her beautiful pink fingers with manicured nails surprised me. I was amazed to see this child, who looked like a fairy. *God had taken time to make her*, I thought. My eyes teared up with joy and gratitude for giving me this moment of bliss.

Vijay came in the late evening to see his daughter. Watching him approach us brought back the unpleasant, accumulated memory of his kicking me in the stomach. I cringed.

His face brightened as he gazed at his beautiful daughter, held her hand, and touched her feet and her cheeks. He was immersed in her and kept smiling at me, his eyes filled with appreciation, as though I presumed, he said, "Thank you for giving us a daughter."

I felt the genuineness in his affection and finally allowed myself to feel happy. I sighed, and with that sigh a deep respite settled over me. He was my daughter's father, and we were going to be together. I once again let the dream of our future together flourish.

Customarily, a woman stayed with her parents for the first forty days following her delivery. This gave her a chance to completely recuperate before she was sent back to the in-laws, where she was expected to dive into the daily chores. I thought the underlying reason was for the husband to sleep away from his wife during that period, which distance ensured. During this time, women were massaged each day with mustard oil by either a masseuse or the maidservant and fed a special nutritious diet full of protein and good fats to restore her energy and stressed muscles.

On our first day at home, and for many days after, Mom massaged Nina with mustard oil and gave her a warm bath, not allowing her to be touched by the maidservant for a massage or bath. This was my mom's love toward her grandchild.

While Nina and I were at my parents' home, Vijay visited us most days after work and sat next to Nina. He adored her, held her hand, and played with her.

During those forty days, Vijay told me he was looking for rental apartments in South Delhi. By January 1982, the forty-day recuperating period had ended and since Vijay hadn't yet found a place for us to live, which didn't surprise me, we left for Gurmandi, Old Delhi, to stay with my in-laws until he got the apartment. I had no issue with staying with them for a while to let them enjoy Nina, who'd bring joy to their quiet home. I had no prejudice against them.

Everyone, including Shiela, was delighted to have the first newborn in the family. It made me happy to see everyone enjoying the new addition.

This was a new beginning. Vijay and I were starting over in the same room we had when we were first married. I tried not to think of the big rats. But the small room was overstuffed, as it was apparently being used as a storage room, which suffocated me in the night when the doors were closed. I was claustrophobic.

Nina kept me up every night, then slept in the mornings, which made things difficult since I was expected to get up at 5:30 a.m. along with the rest of the household. Each morning, I'd cover my head, come out of the room fully dressed, and look for my father-in-law, so I could touch his feet. Whether he was in the kitchen, in the bedroom, or on the veranda, sitting or standing, I'd bend to touch one foot and then the other with my right hand while he'd touch my head as a gesture of blessing. This had been the norm observed for years, and I was supposed to follow it, as my sister-in-law had told me when I first arrived after my marriage. Only after I fulfilled this duty, would the day start for me, whereas in my parents' house, the old ritual was not followed, luckily for their daughters-in-law's.

Each morning, after the four men had left for work, I helped my sister-in-law with household chores, dusting and cleaning, though I never met her standards. Anything I did, whether it was cooking or washing clothes was not good enough. I wouldn't get far before she'd snatch the duster from my hand and tell me to go sit down, since I obviously didn't know how to perform the task correctly. Day after day, my fear of her increased.

Shiela clearly envied me. Sensitive to her insecurities, I wanted to show my compassion, but she gave me no chance to open up with her. Instead, she subjugated me to the role of her helper, as she took the traditional, societal role of an older sister-in-law. Her overpowering tone and taut body language troubled me. I wished she would have taken me under her wing and mentored me as an older sister.

When the men came home at the end of the day, she magnified my smallest errors. When I ruined a dish, Shiela would not only blame me but also not let me fix it. If I made lentil curry in a pressure cooker and all the water evaporated, she wouldn't let me boil water separately to add to the lentils to make it into the right consistency. Instead, she would serve the lentils as they were, mashed and lumpy, so everyone could see my unworthiness. This was all to embarrass me, to show Vijay she was the expert. In doing so, she maintained her control. Slowly, her attitude toward me, the constant scrutiny, growing criticism, and persistent intimidation created severe anxiety in me.

On weeknights, the men would return home, one by one, my husband being the last to arrive. I soon realized he'd stopped off for a drink after work. He was careful not to appear drunk in front of his father. If not for my sister-in-law's malicious attitude toward me, I might have found this a more hopeful sign of Vijay drinking within his limits.

The doorbell rang late one evening. Vijay must have arrived. I got up to open the door, but before I could, Shiela did. Vijay looked at me, handed me his briefcase, and followed Shiela to the covered patio. I went back to our room. Shiela had a habit of talking in whispers. I let them talk. The brother-and-sister sharing were okay with me. Vijay would come to our room at his will after seeing his father and brother. Often, he wouldn't say a word. He would just stare at me, eyes cold yet filled with unpleasantness. Used to his stare, I sensed he was angry, and I'd try to stay out of his way. Since it was his father's house and close quarters, Vijay couldn't shout at me in front of them. Instead, he would broadcast his hostility through his long, ghastly, intimidating, hateful stares, which were quite frequent.

When he tried to level me with that stare, I would know my sister-in-law had said something against me, or that he was annoyed about some issue unknown to me. I understood his sister was making him feel guilty for getting married before she could. As a result, he treated me as though I were invisible, to show his sister and others he wasn't enjoying our marriage. Dev had tried finding a suitable boy for Shiela for many years, but he and her brothers had remarkably lofty standards set for Shiela and rejected any proposals.

One morning, after Nina had kept me up all night, I overslept through the morning hustle outside my room as the four men used the facilities to brush, shower, and get dressed for work.

My father-in-law knocked hard on my door. "You need to be awake on time!" he called.

"Bauji," this is how we addressed him, "Nina has kept me awake all night."

"No arguments with Bauji!" I heard Shiela's assertive voice.

The door to our room was expected to stay open all day. I wasn't given the freedom or privacy to be in the room with closed doors and enjoy baby talks with my daughter or be with my husband on the weekends. No one, including Vijay, cared that I was a new mother, which was also taking its toll, especially when Nina kept me awake all night. I couldn't carve out even a moment for myself.

My life was in reverse gear. Instead of progressing, I was regressing. My laughter had vanished. I walked around the house with my eyes downcast, my shoulders slumped. There was no love, laughter, or romance. The Prince Charming of my dreams was lost, as were my dreams. I was choked in that environment, and I would look for ways to remain cheery.

When Vijay came home from work, I asked him to take me out for a glass of juice to revive my utterly low energy. I was desperate for fresh air, away from the four walls of the house. I also planned to buy some essential baby things for Nina. Vijay looked at his sister to get her permission. After she nodded yes, we headed out to the shopping center on his scooter, me sitting behind him, my arms wrapped around him to get a feel of intimacy and closeness. It felt so good to be out, to be alone with Vijay. I didn't want the ride to end, but the marketplace was less than ten minutes away. Vijay stopped at a fresh juice stand and ordered a pomegranate juice for me and an orange juice for himself. We both were quiet. I wanted Vijay to say something but perhaps he didn't have anything to say, either. I sensed a void getting created between us.

We walked through the market toward the kids' clothing store. While I was inside the shop, I looked for Vijay. He stood by, pacing and impatient, in a hurry to go back home. I wanted him to participate in buying dress for our little princess, but he seemed remote. I paid the cashier and came out.

I said, "What's the hurry?" and, once again, he fixed me with his cold stare, so I kept quiet.

I was in need of menstrual pads for my monthly cycle, so I ran in and out of the store quickly. I'd noticed Shiela didn't use pads. Instead, she used cloth strips cut from worn-out clothes.

On the way home, I sat behind him, maintaining my distance, and not holding him anymore. I was angry at him for giving me his stares for no fault of mine. I took the bags containing my purchases to our room. And then I heard a commotion from the living room.

"Why did she take the bags inside?" I heard Shiela ask Vijay in a loud tone. "She thinks she is not one of us. She thinks she is better? She thinks we will eat all the chocolates she has brought for herself and kept hidden from us."

I stepped out of my room to clarify my stance. I saw my father-in-law, both brothers-in-law, and my husband letting Shiela scream. Before turning to go back, I said, "I bought essentials for Nina, and sanitary pads for me, which I did not want to keep out in the veranda."

She glared at me, her hands at her waist, her voice raised as if she wanted to hurt me. I had no idea from where her anger had erupted. She then turned her gaze toward Vijay and said, pointing at me, "She thinks she is better than we are," and thudded out of the room.

I kept looking at Vijay, silently urging him to support me. I did not deserve this. He didn't say a word in my defense but rather gave me his hateful stare with his eyes wide open and nostrils flaring, which always fluttered my heart and gave me pain. And then he simply rushed out of the room. An easy escape.

I looked at my father-in-law for consolation.

Without looking at me, he said, "You should have kept all the shopping bags on the table in the veranda, as we all do," and walked away. My embarrassed gaze turned toward the two brothers left in the room. Ajay and Sanjay glared at me, as if I had committed a horrendous crime by taking the bags to my room. I walked out, straight to my room, helpless and hopeless, my sobs stuck in my throat. I was still a stranger in this house. I was not a part of the family yet.

I was at fault either way. If I had kept the bags out with the sanitary pads in them, then Shiela would complain I had no shame in keeping sanitary pads in front of her widowed father and unmarried brothers. I felt dejected and insulted in front of five people standing against me. They were all on the side of the dictator.

Vijay entered our room after an hour. I was waiting for him, not with any hopes but to once more clarify my intentions. He came in with a clenched jaw, furrowed brows, and intense eyes. He raised his finger in front of my face. "My family is my first priority. Make sure they feel respected. I do not want to see them upset."

There was no need to waste my words on deaf ears and a closed mind. I turned and lay next to my lifeline, my Nina. I held her to my chest, and wrapping my arm around her, closed my eyes to sleep.

The constant anxiety from treading cautiously every day had turned into severe anxiety and depression. I started to contemplate what method might be least painful to end my life. I missed my parents and my siblings. There was no phone line here to call them unless I walked to the nearby marketplace and asked a shopkeeper to use his phone. However, I was fearful the shopkeeper might know Vijay's family.

I started to write a journal in a blank, old, pocket diary, which I had found in one of the drawers in the room. My first sentence was, "Dear Diary, you are my only friend in this big vast, wretched world." I could not continue writing in the journal for long due to the fear of someone finding it and reading it.

The next morning, after the shopping bag incident, after Ajay, Sanjay, and Vijay left for work, Shiela and my father-in-law also went out to visit his brother's family, to nearby town. I was relieved to have some space. I wore my comfortable jeans and shirt, from my college time which I had quietly stored in the suitcase. I switched on the radio to my favorite radio station and hummed the songs while playing with Nina. In the background, my mind did not stop chattering. *What will happen next? What does my future hold? How did I land in this mess?*

At 2:00 p.m., I put Nina to sleep and took a nap myself. I got up with a jerk, at 4:00 p.m., and quickly changed back to Indian dress. I thought of preparing some dinner in case Dev and Shiela took longer to be back. I put lentils in the cooker and started dicing the vegetables. Ajay and Sanjay returned from work, and without saying a word to me, went into the living room. I went back to the kitchen and brewed tea, but when I brought it to them, they said they did not feel like it.

It did not seem normal. When I had finished cooking, I again went in to ask them if I could set dinner, but once again, their tones were short, and both said they weren't hungry. Neither looked at me. I could sense the tightness in the air, perhaps lingering anger from the previous night.

Then the doorbell rang. Vijay staggered in. Without looking at me or having a word with me, he lurched to the living room, his head bobbling.

I brought Vijay a glass of water. I didn't want any scene to be created for not bringing him water. He raised his arm to signal me to keep it at the table. Both brothers looked at Vijay disapprovingly, suggesting that coming home drunk was unacceptable in that house, that their boundary was threatened. They were both teetotalers, at least in the eyes of their father and sister. I was not certain if they ever consumed alcohol in society.

However, Vijay took my arm and squealed, "Tell them why I got married. Look at me and tell them why I got married!"

My heart raced, as I knew where this was going.

He blabbered, his head still moving up and down, gaze on the floor, hands dangling in the air, he said, "Because they all wanted me to. I never wanted to. But I thought you would support my family." He looked at me with contempt, his eyes enraged, his jaw clenched tight.

I stared back into his eyes, breathing heavily.

He sprang toward me and said, "How dare you stare at me?" He caught me tightly by the wrist, dragged me into the bedroom, and slapped me hard.

My ears rang from the force of the slap. I put my hand on my burning cheek, recoiled, and released my arm, almost ready to slap him back. His eyes moved fast from one object to the other: a paperweight, a book, a brush. While my gaze moved with him, trying to see what he was going to pick to hit me with, he raised his arm again and slapped me one more time.

That was it. I was done! Pressing my hands to my burning cheeks, I slowly shook my head from side to side. I kept my tears from falling and held a big lump in my throat. No more. I would not shed my tears for this incorrigible man. I was not going to tolerate this injustice.

He clearly hated me. I was done with this unscrupulous and uncouth man!

Sanjay and Ajay heard the commotion and had not come to my rescue. I picked up Nina, who was profusely crying, and went out, down the street, straight to the marketplace to make a call to Neel.

As soon as I heard his voice, the dam of tears broke, and I sobbed over the phone, "Neel, come and get me and Nina. Now!"

No questions asked, he said, "Wait there. I am coming. Just hang in there."

Then I hurried home in the same breath. I did not find Vijay in our room. I gathered all that Nina would need the first night—milk bottles, her clothes, her nappies, my change of clothes—and threw them all in a stroller. I dressed Nina and waited for Neel in the room.

The headlight of a motorbike appeared down the street. It was Neel, with his friend. His friends were respectful of me. I held Nina tight in one arm and dragged the stroller with another to walk out as soon as I heard Neel knock.

As I opened the door, Vijay appeared and snatched Nina from me, pushed me out of the door, and ran inside shouting, "You get out. Nina will not go with you!"

I was hysterical.

My brother yelled, "Don't touch my sister!"

I went back in. Vijay had locked himself in the corner bedroom. I could hear Nina crying inside.

Meanwhile, Sanjay came to the door and pushed my brother out of the way when he tried to follow me inside. Then Ajay ran to the kitchen, filled his pants pockets with red chili powder, and raced back to throw it at my brother and his friend. My brother ducked, but his friend got it in his eyes. He ran, almost blind with the sting of the powder, from the stair toward the lawn in front of the house, crying for water. Neel and I came down the stairs.

The next-door neighbors, hearing the noise, came out of their house. Someone had called the police from the local station by the corner, two policemen arrived on a two-wheeler scooter. Dev and Shiela entered the community gate at the same moment, astonished to see the police and their family members within the crowd. The police wanted to take my statement. I was afraid to say anything against Vijay or my in-laws, afraid they might harm my brother, if I lodged a complaint. And if Vijay was arrested and put in jail, his brothers were capable of hurting my family or me, even fatally through their contacts. The legal system was very much pro-men and run by men, who would never come to the aid of a woman or even listen to her. I was shaking and crying with the fear of the unknown. It was too dramatic to be real.

A policeman came forward to take my statement. I told the policeman it was a family matter and that no formal incident report (FIR) should be lodged.

Dev and Shiela stared at me. From a distance, I could not read their expressions, but they looked threatening.

The family was not oblivious to Vijay's temper. He was their child, and I had told Shiela he was full of anger and unpredictable.

Shiela's response was careless. "Oh, he is a *kaleshi*. He creates misery in the house. He doesn't have good relations with both his brothers. He argues with Bauji. We have tolerated him anyhow. Now it's your turn."

"But that's not fair," I had said.

"My father's brothers' wives have also been beaten, but they have learned to accept their husbands' ways. That's how men are, and that's how women have to adjust."

That was her normal.

The police asked me what I wanted.

"I would like to take my daughter and go with my brother," I said, wiping my tears and still sobbing.

The policemen walked over to Dev. After a conversation, Dev went to Vijay and asked him to hand over Nina.

Nina, my six-month-old baby, was in shock and moving her head everywhere. She cried, wiggling out of Vijay's arms to come to me. A neighbor came and handed her to me. I held her to my chest, petting her back to be quiet, kissed her a hundred times, and sat in the motor rickshaw the police had called. The motor-cycle and the motor rickshaw pulled out of the street and onto the main road.

I had already started to feel safe with my daughter on my bosom. I blocked my brain chatter for a bit, comforting my child. I arrived at my parents' house holding Nina tight as she had fallen asleep. I was still in disbelief, not able to decipher fully what had happened. I straightened my stooped, distraught shoulders. I hugged Nina tighter and took a deep breath of reprieve, my body's reaction to being back in a safe place where no one could bully me, hit me, undermine me, or snatch my child from me.

My parents were both waiting on the balcony. Parents always had that sense of knowing—the sixth sense. They hugged me without asking any questions. Dad looked at my face, my cheek was still warm, perhaps the slap had left an imprint on my cheeks. He turned to look at Mom. I was still in shock from the blows, and we all cried.

Dad took Nina from me. Mom served me food, but I had no appetite. All I wanted was to be in bed. I was extremely exhausted, entirely hollow, and downright numb.

I woke up, startled, in the middle of night to see Dad standing next to my bed, quietly sobbing. "Why did it happen to my darling daughter?" I heard him say.

I was so cold, traumatized, and devoid of emotions. I glanced at him and closed my eyes. I desired for my parents to have pride in me, and I gave them pain and agony. I was so hurt to bear my own trauma and worry my parents. I needed to empty my mind, to be peaceful, even if only for a moment.

I visualized my guru's image in front of my eyes. Maybe my faith in him would help me. For me, it was never *why* but *how*. Not, "Why me?" but, "How can I overcome this? Please give me direction and strength. Give me a sign."

A quiet agony filled the house. For the next few days, my parents could do nothing to change my mood. I was not only sad but also deeply depressed. I wanted to be left alone. To add to the grief, I missed my period. I was pregnant. Again! This was an unbearable ordeal. I would not tell my parents. I would not let them go through an added mess. I secretly called Leena and asked her to accompany me to AIIMS. I had no money to go to a private hospital and was hoping to see Dr. Thakkar. This time, I didn't want to keep my baby, so Dr. Thakkar performed an abortion.

As the days passed, my anxiety and melancholy deepened. I had the added pressure to constantly wear a mask in front of my parents. And my little daughter needed my attention. I had to come out of the depression before it became acute. I felt the need to talk to someone outside my family, a stranger with whom I could let out all my deeply buried hurt and pent-up emotions.

Counseling and therapy were unheard of in India in those days in the early '80s. But I'd learned about Sanjivini, a counseling center started by alumni of my MSW program. Sanjivini was the first institute to recognize professional counseling for mental health in India.

Neel offered to give me a ride to the Defence Colony flyover, where Sanjivini was located. Kiran, my counselor, was kind, compassionate, and experienced. She also was a great listener, and I was vulnerable. I shared my story and as I unveiled each scene, my tears flowed endlessly, and my crying became louder. She held my hands and hugged me each time I howled. I was blessed to have her. She was my angel in distress.

"Kanchan," she said at the end of our session, "you are just like a frog inside a well, scared to look outside. Crawl to the periphery and look over the ledge. There's a whole world outside. You may keep falling back into the well, but do not give up. Try, try, try again."

It made a lot of sense. The hurt was still etched deep in my heart, but I came out of the counseling session lighthearted, even hopeful of my future.

I just needed to look outside of the well.

Chapter 6

Out of the Well

1982–1983

Kiran's compelling words continued to resonate, giving me a push to get up and get out of the daze and help myself for my daughter's sake and my own. I couldn't sleep that night. I kept brooding, praying, and visualizing myself as the frog sitting on the periphery of the well, looking at the world and then jumping back into the same well. I needed to force myself to jump out of the well to see the world and the opportunities it had to offer. I resolved to do it the next morning when there was more clarity of mind. I needed to stand up on my own, resume my responsibilities, make my own decisions, and earn my own money to feed Nina and myself.

It was a brave thought. However, I needed to work on myself first, which would take some time.

My parents' continuous endeavors to change my mood made me plaster a smile on my face. Mortified that I was still a liability to them, I carried a heavy weight on my shoulders. My dad had always talked of vacationing and traveling with Mom once their duty of raising and marrying the kids was over. And here I was, back with them, now I was a hindrance to them living their dreams. They had just finished bearing the expenses of my delivery and hospital charges and would have to continue carrying my burden. Although the hospital bills were a husband's responsibility, legally there was nothing I could do to make Vijay pay. No law existed about garnishment for childcare. I didn't want to take any money from Vijay's earnings, so it never occurred to me to pursue the issue.

Mom used to say a parent's responsibility is never over. Growing up, I had been hell-bent on defying that adage. I ached that I couldn't.

The sulking and pitiful thoughts were feeding rather than fighting my depression. I needed to rebel against any desolation and throw it out of my system. I did not have the luxury of sitting idle in my wretchedness. I had my daughter to fend for. She needed to be brought up exactly like I was brought up—a princess.

The next morning, I approached Dad to see if he could find any employment opportunities at the Institute of Technology for me. He smiled and his eyes brightened, a sign of some hope visible on his face.

"So, you are ready to step out. I am glad. I'll most certainly find out, my darling."

IT as an organization was huge and because of Dad's position and reputation, there was a possibility. I smiled at him, feeling lighter. He patted my shoulder, silently commending my courage. I assumed I'd have to take a low-paying, entry-level position to start with and get my confidence back.

In the meantime, I had to plan where Nina would stay when I started working. Mom volunteered to take her vacation days until we could figure out an alternative. I wanted to make sure Nina wouldn't be an inconvenience for my parents if I were to go out and work.

Dad came back that evening with a prospect of an hourly job for me, working as a proofreader for the engineering students' yearbook. The news came as a delight. I signed Nina up for the day school nearby until the time Mom got home.

It felt good to step out of the house and be with people, which I had not done for a long time.

Two weeks into the hourly job, I came across a listing: "Job opportunity in the social sciences department." The job was a perfect fit with my fieldwork experience during MSW.

Excited, I hurried down a seemingly endless hallway toward the social sciences department to meet Professor Prasad. I walked into his office and introduced myself and my purpose for seeing him.

The job, he explained, was for facilitating projects in remote rural areas on the outskirts of Delhi. These projects were to aid in the social and economic development of villagers living below the poverty line. The department had government grants and donations from large industrialists to implement these projects, which included mushroom farming, opening handloom centers, and converting cattle waste into biogas energy.

I shared with him my fieldwork experience during MSW. He asked questions to fully understand the role I'd played. I shared my skills, most importantly of forming a quick rapport with villagers, panchayats, town council members, and banks, which were the requirements of the job. When I finished outlining my experience and willingness, he sat back in his swivel chair, silent for a minute.

I watched him closely for a sign.

After a minute, he said, "I'm so relieved to meet you. I've been awaiting a suitable person for this job."

I wanted to smile wide and show my own relief but hid my exhilaration. This opportunity seemed great, although it wasn't what I'd planned on doing if I'd pursued a career immediately after my graduation.

After leaving Dr. Prasad, I walked straight to my dad's office, excited to give him my news. He was pleased for me, especially since I'd landed the job on my own merit. He hugged me. I needed that hug.

The next day, after interviewing with two other professors on the hiring panel, I received a verbal offer. The proposed salary was enough to take care of my daughter and me while still living in my parents' house. I couldn't believe it. That evening, I came home with an offer letter and tears of thankfulness streaming down my cheeks while standing with my dad and mom in front of my guru's picture with folded hands.

Gathering my remaining strength and still containing my deep-rooted sadness, I began the new job. My workday started early at 7:30 a.m. and ended late in the evening, due to the field-work and traveling long distances.

The initial visits to these villages, meeting the panchayats, other seniors, and government officials, were empowering. I felt as upbeat as I had three years earlier while earning my master's degree.

My boss, Dr. Sarkar, was a short, stout man from Calcutta, in his midfifties. He was highly educated and seemed kind and gentle. I traveled to these villages with him in his chauffeur-driven company car. He felt like a father figure to me due to his demeanor. I started to trust him.

As we rode to and from these villages, Dr. Sarkar talked about his work and his family, especially his wife, who he said was bed-ridden. He seemed curious to know about me and my family, especially my husband and daughter. I didn't go into much detail, but he could surely make out from my responses that, although I was married, my daughter and I lived with my parents. On longer trips, since there was only so much I wanted to share about myself, we were silent most of the way.

As the days passed, I was happy being on my own, earning money, and exercising my independence. I started regaining my confidence. Although I didn't miss Vijay, occasionally I felt sorry for myself, doubts swirling through my mind on our long trips through the countryside.

What did my future hold? Was I happy in Mom and Dad's place? Would I be able to move out on this salary? Would I feel compassion toward Vijay again, if he comes back? If so, would it be a good idea? I had no answers.

Toward the end of the first week, as Dr. Sarkar and I walked into Jharsa Village, I held up my sari to keep the hem out of the dust. With my hem pulled up, my feet inside my delicate sandals were naked and visible.

Dr. Sarkar said, "You've got lovely feet."

I wore a sari and sandals like any other woman. I was young and lean, so maybe my feet did look nice. Still, I assumed he was just being friendly. I smiled and didn't think much of it.

Two days later, as I rode in the car with Dr. Sarkar, he opened his briefcase and took out a new Adidas hairbrush, still in its packaging.

"Keep it in your bag," he said. "You can use it on the way, since I've noticed your hair gets blown by the wind."

I was twenty-four at the time, vulnerable and naive in many ways, but I wasn't stupid. My sixth sense was sharp. I'd gone to school and studied with plenty of boys and braved public transport. My gut sensed a red flag. This man of my father's age might be testing me to take advantage of my vulnerability. But I remained calm, as the situation did not demand a strong reaction.

I opened my bag and took out my comb. "Dr. Sarkar, please don't bother with gifts. I use my comb when needed." It was the personal nature of the gift that offended me. And it meant he'd been watching me and thinking about me.

The hairbrush incident made me uncomfortable. Soon, I found an opportunity to speak with his driver in confidence during my lunch break. When I asked him about Dr. Sarkar's wife, the driver said she was a university professor, a nice woman who was extremely active and involved. Both the driver and I now knew Dr. Sarkar had lied to me about his wife. She wasn't ill. There was no need to confront him; I chose not to. I became even more reserved in my conversations with him.

A week later, when we were returning from the field, he opened his briefcase again. This time, he took out a packet and set it on my lap.

"These are for you."

Again? Why couldn't he get it? I looked at him with crunched eyes and puckered eyebrows.

On my lap were two Banarasi silk saris with gold borders, one red and one blue. They looked expensive, as any Banarasi silk is, elegant and delicately embroidered. Furious and nervous at the same time, I didn't yell or shout because the driver was there.

Instead, I pushed the envelope back on Dr. Sarkar's lap.

"Don't do that!" I said. "What are you thinking? Why would you give me saris?"

I found it difficult to control the sudden adrenaline upsurge. For one moment, I imagined slapping Dr. Sarkar across his face with the same force Vijay did to me. Fists clenched, I talked myself down, my desperate need for the job holding me back.

My voice came out assertive and harsh. Proud of myself, I wondered why I couldn't do that with Vijay or Shiela when they demeaned and insulted me and when Vijay hit me.

"Oh, I was buying saris for my wife," Dr. Sarkar said, "and I bought a couple for you, too." His gaze was sheepish, and his voice quivered.

He was clearly lying. There had to be a motive, a sleazy one, to give such personal gift. He was far beyond his boundaries.

He could see that I was visibly upset, so he quickly put the saris back in the briefcase.

Dismayed, I headed to the bathroom to shower when I came home. I didn't even see Nina. I didn't tell my parents, as my dad would either forbid me from going back or demand to go in with me to sort it out. I was an adult now and needed to handle this myself.

If I shared what had happened with anyone else, like a colleague at work, all of the men would not only make fun of my naivete but also want to know, mindlessly assuming, what signals I had given Dr. Sarkar, which had encouraged him to buy saris for me.

I even questioned this myself. Did he think I was desperate to get this job that I'd sleep with him? Quid pro quo? Or did he take me to be a foolish, vulnerable young woman to be taken advantage of? How could I resolve this? Possibly, I had to be in control and absorb this without telling anyone or risk spoiling my own reputation. I did need this job.

The next day, Dr. Sarkar and I had an appointment to see a well-known, highly reputed industrialist who was financing the bio-gas project. On the ride to his office, a knot of dread cramped my stomach. My heart racing all through the journey, I was ready to jump out of the car if he tried a new trick. I checked the handles and door locks just in case. But so far, he hadn't touched me. He'd kept a professional distance between us. Although I felt I could trust his driver, an elderly village man who occasionally looked at me with empathy, I could not completely trust anyone.

When I entered the front door of the long office—an open hall with rows of desks—all heads turned toward us. Several young men looked right at me. Usually when someone entered an office, a few people might glance up. My gut told me Dr. Sarkar had a maligned reputation in this office, perhaps he is known to bring young woman to meet the industrialist. All of a sudden, all my desperation to keep the job left me. My body reacted as if I were on a warpath. I planned to shout and scream loudly if the industrialist tried to make any kind of advances toward me.

Thankfully, the industrialist had to leave for an emergency meeting. He met us in the hallway, waved at Dr. Sarkar, and signaled to come another day. Once we were back at the car, my heart seemed ready to explode. I felt my head being hammered, my shoulders and neck ached and caved under the weight of blows, the intense fear and anxiety of insecurity weighed on me. I was carrying more than I could. Was this the plight of a single woman? I was in a quandary. I was reminded of the safety I had in my husband's house, at least from outsiders. As we drove back to the office, a lot of thoughts about Vijay arose.

I had not faced any of such issues being the cause to walk out on him. Out in the world, without the presence of a husband, I was an object. Anyone could look at me in any way they wanted. They could make advances, give me inappropriate gifts, and use me at their whim. It was a man's world. Society found fault in women only. At least with my husband, there was only one man I was expected to give myself to, even if he caused me pain and hurt. Without a husband, it seemed anyone could try to claim me. There would be a Dr. Sarkar no matter where I worked.

However, I needed to report him, to save myself and many other women like me. It had to begin somewhere. My feminism had not completely died—it was alive. Upon returning to work, I headed to the CEO's office. I told him about Dr. Sarkar's unwelcome behavior amounting to sexual harassment, quoted the gifts he bought for me, and asked Dr. Sarkar be taken to task. The CEO fixed his piercing gaze on me, which made me squirm.

This tall, sixty-plus, gray-haired man seemed like a sincere, serious man. Taking my grievance to him felt right. Instead of some compassion and empathy, I met a poker face with an intensely suspicious gaze on me. Tears of helplessness swelled in my eyes, and I could not keep them from falling down my cheeks.

The CEO got up from his chair, which startled me a bit. He came around the table, picked up the tissue box, and handed it to me. Embarrassed, I wiped my tears, got up, thanked him for listening to me, and walked out of his office.

The next morning, the CEO called me and asked for a written report. I wrote and submitted the report, though hesitantly, as I didn't have a grasp on the extent of organization dynamics and the political environment prevailing in this state-run organization. I suspected my complaint wouldn't remain confidential for long.

I had just submitted a written allegation of sexual harassment. Would Dr. Sarkar send someone after me?

In India, money could buy anything. One could pay and hire con men to harass, kidnap, and murder with no fear of retribution by law, society, or God.

The following day, I went to work as usual, apprehensive about what would happen. By this time, the news of my grievance had spread like wildfire throughout the office. All eyes stared at me, and plenty of them—from the security guard to the receptionist to colleagues—smirked when I walked past.

The CEO, it seemed, had been waiting for such an opportunity to avenge his own professional differences with Dr. Sarkar. He used my complaint as an excuse to suspend Dr. Sarkar for four weeks. The prying looks of the office staff made me feel as if I were the guilty party rather than Dr. Sarkar. This left me bitter. A strange fear filled me. Was it even possible to survive in this world with dignity and respect? I was drained. I desperately wanted all the bullying and harassment to go away and leave me in peace.

Once again, I found myself thinking maybe life with my husband was far better. At least there was only him to deal with. He loved me in his sober moments. He had expressed it to me several times. He loved his daughter, and my love for him, in some corner, had not completely left me either.

I could have made things better between us if I had just tried harder.

At work, it was like a punishment for me to sit at my desk through the day. Several times, the thought of escaping this caustic environment crossed my mind, though not an option given my circumstances.

Later in the day, the security guard approached me. Someone waited for me downstairs at the reception desk. I had no idea who would come to see me at work, but I was eager for any distraction. I took the elevator down to reception.

When the elevator door opened, Vijay stood there, immaculately dressed in a dark-blue suit and a light-pink shirt, with his charming smile and twinkling eyes—suave and definitely at his best. I'd never seen him so gorgeously dressed, smiling in a way I'd never seen, and his eyes were full of love, just for me.

Vijay came toward me with open arms, and without hesitating, I walked straight into them and hugged him tight. It was all a reflex. He engulfed me tightly in his warm hug. I needed nothing more than a compassionate face at the time. I needed the comfort, and there he was, ready to provide it.

My inner voice prompted, *My prince charming has come to rescue me and take me to a safer place, where the harassment came only from him. I will not have to go out to work and face any molestation or ravaging eyes.*

Vijay took me to a small boutique hotel in Greater Kailash, in one of the posh areas where he was staying. Amrit Guest House was owned by a retired Major Singh, a very graceful ex-army man. I followed Vijay to the room he rented. We talked, but not about any incidents of previous abuse. He said he was moving to Kanpur, nearly four hundred miles north of New Delhi, and working at Paramount Machines as a consultant.

"I am deeply ashamed and sorry for what happened in Bauji's house," he said, holding my hand and showing remorse in his eyes. "I have learned my lesson. Please do not penalize me by going out of my life. I cannot take the burden of life, alone. I want Nina, my daughter, in my life. Come back to me in Kanpur, not Bauji's house anymore. I want to build my own family. You know I cannot live without you. You are my only love."

His words did not melt me but certainly took a weight off my shoulders. The stress of the job vanished. This could be the option for not going back to work and being vulnerable to such horrendous behavior. I could go back to him, where I could feel safer than at work and without the guilt of staying with my parents. He seemed like a new person, with warmth and love in his eyes. His manipulation was once again working on me.

The very next day, I sent my letter of resignation. I told my parents Vijay was in town. I knew they would have mixed reactions, and rightly so. Because I was not steadfast on my resolve. I did not wait for their response as I did not want to get prejudiced. Come evening, I carried Nina with me to see her father.

He was excited to see her. He held and played with her all evening. But he did not want to come home to see my parents. Neither did he want the Behls to know he was in town. Presumably because he did not want the news to reach his family.

My parents were concerned. "What if you get pregnant?" Mom asked.

They didn't want the neighbors to gossip. I listened to them, but once again, my arising hopes at starting back with my husband eclipsed their concern.

Vijay went back after a week, saying he would take some time to settle into the new job, then look for a house and come back to get us.

In about two months, Vijay came again and asked me to stay with him in the guest house during the week he was in town. The romance was back. Happiness prevailed. Life had hope, and the future was no longer bleak.

Except now I had missed my period.

I felt nauseated and bled in the bathroom of the guesthouse. Vijay ran out of the room to get Major Singh, who called for his wife, Amrit. She came in no time to check on me and said it sounded like an early miscarriage. She took me to a nearby clinic, and the doctor recommended a D&C to make sure everything was back to normal.

Vijay returned to Kanpur, a day later, as he had yet to look for a rental house for us. He called in three weeks to ask me to book my ticket. I was again excited to start a new life filled with anticipation that it would work out this time.

After a six-hour train ride, I landed at Kanpur station around 9 p.m. with Nina, who was less than a year old. Vijay was nowhere to be seen on the platform. Arms loaded with Nina and our luggage, I panicked. I then recognized him from a distance by his familiar wobbly walk. *He is drunk.* My heart skipped a beat and my eyes teared up.

He made his way to us, all smiles, and gave me a quick hug, trying to keep a distance so I wouldn't smell the liquor. He took Nina from me and started to baby talk her as I followed the porter toward the parking lot. He stopped in front of a jeep, where a young man sat in the driver's seat. It seemed the young man owned the jeep, which obviously was not a hired taxi, so maybe he was Vijay's acquaintance or a colleague from work. He appeared sober but smelled of alcohol as well.

The city roads were jam packed with highly-disorganized traffic. It was a big hotchpotch of all kinds of vehicles, buses, trucks, motor rickshaws, cars, bicycle rickshaws, motorcycles honking, trying to overtake, and slowing down the traffic. The cows squatting in the middle of the road could not be missed, creating more chaos. Everyone was in a rush of reaching some-where. After an hour of extremely noisy and overloaded traffic, we entered an industrial area. The jeep stopped in front of a four-story building. I wondered why we stopped.

"This is it," Vijay said.

With the young man helping us with the luggage, we climbed the stairs to the third floor. There was no elevator in this old building. We landed on a large central veranda. One of the doors opened into a hall, which was furnished with tables and computers. It looked like a large office space. Next to that was a small kitchen, more like a pantry. At the far end of the veranda were four steps leading to a platform, a door opened to a kitchenette, and another to a room with a king-size bed, a study table, and an attached bathroom.

We followed Vijay to that room where he had his stuff. *Oh, so this is where he is living.* This was the house. Suddenly my energy gave way just like the air exits an inflated balloon, leaving it limp, devoid of air.

I felt the hairs on the nape of my neck rise as the young man stared at me. Vijay's eyes were distant, like a stranger—a man I did not know. I held Nina close, with two drunken strangers in the room.

"Why are you so drunk?" I asked him.

"I was so happy to have you back, I wanted to celebrate."

"And how about this man?"

"Oh, he is my new friend. He will leave. He gave me the ride."

Vijay was a weak person who needed a crutch to perform any task. I had known that before. Had I made the right decision by coming here? I'd been back with Vijay for less than an hour, and already this thought haunted me.

He almost raped me that evening without waiting for the night, acting like a beast, leaving my cheeks black and blue.

The next morning, I met Bilal Fayez, who lived in the room opposite the office hall. Bilal was a polite and kind gentleman. He wouldn't even lift his gaze to look at me, which I found refreshing after everything with Dr. Sarkar. Bilal treated me as one should a sister or a friend's wife. I thought of him as a rescuer. If something strange happened, I could approach him for help.

In three weeks, we moved to a residential town farther down the industrial area, to a two-bedroom apartment. The office had taken objection to Vijay's family living on the premises. It was a blessing for both Nina and me. We would have our own space where Nina could play out of the room at her own will.

This change of venue brought good days with it. Vijay came back home on time and spent time with Nina while I cooked dinner. I could see his love for her. We would go for a stroll after dinner. A couple of his colleagues invited us. It seemed like an ideal household. He expressed his love often. However, I did not want to think too much into it and kept my fingers crossed.

A few weeks later, Vijay began to come home late, the smell of alcohol lingering on his breath. This was not a good sign. Questioning him would trigger fights and verbal abuse. I panicked. He might become violent at any time. He looked for triggers, and I was careful. Till now, I had not realized his anger episodes were cyclical.

Every evening, after cooking dinner, I stood on our balcony, which overlooked the approaching road, with Nina in my arms, half-balanced on my hip, as she had become heavy. We waited for Vijay to come home until late at night. He would come home drunk and start to push my buttons each day to rile me—anything to give him an excuse to relieve his frustration.

One Sunday, lounging in his boxers, he started drinking in the afternoon. By evening, he started to fight with me for absolutely no reason. He began shoving me and pushing me, with much strength and power. I could never match his strength.

"You shouldn't have married me!" I said enraged. "You've ruined my life, and now you're ruining Nina's."

He started punching me, twisting my arms until I shouted in pain. He dragged me around the room and punched me in the stomach, verbally abusing me. When he wore himself out, he drank more whiskey. By then, it was late at night.

As the liquor hit him once more, he ran downstairs in his boxers, after midnight, shouting, "I will kill myself under the train!"

I went out on the balcony to watch him run off into the dark. The main iron gate to the building was locked. He scaled the ten-foot gate, then hauled himself up and over like a werewolf in the movie and ran toward the main road in the middle of night.

I stood in shock, trembling and cold—all familiar feelings. I was also so scared of where he'd gone. All scenarios came to me:

Vijay lying dead on the train track. The police coming to deliver the news, take Nina away, and take me to the police station.

Nina was crying. I held her tight. With his strength and power, he changed into a voracious beast who could kill either me or himself. It was dangerous to live with him for my daughter and me. I should take her to a safe place.

The next morning, I saw Vijay sprawled on the floor snoring. After he left for work around noon, I threw Nina's stuff in a suitcase. I could barely fit mine, as I could not carry heavy luggage. I left the building and hired a rickshaw to take us to the train station. The station was crowded. I bought a ticket on the 2:00 p.m. train, leaving soon for the New Delhi railway station—the only place I was familiar with, to go back to where I'd taken the train to Kanpur three months before.

Chapter 7

Trapped

1983–1985

We reached the New Delhi railway station 11:00 p.m., completely exhausted. I walked out of the platform to the motor rickshaw stand, holding Nina in one arm and dragging the suitcase with the other. I was nervous about riding in motor rickshaw alone with a toddler at that hour due to my own prejudice and the stereotyping of the auto drivers.

Before hiring one, I walked up to a policeman standing by the fence and asked him to note the license plate number of the motor rickshaw in case something went wrong on the way. Not that I trusted him more, but I surely trusted the uniform he wore.

The road to IT campus, nearly twenty-five miles away, seemed never-ending. Around midnight, we reached the familiar red-brick, four-story building in which my parents had their apartment.

"Wait," I told the driver. "I'll get the money." I had no fare to pay him.

As I dragged the suitcase toward the staircase, holding Nina, I saw Neel walking toward the building after what I assumed must have been a night out with his friends. As soon as he came close, my heart burst out with trapped emotions.

I hugged him with a flood of tears rolling down, my voice hushed and wailed. "I am back again. I am back again."

He hugged me tighter and wiped my tears with his bare fingers. He took Nina and my suitcase from me and paid the driver. He had a duplicate key to the house. I stopped by my parents' room to see if they were still awake, which they were. If they were shocked to see me arrive in the middle of the night, they didn't show it. Mom came ahead, took Nina from me and gave me a tight hug with her other arm. And then Dad hugged me, putting his arms around my shoulder, and walked me inside into the living room. Neel teared up, too.

I could not look into anyone's eyes. I was ashamed for coming back at their doorstep unannounced after Vijay's violence. Nina was wide awake and giggling, looking at us.

Mom said, "As long as we are alive, we will do whatever is required to be done for you. This is your home, too. Stay as long as it's required, and we will figure it out. All shall be fine."

A big lump in my throat choked me, as I held back my tears from shedding. Mom dad will not be able to hold if they see me crying, so I gulped the lump and chose not to cry.

Exhausted, Nina sucked on her pacifier until my dad reached over, grabbed it, and threw it out the bedroom window.

I bit my lip. "Dad, what have you done? She will not sleep without it, and I am already so drained."

Nina looked at him, then me, and broke into a cry.

"She does not need a pacifier," my dad said. "We shall take care of her." Perhaps that was his way of expressing he was there to look after Nina and me.

As usual, Mom and Dad went out of their way to provide comfort to us, trying to cheer me up, playing with Nina, and straining themselves to take away my strain. Months passed, then one night after dinner, while Mom cleared the table, Dad said something to her in Tamil, their code language they had picked up after their wedding in Madras, now called Chennai, a State in

South India. She left everything in the kitchen and came back to the table. They both gazed at me.

Dad said, "Your mother and I think it would be a worthy idea for you to file for a divorce and get remarried."

I was blindsided. Although it was a sensible idea, my mind was clouded and cluttered.

Before I could react. Mom added, "Don't worry, we will adopt Nina."

"You've already planned this?" I asked.

I got up from the table like a spring. "No way! That will never happen. Nina will not go anywhere. She's mine, and I'll look after her." Even the thought rattled me. Seeing me flustered, they left the matter there, and Mom went back to the kitchen.

Nina was my treasure. Her smiles and twinkling eyes brightened my days when nothing else could. Her constant giggling and crackling filled my life with joy. Motherhood healed my wounds of betrayal and abuse by my own husband. I panicked at the thought of her being taken away from me. There was no question of giving my daughter up for adoption, even to my own parents. I had no interest in remarrying. The idea of trying again with another man was terrifying. I felt trapped in a negotiation. Leave my daughter for another man in my life? In Indian society, a man would want nothing to do with a child who wasn't his. Moreover, even if a man did accept Nina, who knew what he would want in return, especially when she grew older? I couldn't think of fulfilling my own desire for a normal married life if it meant losing the little girl I held in my arms, close to my chest.

This stark truth came as a jolt. Divorce at the age of twenty-four meant giving up my daughter, as I would be expected to remarry. If I didn't, I'd risk harassment of various kinds, including sexual in nature, at all levels of society, not only by men but also by women. This society would not let a young, divorced woman live by herself.

The vultures would prey.

I shivered at the thought. In this patriarchal society, when my daughter grew into an adolescent, without a man to protect us, would I be able to fend for her? My parents couldn't guard us forever. And since I would not give up Nina, did I have to live with Vijay in an unpredictable and unsafe environment? Would that be best for my daughter? How could I be sure? After about four weeks, Bilal Faiyaz, the colleague of Vijay, arrived at my parents' house at Vijay's behest. He conveyed Vijay's message that he was sorry for what happened and requested us back. My answer was no.

A month later, another colleague, Shailendra, and his wife, Shefali, visited to impress upon me how apologetic Vijay was for his actions. But I was tired of his apologies and all the promises he couldn't keep, so I sent them back on their way.

They both returned after two months. Shefali was empathetic. They were a decent couple and very respectful of each other. However, I did not budge.

A few days later, they called and asked me out for a cup of coffee. It was a good idea to step out, so I met them at the coffee place. From the table, my gaze fell on a short, lean man, well-dressed, with black hair and glasses, walking toward our table. He looked so much like Vijay. It startled me. When he came closer, to my utter shock, I recognized the man. Vijay! I looked at the couple and back at Vijay, eyes wide open, a fleeting look. He nodded his head in his typical charming way. He came and bent to give me a hug, smiled sheepishly, and sat in the fourth empty chair.

I was not ready to see him nor to confront him. Each time I came back to my parents, I healed and recuperated some but did not feel part of their house anymore. Something had changed in me after my marriage. I needed my own space. Yet, each time I returned to Vijay, I always felt back at home. I got a sense of relief until, once again, living with him became tormenting and unbearable.

It was not easy to walk out on a relationship, especially when there was a child's life and well-being at stake. The worry of losing my child to divorce hung like a sword in the back of my mind. Every time I left, Vijay came back, full of repentance. He seemed so helpless and childlike. I could never fathom this could be a manipulation, and my compassion returned, in those weak moments.

Without me, he would be all alone. His family never visited him or tried to intervene. His friends were booze buddies. I was the only one who could possibly help this educated and intelligent man. He was wasting his precious life and was in dire need of mending. He needed intervention, but he was not in agreement. I could help him if he'd let me try.

Vijay's violent streak was much more dangerous than his anger issues. His dreadful and cyclical behavior had a similarity to other classical cases. He would control me and start the blame game. Then he would engage in self-violence by drinking and changed into another person entirely. It was like a split personality or a sadist who wanted to hurt me. He wanted to feel powerful by controlling, shoving, and beating me. He treated me like a doormat. During this phase, his eyes moved faster, filled with hatred. His pace increased, and his nostrils flared. The verbal abuse changed into physical violence. After a few days of unpredictable, abusive behavior his maneuvering me would involve tearful remorse, minimizing and trivializing his violence, still blaming me and denying his terrorism as a reaction to my behavior toward him. All of this would be followed by deep apology, proceeded by promises of best behavior, his adoration, and claim of love for me.

During his lucid moments, I told him he should see a doctor, a therapist, or a psychiatrist to manage his anger and delusional behavior, but he always refused to accept he needed help. He would tell me I was the one who should seek help. I was the one who had mental issues. He was in complete denial.

I often thought about my master's program in social work when I had done fieldwork in the psychiatry department of Safdarjung Hospital. I did case studies and group therapy for compulsive or manic outpatients. They were very cooperative and desired to be treated. I developed compassion for them, as they accepted they needed help and sought it.

In my second year, my field work was in the red-light area, close to the university, where sex trafficking took place underneath the authority of police and lawmakers. By the end of my research, I stopped judging the women selling their bodies. I became empathetic to them. I stopped judging people—period. Their horrifying stories brought tears to my eyes. They were compelled to do this work by extreme circumstances, mostly related to poverty. And once they were in that life, there was no way out. They were trapped. The pimps controlled their lives.

I'd begun thinking of marriage, or most marriages, as a kind of legalized prostitution, where the customer knowingly played with the emotions of the woman, felt entitled, and controlled and hurt her. The woman in return got entangled and imprisoned in the torment of her possessor. And then she had no way to escape. She was shackled.

During the rare, good times, I had hoped Vijay would take responsibility for his abusive behavior. However, the episodes increased. I would blame myself up for sympathizing with him or trying to mend him. In these times, I thought he was incorrigible—someone who would never change, never to be mended.

Vijay, Nina, and I now lived in New Delhi's Kalkaji area, as he had taken up a job in New Delhi, back at the consulting company he had worked for earlier. I had moved back after conceding to his pleadings when Shefali and Shailendra arranged our meeting.

After a few days of fun, as per his pattern, Vijay once again took control of my life. He alienated me from my family by strictly prohibiting me from seeing them though they lived only twenty miles away. He tore away my offer letter for a job in the hospitality industry, for which I had interviewed secretly and was selected after three tough rounds. He managed the money, giving me none, not even pocket money. He instilled fear in me through violence and threats to kill himself. I was confined.

He abused and hit me. A couple of times, the landlords came to stop him, but he would cry in front of them and convince them that I was the villain. He would threaten to hang himself from the overhead fan with my sari twisted as a long rope. He swore to leave a note, blaming me and my parents for his death.

Knowing the Indian judiciary system as I did, this was no idle threat. Such a letter could result in me and my parents spending the rest of our lives in jail. There existed no law to protect us. And while these fears worked up my nerves, I felt myself losing my mental and physical health.

Nina, in her formative years, watched this. Her memory stored everything, and I worried how her psyche would be impaired as she became a teen.

The only house I was permitted to visit was Amrit's. She and Major Singh had become our friends. Since Vijay was adept at charming people outwardly, I feared it would not be easy to convince them of his abuse. But Amrit trusted me completely.

When Vijay left for work, I'd dress up Nina, hire a motor rickshaw, and go to Amrit's house, fifteen minutes away. I'd pay the fare from the little money I kept aside from the grocery money. Nina was two now, and Raj, Amrit's son, was a year older. They played while Amrit and I spent time together. She became my confidante, counselor, and friend. She had a good sense of humor and was tomboyish— "carefree" or *bindaas* in Mumbai slang. She made efforts to make me laugh. Amrit was a tall, charming, and confident woman with lots of consideration, which comforted me. She became my safety net.

She'd rescued me when I'd miscarried, and now she was an older sister with whom I could share my heart. She was careful to maintain good relations with Vijay and never let him know what I'd shared with her.

As the years passed, it had become Vijay's tendency to change jobs frequently, voluntarily, and involuntarily, every six months or so, which meant instability and financial worries. Soon, he got an assignment in the same company in Kanpur where he had worked before and moved there. Nina and I moved with him. Within a couple of months, I found myself suffering from discomfort and aches in my lower abdomen. I convinced Vijay I should go back to Delhi to get myself checked out. This was also an excuse to see my parents, whom I had not seen for two years. Surprisingly, Vijay agreed, and I took the train.

The reunion between Nina and my parents and siblings was touching. We hugged and kissed each other, even cried. We instantly reconnected where we had left each other.

The doctor at the IT clinic suggested an ultrasound. I discovered I was pregnant—with twins! On the report, the word "twins" was typed in red uppercase letters and underlined for emphasis. I literally jumped with joy. I'd never heard about any twins in my family. I didn't know of anyone who'd had them. I was thrilled, delighted, and surprised that something so unique was going to happen to me. Twins. My stress vanished. I forgot how distorted and broken my life was. I always desired more children.

I was fortunate to get Dr. Thakkar back as my obstetrician. She again advised strict bed rest and weekly Proluton injections to keep my uterus strong and retain the babies. I wrote to Vijay, and he seemed thrilled, too. His sister was born a twin, although her sibling had survived only seven days. I had not known this. The thought of only one twin surviving stayed with me throughout my pregnancy, creating a lot of anxiety.

I grew superstitious. I would not let my mom knit or sew just one single set of anything. There had to be two of everything, one for each twin. Whether she was knitting baby suits or sewing tiny pajamas, I insisted on two of the same color and fabric.

Lying in bed all day was not comforting. My belly grew bigger. I felt the twins' heads on both sides of my stomach. I could count their fingers. I was advised to lie straight to not squish the heads and fingers of my little babies. Nina was very understanding of her brothers in my belly.

"Two, two *bhai.*" *Brothers,* she would say, pointing at my belly. I was concerned not only for the survival of both babies but also for the gender. I was apprehensive about having two more girls. What if their destiny was as bad as mine?

Vijay and I kept in touch through letters, but he refrained from coming to my parents' house, probably out of shame. Finally, he came to see us in my eighth month. The very next day, he insisted I visit his family, who were sixty miles away. I told him it was not a good idea for me to travel that distance because I was on bed rest, but he would not listen to me or my parents. As a result, during the ride to and from there, my whole body swelled to dangerous proportions due to water retention. Vijay went back to Kanpur, leaving me behind in that condition, and I had to be admitted to the hospital. Dr. Thakkar was worried I might deliver during the eighth month of my pregnancy, which would have increased the chances of delivering the babies before their brains had fully developed. Fortunately, after safe care for five days, I was discharged with strict advice to take complete bed rest.

I did not mention this to Vijay, as I was not expecting any remorse or concern from him.

On New Year's Eve, I received a letter from Vijay. I opened it eagerly. But instead of well wishes for the New Year, as I expected, I read some nasty sentences of ridicule, of me being selfish and of how he wished I was not in his life. I was anguished. I went to the bathroom, as I couldn't hold back my tears, when suddenly a burst of water ran down my legs. So much water! I panicked and shouted for Mom.

She ran in. "Your water's broken."

Dad had just left to buy snacks for the evening to celebrate New Year's Eve. She ran to the balcony and shouted for him to come back, explaining to him in Tamil what had happened. Dad called for a cab. Mom and I sat in the cab while Dad followed us, dropping Nina at my sister's house on the way to the hospital.

Mom panicked that I might deliver in the cab. As soon as we reached the hospital, we didn't wait for the stretcher. Instead, Mom made a beeline for the elevator, and I followed, leaving a trail of water. As soon as we reached the fourth floor, Mom hurried into the hall, shouting for Dr. Thakkar.

I was admitted to the labor room at around 7:00 p.m. Dr. Thakkar wouldn't return until the next morning. I was quite disheartened. She had been a good omen for me. I trusted her and was comfortable with her delivering my babies.

Those thoughts disappeared with the first wave of strenuous contractions. The movement of the twins became so trying due to the loss of all that water. At one point, I was sure I would die from the labor pains. This time, there was no Dr. Saha to hold my hand, or anyone like him to give me a pep talk. Perhaps all of them were celebrating New Year's Eve.

I was taken to the delivery room at 4:00 a.m., after eight hours of excruciating labor pains. Two young interns were on duty in the delivery room, and I missed Dr. Thakkar even more. Then, at 6:25 a.m., the first baby came out into this world.

I heard a little shriek. The nurse brought a beautiful child wrapped in a white towel and announced the baby was a boy. My son's beautiful eyes were wide open. He gazed back at me, struggling to push his little fist in his mouth. *Oh, he is hungry!* Before I could take a second look, my next pain gripped me. Fifteen minutes later, at 6:40 a.m., my second son was born. I was exhausted by this time.

"Wait!" one of the doctors said. "There is a third baby coming."

For a second, I was shocked. The intern smiled teasingly.

"A poor joke, and at a bad time," I said and smiled at them. I lifted my head to see my second baby.

The nurse hadn't yet swaddled him, and as the surgeon held him up for me to see, my son slipped from his hands. I gasped, and my placenta coiled back inside me. Luckily, the doctor caught my son before he hit the ground. I heard some commotion, and then I was moved to the operating theater on a stretcher, where they had to cut me open to take out the placenta that had gone back inside my uterus, which could be fatal if not removed immediately. Since there was heavy blood loss in the process, my older brother Ravi gave two units of blood for a transfusion.

I woke up in the recovery room to Dr. Thakkar gently tapping my cheeks.

"What was the hurry?" she kidded. "You could not wait one more day?"

I opened my eyes and managed a smile. She assured me she would be back after her morning rounds to check on me again. I was shivering with cold. I had two drips in my veins on both arms, and my parents stood at my side. Dad saw my temperature drop suddenly, perhaps because of excessive blood loss. He shouted for a nurse, told my mom to rub my feet to warm me up, and then ran to the nurses' area to get blankets to cover me. I could see the worry on his face until my temperature returned to normal.

Once Dad knew I was going to be fine and that the boys were healthy, he stepped out to send a telegram to Vijay in Kanpur. Mom brought the twins from the nursery and placed them in the crib next to my hospital bed. They were so handsome and more so in their light-green baby suits Mom had knitted. The boys had perfectly round faces and heads with black hair. They were highly active, with fists open, lovely big eyes constantly searching, and made clicking sounds with their tongues.

Both had white tape wrapped around their wrists with "Baby 1" and "Baby 2" written in blue ink. It was divine to watch them. My parents couldn't stop smiling. Ravi, Leena, and Jeej were by my side. Neel was out of town. They held my hand and congratulated me. It was the happiest day of my life after the day Nina was born.

Leena brought Nina with her that evening. Big sister Nina brought her teddy bears and other soft toys to give to her brothers. She kept jumping on my bed and touching the twins in the crib. At three years old, she was full of joy to have two little brothers to play with.

I was discharged two days later because I was concerned about catching an infection in the hospital. I was thrilled to take the twins home to my parents' house. We decided on a nickname for my Kabir and Kuber—my mother named them Huny and Suny.

Mom and Dad were fully dedicated to taking care of the twins and helping me recuperate, also heal from my stitches from the minor operation after delivery. It was an extremely chilly winter for New Delhi, so Mom and Dad made sure the diapers weren't wet. Dad would sit in front of a heat convector to dry the diapers and prepare two fresh stacks for the morning.

Late on the fourth night, there was a knock at the door. We all knew it was Vijay, who was happy to see his two boys.

Rather than waiting the full forty days this time, Vijay came for me and the children sixteen days after delivery. I still had stitches from my operation and wasn't fully recovered from the twin delivery, but he insisted. He took us all to my in-laws' house before we left for Kanpur. They were excited to see the twin boys and took pleasure in holding them.

We boarded a train to Kanpur on the fourth night.

＊　＊　＊

Taking care of the twins on my own, without my parents or any full-time help in Kanpur, was an ordeal. I had to take care of Nina, too, who was just three years old. Vijay did not come forward for any help of any kind. None. Perhaps he decided not to raise my expectations. Although he was loving to the twins, he acted as if he were living in a hotel, coming home to sleep, and then getting up to go to work.

All the domestic helpers I hired quit after a week or two. They didn't want to deal with three young ones in the house. We lived in an industrial area in an old industrial city where workers could get paid higher wages for other forms of menial work in factories. Yet I needed the help, so while still not completely recovered and in a fair amount of pain, every week or so, I'd go to the slums close by and call out, "Hello! Is there anyone here who does domestic work?"

My day was gone in feeding, massaging, bathing, rocking, and cleaning the babies. I would rock the crib with one hand and then the other to make them sleep so that I could relax a bit, but they never slept at the same time. One would hardly go to sleep and the other would wake up, crying for milk. The older twin seemed to be always awake, keeping a constant gaze at me. Their presence in my life was enough to give me courage and keep me going.

In the evening, I had to put food on the table for Vijay, Nina, and myself. For a couple of months, I would just put lentils and rice in the pressure cooker and serve it with a pickle. Every morning, I'd wake up and stay in my nightgown all day and then sleep in it. I never had a chance to change or take a shower. My long hair was always tangled. I was exhausted to the bone.

Nina was admitted to a preschool, which helped, since I couldn't cope with three kids and a handicapped fourth child, as I thought of my husband, who only made demands of me and did nothing to help.

My brother Neel was now working in Kanpur, so he came in the evenings when he could to help with the twins.

After about two months, Vijay started coming home late with alcohol on his breath, which soon turned into coming home fully drunk. And sure enough, he picked fights much more frequently. He didn't need an issue to abuse me and curse, beat and punch, slap my face, twist my arms, gouge my cheeks with his fingers, and push me against the wall. When I tried to protect myself, he'd hit me harder. This was more intense than it had ever been before. He was completely out of control, and I was weak.

❋　　❋　　❋

One evening when I saw Vijay walking into the house flustered and wobbly in his typical walk when he got drunk, my heart sank. I suspected a dramatic explosion coming. I ran and put the twins in the guest room along with Nina, away from our bedroom and bolted the door. Without saying a word, I put his dinner plate on the table. As I turned to the kitchen, he swung the plate in the air, barely missing my head. He was like a madman. His head moved constantly while he blabbered. He cornered me and pushed me into the kitchen wall and battered me with all his strength.

I managed to get away, run down to my landlords' house, and phone Neel. I was afraid Vijay could kill me out of rage combined with power he possessed in that moment. My landlady was extremely concerned, seeing my condition. After calling, I hurried back upstairs. I couldn't leave the kids alone with him.

When my brother arrived, Vijay, hair wild, eyes crazed, and drooling, was punching me.

"Leave her alone!" Neel yelled.

But Vijay didn't stop. Neel tried pulling him off me, and Vijay threw a punch at him.

Neel pushed Vijay to the floor, pinned him down, and said, "Don't you dare touch my sister again."

I begged Neel to get up.

He said, "You and the children need to come with me now. Your husband cannot be controlled."

He picked up Nina and I quickly grabbed the boys in both my arms and ran out, fearing Vijay might come after me or take one of them. Except for the kids, we left empty-handed, all of us barefoot, and raced to Neel's motorcycle parked outside. It was around 8:00 p.m. I held the twins tight, one in each arm, sitting cross-legged on the back of the bike, and Neel set Nina in front of him. Then we drove off, the neighbors downstairs and across the way outside, watching.

Neel bought milk at the only shop open. I didn't nurse the twins for long, as I was unable to manage them both at the same time and they would go red and blue from crying of hunger, so I had introduced bottle feeding very early on. But we had no bottles, so we fed milk to the twins with spoons. We both decided that I should go to my parents' house, by the morning train going to Delhi.

It was a long ride in the hot and humid July weather. I bought bottles before we left, but the milk ran out on the train, and the twins cried from hunger and the heat for the remainder of the trip, with Nina watching. She joined me in cajoling them but to no effect.

The train reached Delhi late that afternoon. I hailed a motor rickshaw, but the driver refused to go to Gurgaon, crossing the Delhi border. We walked to the bus station instead. I got into the bus with all three children, holding one twin on each side. A compassionate woman tried to help with the twins, who were continuously crying of thirst, hunger, and heat.

Finally, the bus reached Gurgaon. A rickshaw was parked at the bus stop. I hired it, even though my parents' house was only walking distance away.

Dad opened the door. His eyes showed surprise, and then empathy replaced surprise. Perhaps he wanted to say, "Oh my poor children, that devil again pushed you out."

Mom was not far behind. "Come in, my children, Nani [Grandmom] is here."

Dad had already lifted Nina in his arms, kissing her cheeks, and Mom took the twins for me.

Dad said, "And Nana [Granddad] is here, too." He embraced me and took me in with him.

Chapter 8

Give Me One Last Chance

1985–1989

Once again, I found myself back in my parents' house, this time at their newly-built house in Gurgaon, built after Dad's retirement. I was smothered and oppressed by my own husband, and was an encumbrance on myself and to them, especially with my three children now. They loved me dearly and would do anything for me, which made me feel guiltier.

My parents' perception was different from mine. I was still their daughter, and my welfare was their first concern. They were fond of my children, their joy. They never considered me and my children a burden.

Mom suggested we put double mattresses on the floor so the twins wouldn't fall off the bed. They were now at the crawling stage.

During the day, I was left alone with the children—Nina, three and a half, and the boys, six months—while Mom and Dad were at work. Dad had taken a consulting job, and Mom was a school principal at Mahipalpur, on the Delhi–Gurgaon border. The thought of me being employed was not even a legitimate question with three toddlers who needed a parent's attention.

113

It was an extremely tough time, as there was no help with the children until Mom was back from school. The days were long, hot, and humid, and the ceiling fans were of little help. I was devoid of any energy, angry with myself, and filled with self-pity.

One evening, as I was out on the veranda with the twins who wouldn't stop crying, I felt so helpless and weak, I started crying, too. I looked up to find my dad watching me.

He came up and put his arm around my shoulders.

"How will this work out? It's not going to work out!" I sobbed.

"It's just a matter of six more months," he said softly. "The twins will become more manageable soon."

This made me cry harder. "I can barely get through one day," I said, "and you're saying six months?" A mountain-like load weighed me down.

He held my shoulders with both hands and peered into my eyes. "Wait and see. These boys will be your gold mines one day. Mark my words."

Dad always said the truth, I thought. But this meant my solace was still so far away!

After a few weeks, out of sheer despair, I wrote to my guru. "Master, you must know what life I am leading. I would like to dedicate myself to the services of the ashram. I want to come and stay there with my children. I could take up an admin job in your hospital or library and earn some money to send my children to school."

The reply came a week later, signed by the Master himself. "My child, the ashram does not have a paying job or a place to live with your children. If you love God, love your children first. They are sent by Him into your lap, so look after them and do your duty."

His reply disheartened me, but the idea of putting my children first stuck with me.

Now, Nina started going to a preschool, and the boys were standing and walking in their walkers. Mom hired a helping hand for the boys.

One evening, when Mom and I sat in the living area, my dad looked at my mom and said in a morose tone, "I wish I would have thought deeper about Dev's response to me when during

Kanchan's engagement ceremony. I had said to him, 'From today, my daughter is yours and your son is mine.' His comment was, 'He could not become ours. You may try.'"

Dad said those words had bothered him for years. He couldn't make sense of it and didn't share it even with my mom. He kept it to himself, buried deep in his heart, and berated himself for not knowing better.

I had made up my mind to get out of my marriage, but I didn't know which resources to tap. There were no computers yet, no Google, no online search. I didn't want to talk about it with my parents until I was sure and had sorted it out. First, I needed to know what divorce entailed: the laws and the trend of verdicts regarding the custody of children.

I discovered I could get free counsel at Patiala House, one of the five courts in Delhi, where advocates were available to provide legal advice. Leena and Jeej accompanied me. Leena thought it would be a good start.

I walked into a cramped, cluttered room filled with old, tethered files, papers hanging out, and stacks of thick, yellowed law books covered in dust.

The young lawyer sneered at me from behind his thick reading glasses as if saying, "What's this young woman doing here, where men belong?" His scorn changed into contempt when I told him the reason for my visit.

He rolled his eyes from his thick glasses and in a sarcastic tone said, "Tell me your side of the story. What do you do to him that he drinks so much and becomes violent?" His question was direct and had the malignant tone of an egotistical male chauvinist, who had no respect for women.

"Divorce proceedings take a lifetime, Madam," he said, stressing the word "Madam" sarcastically. "After two years of separation, if the desire for divorce is not mutual, there will be years of court hearings, which may feel like harassment to a young woman. The children will surely be separated from each other, as they are minors. The court will decide their custody." He further added, moving his hands in the air, "And Madam, there is no law stating a husband cannot beat his wife or that he is to be punished if he does so."

My already faded hopes were doomed, and I returned home with a heavy heart and a sense of failure. I was so ashamed of how I was treated by lawmakers and so-called protectors of society.

❊　❊　❊

Six months later, Vijay left his job in Kanpur or most certainly, was let go, and was back with his family in Delhi in search of a new job. Since he couldn't gather the courage to visit me at my parents' house, he knocked at Leena's house. He pleaded with her, visiting every evening. After several such visits, my sister, being a trusting person, was easily manipulated by Vijay.

"If you could just ask her to give me one last chance," he said yet again, "I will never repeat my condescending behavior. I am filled with shame. I love her and my children."

Soon, she found herself caught in the web of his mind games. Empathy and compassion for him were not far behind. She talked to Dad and Mom, and they called me into the discussion. I had no views, hopes, or desires left. I was totally immersed in self-loathing, demoralized, physically weak, and, above all, filled with guilt for diminishing my parents' retirement savings. I lived in a black hole with no way out.

Living with Vijay would at least free me from everyday guilt. We would live on his earnings and not my parents'. He had affection for his children. There was the hope of some days to be good. I just couldn't think of a life on my own with three children to feed. My employment was not an option until the children were a certain age. The chances of divorce, with custody of children, seemed very dim, so maybe I should give him one last chance.

At his repeated visits to my sister's house every evening, on my sister's request, I went to her house to see him. On seeing him, I thought of him as a faraway stranger, whom I had never known, for whom I had no feelings or emotions, while he was, undeniably, on his best behavior.

Predictably, the imploring started in front of Leena and Jeej, asking me to give him one last chance. When I did not respond or look at him, he sobbed.

"I will die without you, I don't have anyone else in my life, you are the only one. I have taken up a job in Vista's in New Delhi. There is a waiting period of one month till the current director retires."

He kneeled in front of me and held my hand tightly. "I have resigned and am back to Delhi. We can live in Gurgaon so that you are still close to your family."

He knew I needed my parents' help with children or else he would not want me living close to them. I freed my hand from his grip and looked at Leena and Jeej. They nodded their heads, as if to say, "Forgive him this one last time. He is really repenting."

Immensely confused and susceptible, I got up, ready to leave. "Let me talk to Mom and Dad. I am going to consider their views. I will let Leena know in a few days."

When I went back home, my parents said, "What do you want?" They were not asking me to leave him now—they would look after us till I became financially independent. They neither had the resources nor the thought anymore. I had no malice about it; I understood their situation.

With an exhausted and sullen face, I gathered the guts to tell them I could perhaps take another chance with him if we could stay in their house until he started his new job or maximum of two months until we found a rental. I saw some promise in this proposal, as he would be living under their vigilance. We could decide on certain boundaries: no drinking, no coming home late, no abusive language, and no outbursts. Laying his hands on me would be out of the question. They nodded in agreement but with some apprehension.

The master bedroom was given to me with a small cot on the side for Nina. The kids in India are not weaned away in a separate room till they are of certain age. Vijay behaved well with my parents and so did my parents. One month passed quickly. He was on his best behavior, respectful to my parents. There was no drinking, no bullying, and no anger outbursts.

Vijay started his job. He drove back home in time to have dinner together, but I didn't trust it would continue. *Do people change unless they are committed?* Then one night he betrayed trust of my parents and me, knocked late at night, and quickly walked to our bedroom. He asked me to serve him dinner in there.

My dad smelled alcohol in the air but didn't say anything. Vijay took advantage of the situation and the nicety of my parents. He not only frequently came home after boozing out with his buddies but also did not respect the boundaries of coming home at a decent time. His ridicule and abuse were not far behind. He started the bullying inside our room. His hostility created fear in me, and I worried his voice would reach my parents or Nina would say something. This was my own fault. Staying with my parents was a bad idea when Vijay, who continually failed his promises, never changed. I should have known better.

One evening, dispirited and limp, I stood outside on my parents' veranda, clutching the twins tightly to my chest, my daughter clinging to my legs. Vijay had fought with me and ran out in his flip-flops, shouting over his shoulder that he wasn't coming back. My parents were unaware of this incident. Standing outside on the veranda was a way to let go of my agony, out in the open, away from my parents' peaceful house. I was suffocating and choking. *When will these atrocities end, oh God? When will You look at me? I always thought I was Your blessed child and you my Father, so how can You see me suffering in the hands of this man? How can You see me in so much anguish and pain?*

I stood there still, gazing at the sky turning gray from evening to night. The children dead quiet, as if they sensed my worry. And then, I felt a shadow at the back of my neck. I turned to find a woman by the fence between my parents' house and the house next door, in absolute silence. I hadn't heard her approach. She smiled at me, and I forced a smile back still holding the twins.

"You must be Mr. Bhaskar's daughter?" she asked. I nodded.

She introduced herself, then asked, "Are you all right? You look sad."

The dam of tears waiting to burst, broke, and I let them flow. She was beautiful, with big eyes, jet-black curly hair, and her face glowed under the light filtering from the street pole. She was probably in her mid to late forties. She said she was visiting India from the United Kingdom and staying in her brother's vacant house to rest before leaving the next day.

With boys on my both arms, I could not even wipe my tears. I shared my plight with her.

She listened carefully. "But you seem like an educated girl to me."

I nodded again.

"So why do you continue to live with him?" I continued to be quiet. My eyes cast down.

"The first step toward your survival is to stop the self-pity and become financially independent," she said with an assertive tone.

"But how can I go to work with three little children?"

"Those are excuses. You have to stop making excuses and start to take action for the sake of your three children and your-self. Do whatever it takes. Put them in day care and go to work. Money will bring you confidence and make you self-reliant." She wished me good luck, patted the children from across the fence, and returned to her brother's house.

I had goose bumps. Her words touched my heart, as if I'd been waiting for her to come in my life to show me the direction. All these years and no one had spoken those words in such a direct voice to me, including my own parents. No one had put me on that path. She must have been an angel, sent in response to me beseeching Him.

I contemplated her words and felt an instant change. I heard me saying to myself, *You are educated and employable. You had always been a confident girl, the pride of your parents and teachers. Why have you become a vegetable? Where is the girl who was a feminist during her college days, who signed papers against the dowry system, and violence against women? Where is that girl?*

I had a rush of adrenaline pumping into my blood. I walked back into the house with the children and asked my mom to watch them. I locked myself in the bathroom and let the warm, wet tears wash away the victim in me. Then when I was left with no tears, I splashed water on my face, looked into the mirror, and raised my chin. I straightened my limp spine, stood erect with a long neck, and ran my fingers through my lengthy, disheveled hair, twisting it into a neat bun. I applied kohl to line my eyes to pour some life into them. My inner voice said, *You can do this. You are certainly capable of doing this.*

The image in the mirror echoed back at me, *I can do this. I certainly have the capability to do this.* My Master's words resonated in my heart. I had to do this for my children's sake. I then walked out of the bathroom with a fervor, head held high.

Overnight, a miraculous transformation in me followed. I knew this was the Universe coming together to help me. I became like a tigress who would take care of her cubs. I resolved to get back to my old self, fighting for my rights and making my own decisions—the fierce and confident Kanchan. I kept myself awake and firmed up a plan that night, a mission with a strategy, aligning with my end goal. I was going to achieve it by taking small steps, one by one. I didn't assign timelines yet.

I first had to reduce my anxiety and guilt. I needed to rent a separate house and stop being a burden on my parents.

The next morning, over tea, I told Vijay without divulging any of my long-term plans. "It's been a much longer stay with my parents than we discussed, and you haven't mentioned moving out. We need to do that now! I'm going to the property agents in the marketplace today while you are gone for work."

※　※　※

It took us a month to get a second-floor rental three blocks away from my parents, so they could continue to help me with the children.

Once moved out, my focus shifted to finding a job to become financially independent. I had not gone to work for years. I was nearly thirty at the time, eight years behind for an entry-level job in an office space. My angel's words reverberated.

"Don't make excuses."

A teaching job would be best, since I had kids at home and the hours were reasonable. I told Vijay about my job plans, and he didn't object this time with a protest or tearing up of an offer letter. With his spotty job history and children to support, it worked in his favor.

A few weeks later, after a lot of thinking, the idea of meeting with Mrs. Gulati, the principal and owner of Nina's school, seemed feasible. A stern woman and typical businessperson, she responded positively to my surprise. She said she was very fond of Nina. I was offered a substitute teaching job for an English teacher on maternity leave for classes IV and V. The salary offered was below minimum wage: six hundred rupees a month. In addition to not paying well, the job required extra hours after school, but this would be a good start. Despite the low salary and additional hours, I came home happy and successful in my endeavor.

A month later, I enrolled myself in a teacher training program, which would qualify me for a higher salary. The classes were held on weekends at Sanatan Dharma College in Delhi, which meant traveling on overcrowded public buses. I didn't ask Vijay to drive me, nor did he offer.

On the first day of class, I saw a familiar face, a woman who lived in the same neighborhood that I did in Gurgaon. At the end of the day, Rekha, the woman, offered me a ride home in her car and to come pick me up next morning.

Atul Srivastava, her husband, was in the driver's seat when they came next morning. We casually chatted on our way, and I shared I had an MSW degree and a postgraduate certificate but was doing the teacher training course out of the need to earn money.

Atul said, "Can you give me your resume? Our managing director has been interviewing candidates with similar qualifications, but he has not yet approved of any."

That night I updated my resume to hand over next morning.

Two days later, my landlady received a call asking for me. It was a call from Niki, the managing director's secretary. I was invited for an interview by Mr. Sumit Bose at Air Carrier Inc.

There was no job description or title mentioned. *It has to be a mere exploratory interview,* I thought.

The name Air Carrier sounded like a travel agency or a courier company. I hadn't realized I was going to interview for a Fortune 500 global company. Excited, nervous, and apprehensive, my mind chattered. *I might not get the job since I lack work experience, but I will still ask them to consider hiring me. And I will ask for a minimum salary, a little more than the school pays me.*

I dressed in a white cotton sari with a red border and a matching red blouse. This Bengali sari was gifted by Leena when she visited Kolkata. I wore my old pair of heels, applied subtle makeup, and bowed in front of my guru's picture before I left the house. I walked with my head held high, as Dad had taught us. I prayed, gathered my courage, and repeated to myself, *I can do this. I have to do this for my children's sake. I must do this!*

When I arrived, Niki, Mr. Bose's secretary, ushered me into his large plush office. Mr. Bose was polished and suave, his diction clear and precise. He created a relaxing interview environment, relating my replies to his own life. He had been educated at the IT College where I had lived all my life, and he was originally from Kolkata. His daughters had studied in the same school I had.

There was an instant rapport between us. I felt as if he could read into my soul and see my honesty.

After interviewing for an hour, he asked, "So what kind of a job are you looking for?"

"Anything in general administration or office support," I said.

Surprised, he said, "But you have a higher education in human resources. Why would you do a general administration job? I have an open job, for which I interviewed several candidates in the past couple of months, and I find you the best qualified." He explained the job responsibility, which was to look after and manage performance-related and compensation-related confidential matters of his direct reports, named as unclassified staff. Another responsibility was ensuring the well-being of the all the staff.

He then picked up his gold Parker pen and a yellow Post-it note, thought for a bit, wrote down something, and handed the paper to me. The note listed my salary, all the numbers clean and clear. My jaw dropped. The base salary was four times the school's salary. In addition, there was a generous benefits package, including an allowance for child education, and one for house rent. I was not only surprised but almost shocked. Perhaps he mistook my surprised look as not happy because he immediately explained after completing a six-month probationary period, I might get a raise or a promotion to a manager position based on my performance.

He called Niki to draft the offer letter and handed her the Post-it.

"When can you start?" he asked me.

I flustered a little since this was happening too fast. "I have three children," I said, "ages five and two. I'll have to find a nanny for them. I can start in two weeks."

He nodded. "You may accept the offer letter before leaving today and start in two weeks."

Niki brought the offer letter, and I signed it. I shook hands with him and then turned toward the door in a confident gait, spine erect. As soon as I passed the exit door, I leaned against the corner of the building before my legs caved in out of exhilaration. I had joined a large conglomerate, headquartered in the United States, a wholly owned subsidiary of Global Technologies Corporation. Air Carrier, an air-conditioning company had just entered the Indian markets.

I pushed myself up and rushed to my parents' house. I jumped out of eagerness when I saw them.

"I go it, I got it!" We held each other and shed some tears of joy and relief. I was filled with love and gratefulness.

I walked home with a sense of pride. Vijay sat in the dining area, disheveled, in his pajamas and an undershirt, unemployed once again after not getting along with his boss. He looked at me with questioning eyes.

I smiled and told him they'd hired me. He pulled me into a shallow hug. "I knew my wife would get the job," he said. "She is so smart."

I didn't know if he was truly happy for me or just relieved. We hadn't paid rent for a couple of months, and I was leaving apologetic notes under the door of the owner, ashamed to face him. However, our lives were going to change from this point forward.

The magnitude of this victory hit me when I sat down in my chair, removed my heels, lifted my legs, and sat crossed-legged. I paid my humble gratitude to the higher power who made this happen and the angel who had brushed past my life for a few moments, whose words of wisdom changed our lives forever.

I was going to be financially independent.

The next day, I visited the day school for toddlers run by an unpretentious and respectful army general's wife, to enroll the boys. I hired domestic help to cook and look after the kids when they returned from school in the afternoon. I was ready to start my job. My first day was to be July 12, 1987, coincidentally or by His design, the day my mom and dad married.

❊   ❊   ❊

My first day at work, I was prepared and well-practiced. I collected my energy, and my will came along. Mr. Bose's big office opened to a large foyer on the second floor, where two desks were placed. One of them was my desk, parallel to Niki's.

It was a long, unpaved road for me, from a physically-abused woman and a homemaker to a white-collar employee at a highly professional company run by its US board of directors. The reality dawned on me within the first few days. Sitting at home in that tumultuous environment for seven years, I'd forgotten how to speak a complete sentence of good English, my memory had diminished, my confidence was at an all-time low, and my anxiety levels were high. I'd never worked in a corporate environment or on a computer before.

Niki envied me from the beginning. I had a more promising career path than she did. The other two lady secretaries followed Niki's lead and were aloof. They were overconfident, strong-headed, and egotistical, having been hired from the same hospitality industry as the chairman and managing director.

The chairman and managing director were both picked from the highly-reputable and revenue-generating India Tea Company. Both were extremely capable high-level executives hired by Global Technologies Corporation to establish an American company in India, during the time when globalization entered Indian markets.

In the initial weeks, Niki would highlight and circle my typing errors, since I had never typed on a computer before. She showed them to Mr. Bose, but he knew I had no office experience, and he was also aware of Niki's attitude. He became a mentor, teaching me the basics first: how to send a fax, how to answer the phone and say, "Kanchan speaking" instead of "hello" and how to pronounce certain words "it's not *almeerah*, it's *almiira*," he would say.

He was educated in the UK, a professional CPA and belonged to an affluent, well-respected family in Kolkata. He was polished, par excellence in behavior and mannerism, and always exquisitely dressed. And while things were wrong with Dr. Sarkar, everything with Mr. Bose felt right. I vowed I would never let him regret his decision to hire me.

However, to survive in the fast-paced corporate world, I had to not only speedily learn the job but also excel at it, not giving anyone a chance to find fault with my work.

The environment was challenging, as well as the metamorphosis into a professional while continuing my role as a homemaker and mother. To add to the stress, Niki joined forces with another group of ex-India Tea Company professionals inside the company so there was more ridicule and harassment.

❉ ❉ ❉

The stress was overwhelming the first year. I would come home after a day full of disappointments and cry behind closed doors in the bathroom to loosen my heavy heart, embarrassments, and hurt. But then I would wipe my tears, open the door, look at my children's faces, and feel a bit stronger, ready to face a new challenge the next morning.

Since this was a rare opportunity, I learned and grew from every conversation and interaction with the management. I became more confident, stronger, and adept at corporate dynamics. I stopped taking things personally and learned from the managing director, other managers, and even Niki, my opponent, whose envy bestowed me with daily encounters. They all helped me see it as an opportunity to transform myself in my profession.

Mr. Bose's consistent support continued. He saw my willingness and drive to succeed, and he nurtured me to allow my suppressed potential to flourish, frequently calling me into his office to introduce me to the vice presidents and managers. It took me a year or more to gain confidence and be at the level I needed to be.

I established a routine to get up early, dress the children, pack their lunch bags, see them off to school, and quickly-but-flawlessly dress myself. I understood, early on, that presentation matters in the corporate world.

In the evening, after a busy day, I would walk to my parents' house to hold my children who were waiting for me, and then walk them home. Once at home, I'd serve dinner on the table. We had nice interaction about their day, the school, and their homework. Then it was time for their showers and tucking them in their beds. I would listen to their nursery rhymes, rhyming together before switching off the lights.

I would then wait for Vijay to come home from work if he was in a job or wherever he was, apprehensive and anxious about what mood he might be in.

At night, I'd take a sleeping pill to rest my mind and to get up fresh next morning. To remain sane, I had to divert my mind to some good things in life. Of course, the children were one big part of my joy, but I needed to create my own space where it was just me and my blank mind.

I started conditioning my brain to create my own environment. I would create virtual images, visualizing snow-clad mountains, gushing waterfalls, infinite sky with seagulls gliding, forests filled with wilderness, and flowers blooming in all colors.

These images calmed me. It was relaxing and therapeutic for me and helped me nourish my brain. I was able to rewire my brain and felt happiness in tiny things as I did when I was a child, seeing a bud blooming, a squirrel running on a tree, a hummingbird static in the air, butterflies outside my window, or the moon appearing every day in a different shape. This helped me remain in the present and be mindful.

With time, my commitment and dedication at work paid off. The attitudes of two secretaries closest to Niki became better. Niki's attitude softened, but she remained assertive with me.

The children never troubled me, their behavior was excellent, and so was their health. They were wonderful kids. Vijay was oblivious to this. He was in his own world, his situation worsening. He was in and out of jobs several times due to his anger issues erupting out of his insecurities. However, he had no problem with me going to work dressed up, attending office get-togethers, or getting dropped off by my male colleagues. I brought home a steady and stable income.

It took me long time to understand Vijay's "man role" belief system and his heinous male narcissist ego which made him believe man was at the top of human hierarchy. He was to be obeyed, he was superior in gender, and he had the authority . . . where a woman was to be submissive, obedient, serving, and dumb with no voice of her own except to move her head sideways like a cow. A woman, if shouting to protect herself, was prone to be called "drama queen," never a man.

I tried to keep the children away during any violent episodes but sometimes I heard the twins crying inside their bedroom, Nina refusing to let them open the door. Then there would be silence, perhaps because they were fearful their dad would beat them, too. But he never raised a hand to the children, except once to Nina when she tried to protect me.

His rage fueled the strength in his lean frame so that when he pushed and shoved me, managing him physically was unthinkable. One time he choked me so hard by inserting his thumb in my throat that I couldn't breathe and felt as though my eyeballs would pop out. That night, I decided I would make an appointment with the doctor for a medical exam, but the next morning I had to go to work. I didn't want the news to spread to my work. I couldn't jeopardize my job and my financial stability, both of which allowed me to hold onto my sanity.

And I didn't want the complications. The police, which would be the first point of contact in any emergency, were mostly hired from villages with strong roots in patriarchy. Beating women was a widespread practice. And they were not supposed to talk about it. It was an accepted norm. Vijay, being a very logical man and a business consultant by profession, was skilled at influencing and persuading people in organizations, problem-solving their issues, and making plausible and convincing arguments.

During the next few years, Vijay was unemployed for prolonged periods, which caused financial difficulties. We had to move into a cheaper rental in the same community. During one of his makeup phases, when he pleaded with me to forgive him, I convinced him to consult a psychiatrist. Fortunately, he agreed this time. Not wanting him to change his mind, I quickly found Dr. Kothari, a reputable psychiatrist in Defence Colony, and went with Vijay to the appointment.

After talking to Vijay, the doctor called me into his office and handed me a thick textbook marked to the chapter on what was then called manic depressive disorder, now known as bipolar disorder. He asked me to read it and advised that Vijay's episodes would only increase unless he could control them with regular medication, which he would prescribe. That night and the next morning, Vijay refused to accept the diagnosis and take the medication.

I called Dr. Kothari. "So, what's the alternative?"

"Divorce is the only solution to this," he said. "The earlier, the better. This is the only way out if he refuses to take responsibility for his behavior. His situation will only worsen as time passes."

But with divorce, I would lose my children. I was back to square one.

Vijay behaved sanely the next few days, as was his cycle. During these periods, he was the best husband and father. He cooked, joked, watched television with us, pampered the kids, played with them, and romanced me. He took me to the best stores to buy a pair of heels, a nice bag, or a silk sari of his choice. He would watch me when I dressed up in the morning, standing against the dresser with me when I applied makeup. He would say "I love you" a hundred times. I loved the feeling of being loved by a man and learned to relish those moments of love to live my fantasy. I wasn't sure if alternately loving someone and loathing them could be called love, though.

Each time he hit the sane phases, I'd think, *What if he can mend himself? What if he accepted the diagnosis and took the medication?* Life would be wonderful. I wouldn't have to struggle and stress about our safety or divorce, adversely affecting my children.

Every time things were peaceful, I'd become hopeful. Maybe things would change this time. Maybe he wouldn't hit me since he'd made love to me two days earlier. He had certainly learned the art. He would sleep with his head on my bosom as a child would, which would wake my compassion for him. So, I was always on a roller coaster.

One night, I stood on the balcony after tucking the children in. It was midnight, and Vijay still hadn't come home. Worry had turned into fear, fear for myself and my children. I knew the aftermath of his arriving home this late. It was almost 1:00 a.m. when his lean figure staggered down the dimly lit lane toward our building. I swiftly went inside, not knowing whether to take care of him first or myself or if I needed to protect the kids.

I quietly closed the door to the kids' room and unbolted the front door. I waited in the bedroom, holding my breath, but I couldn't hear his footsteps approaching. Perhaps he was walking stealthily up the stairs so as not to wake up the landlord. Despite his being drunk, he could gather his senses when he needed to. Finally, the front door creaked open. He entered the bedroom and stuttered his excuse.

"No transport, so hitched ride a truck," he managed to say.

It was all a story. He'd been most likely dropped at the corner by one of his booze buddies. This was not the first time.

Vijay left the bedroom and I followed and stopped him from opening the kids' door and waking them. Nina was most affected by the violence and abuse, both physical and mental. The boys were still too young to understand, or at least I hoped against hope. Nina not only had to make sense of what was going on around her but also wanted to protect her brothers and me on some level.

He peered at me. "Where's my whiskey bottle?"

"I haven't seen it," I said.

He held my arm and dragged me to the living room. "Go, find it," he ordered.

I stared him down and tried to free myself. He pulled me to the floor, pinned my arms, and straddled me, his knees on my chest. I tried to turn my head, but he dug his fingers into my cheeks and demanded that I keep my face straight and keep looking at him. This modus operandi repeated itself over and over.

"I can't breathe," I said. The weight of his body with his knees on my chest hurt my ribs.

But he didn't care. He was in control—I was his slave. He was having delusions of grandeur. I would have to do whatever he wanted me to do, and he wanted me to choke while looking into his eyes so that he could see my fear. So, I gazed right back. He pulled me up and dragged me into the bathroom, where he shoved my head in the toilet. He tried to push it toward the water like he was going to drown me while I tried shouting for help.

When Nina came running out of their room and the boys followed, he let me go. Then he pushed us all out the front door. He sent the children out first, and then he caught hold of me and pulled my blouse with such force that the buttons popped off. I was scared he would kill me. The children were silent as he shut the door on us.

It was almost 2.30 a.m. I held the twins, one in each arm. We heard the door lock and we waited, but he didn't open it. And I didn't want to knock and risk igniting his anger or waking the landlord or neighbors. So, I asked Nina to go down the stairs and walk with me to my parents' house. She was six and the boys were three.

I picked up the boys, one in each arm, and climbed down the stairs. We walked as fast as we could to my mom and dad's. I had no other option. I was helpless and in tears. We kept walking in the dark. I kept turning to see if anyone followed us and checked to make sure no one was hiding behind the bushes to jump out and snatch my children. The distance was only three blocks, but it felt like thirty.

I kept consoling the children. "Mom is here. Don't worry. We will be okay."

We were all barefoot and frightened when we knocked on my parents' door. They ushered us in, no questions asked. Dad and Mom took the children into their bedroom, while I settled on the sofa, eyes wide and awake.

In just a few hours, daylight broke. I went to work dressed in my mom's sari.

Chapter 9

Building a Ramp

1990–1994

Before signing a contract with a divorce lawyer, it was pertinent to corroborate the facts, the legal angle, essentially around child custody, from a more learned and experienced attorney. Mom obtained the contact information of a retired sessions judge in Gurgaon, a highly-influential judge who practiced from his home office. His private chamber was not far from my house.

Neel was no more in my life. After his marriage, he had to distance from me to make his marriage work. I sensed his dilemma and set him free from any expectation of him. I wanted him to be happy in his life, with his family.

After work, I stopped by the judge's sprawling bungalow around the corner from the Gurgaon circle. I had eyed this massive, quiet bungalow surrounded by huge trees hiding it from noisy traffic and dust from the road, not knowing I would be visiting it one day.

Judge Mehta was gracious enough to see me without an appointment. He greeted me at the door, and we headed toward a long corridor leading to his office at the back of his house. He was of average height, heavily built, in a clean but wrinkled white shirt and white pants, his oily, salt-and-pepper hair well combed backward. He wore thick glasses in broad black plastic frames. He had a firm, assertive voice, and a heavy demeanor. I refrained from judging the judge, as that was his job.

Once seated, he was prompt and did not want me to waste his calculated paid time. I summarized my story quickly and asked him to explain the divorce process and the likely outcome, specifically regarding the custody of my children.

After listening to me intently, he asked a question that caught me by surprise.

"What do you do to make him beat you?"

Astonished, I tried absorbing what he asked me. This highly reputable and experienced attorney was no different from the young, inexperienced Patiala House advocate. This was how men were conditioned in India and, regrettably, only men held positions of power.

Judge Mehta told me according to divorce laws, there would need to be a separation of at least a year or two and no visiting rights before a divorce could be filed for. Divorce proceedings could be a lengthy and harassing process, especially for a woman, as the courtroom environment could be discriminating as well as intimidating. Undoubtedly, the children would be split up, divided between the two parents. And if, by any chance, even if falsely, Vijay implicated me for infidelity, which was easily doable by hiring so-called professionals, Vijay could then become sole custodian of all three children.

In the eyes of the law, beating one's wife under the influence of alcohol was not considered a crime worth asking for divorce. But infidelity by a woman was!

I left his office demoralized. How would I ever be legally free? If the session court judge, a senior most authority in the court system thought so narrowly then how would society at large declare a different fate for a distressed woman who was prey to a violent man?

When I arrived home late that evening, Vijay was already there, sitting with a glass of whiskey in his hand. I looked at his questioning eyes and told him about my visit to Judge Mehta. He showed no surprise, as if he had an inkling. Instead, he asked that we go to see Judge Mehta together the next day.

In front of the judge, undeniably, Vijay was at his most charming self and came across as grounded, logical, and innocent, which made me appear conniving and untruthful in an attempt to malign and manipulate him. Vijay said he loved me, and the fights happened only because he sometimes drank a little and I provoked him.

"But that is hardly any grounds for divorce," Judge Mehta said.

Although Judge Mehta knew my story from our conversation the day before, he nodded when he heard Vijay's side of things. Wife beating was—and to this day is—an unspoken but acceptable norm, more so in backward rural areas, but urban areas and cities were not immune to it. Although Judge Mehta had his roots in the rural areas, one would still expect a judge to be unprejudiced, inquiring and weighing both sides equally, being a man of law.

After hearing Vijay, he advised we should both sign a notarized document stating Vijay would not raise a hand to me.

"The day he does," Judge Mehta said, "will be the day when your separation will begin."

We both looked at each other and without saying a word, nodded as we readied to sign the document.

For a few months, Vijay was on his best behavior. He would come home on time and sober, and then take two or three pegs of liquor at home. He would joke around and play with the kids, and he was well behaved and nice to me. In the evenings, we would watch TV together and then sit down as a happy family for dinner.

I was pleased but fearful. The time for him to revert to his old behavioral pattern was not far off. His snapping at trivial things had already begun. Then he started to pick tiny issues to badger me, corner me into an argument, and try to rile me.

He threw his shirt at my face one night and said, "Don't you see it has no button? Why didn't you see that?" Then he launched into a tirade about how other women respected their husbands and I didn't. That I was good for nothing. He abused me verbally, without touching me.

And his final ace? I had held a sword to his neck in the form of the notarized document. With each day, his anger grew. The shouting and abuse intensified, and he threw objects at me for no reason. I grew frightened, anticipating where this was going. I tried talking to him in the evenings after work, but it made no sense to him. Surprisingly, he would not be angry with the kids. He would wait for them to go to sleep before he resumed his drinking.

One Sunday, the children and I went to a park in walking distance from the house. Vijay wanted to stay home and rest. My parents also joined us, so we had some fun together playing games. We talked about the twins' admission to the same school as Nina, the prestigious Air Force School in New Delhi. It was known for its disciplined curriculum and holistic approach to the development of students. Children of top-ranking officials from the army, navy, and air force were the first to get the seats, and limited ones remained for civilians. Therefore, the competition was high, seats were limited, and the admissions waitlist was long.

The boys' entrance test results were to be out the next day, on Monday morning. A parent's attendance was essential to secure the seat and not lose it to the next on the list, so I was all charged up to go get the results, and so were the twins. My parents were equally excited. I was certain Vijay was, too.

We headed home after sunset, entering the house through the living room door, as it was open, and the children ran to their room. The living room reeked of alcohol. Vijay limply lay on the sofa, completely smashed. As soon as we came in, hearing our voices, he got up and staggered to the bathroom.

When he came out a few minutes later, a familiar chemical smell that I could not quite place clung to him, his white shirt soaked wet across his chest. He lurched into the living room and lay on the ground on the carpet. Something was not right.

"What have you done?" I panicked.

He stuttered that he'd consumed Baygon, a strong chemical poison used for killing cockroaches, commonly found in almost every Indian kitchen. Perhaps he was just acting out and had spilled some Baygon on his shirt to fool me . . . a grotesque manipulation. He wanted me to be his hostage forever. He'd been threatening to commit suicide all this time and had never truly attempted it.

He blabbered, his tongue twisted, pointing at the coffee table. He had written a suicide note.

What? So, he did it, he had been saying it for years. Did he truly consume the killer poison? I panicked and hurried toward the coffee table and picked up the pages to confirm if he was telling the truth.

"I have been pushed to commit suicide." I did not read any further. So, he had actually consumed poison. I spun toward him. I was in shock. I had never thought he would actually attempt to kill himself. He lay there, restless and gasping, his body in spasms. He'd started to froth at the mouth.

My brain fogged. Should I run out to call the doctor, or try to keep Vijay awake? I ran out twice but came back to him. The children were in the other room and must have heard the commotion.

I called Nina and shouted, "Baby, run and get Dr. Manju Bhatia."

She lived close but not close enough. Although it was not a good idea to send Nina out in the dark at 8:00 p.m., there was no option and no time to think. I couldn't leave Vijay alone. His eyeballs slid on the left, his mouth profusely frothing. I talked to him, tapped his face, and lifted his neck to give him some water, but he didn't respond. He was slipping in and out of consciousness, his head tilted to one side, froth continuously seeping out of his mouth.

Dr. Bhatia arrived in about fifteen minutes. She tried poking pins into Vijay's wrists and then his face. Vijay didn't respond. The twins had slipped out of the house quietly to run to my parents.

My dad appeared at my door and saw Dr. Bhatia sitting on the floor next to Vijay, trying to bring him to consciousness.

"Let's get him to the hospital!" he shouted.

My dad, Dr. Bhatia, and I loaded Vijay into the back of my dad's car. In ten minutes, we were in the emergency room of the nearest government hospital, where they immediately put Vijay on a stretcher and took him to the operating room to pump his stomach.

I was shaking. However monstrous a man, I had never wanted him to die. One major reason not to leave him so far was his threats to commit suicide if I left him; I could not bear that. Additionally, his suicide would ruin at least three families. Possible scenarios of ruin if he succumbed reeled through my mind. His family could put the blame on me. His suicide note must have our names. The police would not even investigate. They would simply grab me and my parents and take us away in handcuffs with charges of abetting suicide. My children would be literally out on the streets, with no one to look after them.

Two burly police inspectors, stinking of day-long perspiration, approached me and took me to one of the open rooms in the hospital. They spoke in a Haryanvi accent, atypical of a rural and agricultural state of Haryana from where the majority of Delhi police force was recruited.

"What drove him to consume poison? What pushed him to attempt suicide? Where were you? Who else was there? Did you give him the poison?"

I was terrified. My voice refused to come out, afraid of the loud and mean grilling by the policemen. I wiped my wet nose with the end of my dupatta. My nose usually watered when I cried silently, within. Perhaps the tear glands drained the water out through my nose when the tears refused to come out of the eyes, wary of people around.

I opened my mouth to speak, but I still could not find my voice. I tried again, it came out, raspy, strained, and hoarse. In a low pitch, I narrated them the episode. To my disbelief, they took turns to tell me, in a softer tone this time, "Madamji, we will write a formal investigation report based on your narrative. You can now go and check your husband's condition."

Perhaps they could gauge my honesty and humility when added to my city upbringing.

The doctor came forward to let us know Vijay's stomach had been pumped out and he was out of danger, but we should take him to a major hospital in New Delhi within the next hour for further hospitalization. They loaded him into an ambulance, hooked up a drip, and covered his face with an oxygen mask. We took off for Delhi, red lights flashing, siren shrieking the entire way, clearing the traffic on the jammed Gurgaon–Delhi Road. My dad and I sat inside the ambulance with Vijay. Mom left for home to take care of the children. The entire one-hour ride, I sat quietly, my head down, not looking at my dad. I couldn't meet his eyes.

Halfway through the drive, Vijay opened his eyes, looked at me, extended his arm, and pulled me toward him. "I love you," he said. "I don't want to die." He started to cry.

I was completely drained, half dead, frightened for his life, worried about my children, scared for our safety, my dad running around with his heart condition—all Vijay's vicious doing—and he said he loved me and that he did not want to die. *Is this love or a sadist's hatred? Is this his tactic to scare me? Does he know the poison could take his life and malign the rest of us left behind?* I wanted to run away from him but ironically held his hand instead. I didn't know how else to react in that sensitive moment.

At Safdarjung Hospital, across the road from AIIMS, where all of my three children were born, Vijay was put on a stretcher and taken into the emergency ward. Dad and I waited in the corridor. After a couple of hours of checkups, Vijay was moved to the ICU. We were told he would be under observation for forty-eight hours.

I called his father and told him his son had attempted suicide. I'd kept a lot from his family, protecting the widowed father from the stress of his son, who was bent upon proving his father a failure in ways of raising him. But he needed to know now. This could not be—and should not be—hidden from them. They would blame me if he were to die or be crippled. I was in a rage and prepared to talk in case they questioned me, but fortunately they didn't.

At almost midnight, I asked Dad to go home and come back in the morning. I stayed the rest of the night, keeping an eye on Vijay while my despicable thoughts would not stop.

The long night changed into morning. I sat on a most uncomfortable three-legged stool, barely fitting my hips. It was Monday morning; I would have to leave Vijay for a few hours under my dad's observation. It was the big day for which my boys and I had waited so long. I had to acquire the seats for my boys, even in dire circumstances such as this. If I missed today, the seats would be given to other children and mine would lose a massive opportunity. The school was a big deal for me. It was like getting admission into Harvard. A huge gap existed between this school and any other.

As soon as Dad arrived early that morning, I took a motor rickshaw to Leena's house. I needed to change from my Sunday casual attire, which was stained and smelly, and if I stopped by my house, farther away, I'd never make the deadline. I showered at my sister's and managed to get into one of her dresses. I also borrowed a pair of heels, stuffing the toes with cotton balls to keep them on my feet.

I arrived at the school before 8:30 a.m., heading to the administration building, where I was handed the boys' test results. They had passed the test, as expected, but there was a glitch. The school had only one seat left to offer a civilian. I was not going to accept this defeat. Perhaps the remnants of rage at Vijay and my natural rebellion were ready to surface. I would get both my sons into the same school. The twins couldn't be separated during their formative years.

From the administration building, I walked directly to the school principal's office. On the way, I talked myself into getting my wits and energy for the crucial meeting. It was a make-or-break situation, just like a war zone and I had to win. Although I understood the school's policy, I was determined to present my case to Mr. Nigam, a retired commodore with the air force. I waited outside the office until a tall man in a navy uniform came out with his child.

I barged in before the door closed. "I shall take only five minutes of your time, sir."

He looked at me with surprise that I'd been let in without an appointment, but I suppose he could see the desperation on my face. Also, being from the armed forces, he would be respectful to a woman. He nodded, without offering me a seat.

"The issue, sir, is that I'm being offered one seat for my two boys, who happen to be twins. Where do you propose I enroll the other? Do you really think it would be wise to separate them at such a young age?"

Commodore Nigam tried to convince me to try another school as he couldn't breach the policies of the school.

"I need your compassion in this unique situation, sir." I also reminded him Nina, a pupil of his school, was an all-rounder student and liked by teachers as well as peers. Her teachers thought highly of her. She would soon be unanimously nominated as Head Girl of the school, a valedictorian position, in grade V.

His eyes were frozen on my face but not actually looking at me, as he pondered.

"I have one reserved seat left. It is allocated to Commander Sony's son. The commander is supposed to come in at 10:00 a.m. But if he doesn't appear at ten sharp, the seat will be yours."

That was a reasonable and acceptable response coming from a responsible position. It did not call for a disagreement.

I had an hour to wait. Unwavering, I sat outside Commodore Nigam's office with full conviction the twins would get seats. Each time Commodore Nigam's big white office door creaked open, he would glance at me waiting resolutely outside his door. I constantly looked at my watch, my anxiety going up by each minute. It was 10:00, then 10:05; then 10:10. I had not seen anyone go inside his office, which provided little comfort. My paranoid mind said, *Commander Sony may have talked to Commodore Nigam over the phone and gotten the seat. This is why he is not calling me in.*

At 10:12 a.m., Commodore Nigam's assistant opened the door and ushered me in. Commodore Nigam had a sliver of a smile on his small, fish-like mouth and thin lips, making his black mustache crooked on his round poker face. He picked up his silver Parker pen with a gold tip, lifted his face to look at me for a flicker of a second, and then went back to having no expression and no words while my heart still raced. He then signed the papers lying in front of him and handed two sets to me.

OMG! My eyes opened wide, and my lips parted in disbelief. "Congratulations!"

He stood up, like any gentleman would, to shake my hand. I returned his smile, shook his hand, and full of gratitude, thanked him emphatically. It was a great achievement and a step ahead. I'd stood my ground and fought for what was best for my children. I took a moment to enjoy this success and elation and sighed deeply before going to the admissions office to pay for the twins. My children were taken care of. Time to go back to my other reality.

It was almost noon when I reached the hospital reception, where I was told the patient was doing better and had been moved to the general ward.

My father-in-law, Dev, and sister-in-law, Shiela, came to see Vijay after almost twenty hours since getting the news. They greeted me warmly on the surface, to my surprise, not showing any emotions against me. They knew Vijay's vices and his behavior toward me. Sanjay knew part of the story, and Shiela another, which meant, I assumed, that they all knew.

I told them about the incident. They listened quietly.

Shiela repeated, "Both my aunties have tolerated the violence of my uncles their entire married lives and not uttered a word." My patience with her was giving way. I wanted to give a proper reply. *You should have brought another girl for your brother from the same village, where girls tolerate violence and live their lives as doormats.*

But before I could say it, Dev saw my face filled with anguish, my teeth clenching in my closed mouth, my jaw moving. Dev tapped her arm to stop. I stared her down and then turned away.

The second day, the two police inspectors who had filed the formal investigation report came to take Vijay's statement. They looked at me with the gaze of familiarity. I stepped aside and held my breath while they questioned him. What if Vijay said that I'd forced him to take poison or that my parents had? I didn't trust him. However, he owned his suicide attempt to the police inquiry. He said he was fully responsible, and no one else had anything to do with it. The charge was dropped, and no FIR was lodged. The hospital discharged Vijay after a psychiatric evaluation.

The report said, "Manic depressive" and prescribed medication.

I took him home. Nina never asked me what had happened, and neither did the boys. And I didn't ask my parents what they'd told them. My hunch was the children knew exactly what had happened. I was just relieved it was over. I'd been so frightened to think what would have happened, I couldn't bear to talk about it.

Vijay refused to make a follow-up psychiatrist visit or take the medication. I had no way of pushing a forty-year-old man into it unless he accepted the diagnosis or felt responsible for his behavior.

The episode had shaken me. I was frightened for myself and alarmed about keeping the children in that environment, fearful for their mental and emotional growth at their impressionable ages. If divorce wasn't an option to protect my children, I'd find another way. Vijay wouldn't move out. He was a weak man and needed a crutch. The children needed to be somewhere safer.

But first I had to take care of my own health, which had suffered because of the years of acute stress. I consulted Dr. Wadhwa, my dad's doctor, who became my doctor, too. He was one of the finest male physicians I had known—polite, soft-spoken, patient-driven, and kindhearted. I wasn't sure if Dad had shared my situation with him. I had accumulated various health conditions in the past few years—low blood pressure, anxiety disorder, heart palpitations, severe insomnia, and memory loss—and dreaded a nervous breakdown. Dr. Wadhwa took care of me with B12 shots for energy, prescribing supplements for gaining strength, nerve-relaxing medication to calm my nerves, and Valium at night to sleep and reduce the palpitations.

I did not have a choice to stop and take a break, even if it was medically required. I had to keep going, just like a machine. I had to be physically and mentally fit to look after the well-being of my children and stay on top of their day-to-day homework, their health, and their developing behaviors. I also had to be at the top of my act in my job as that was critical for our survival. I was single focused, as if on a mission, and no one could take that from me. I had to ensure the machine was timely oiled and greased to keep running and not break down, as everything else would come to a halt.

❋   ❋   ❋

The twins were now eight years old and Nina eleven. There was no change in Vijay's behavior and I was fearful of children being brought up in a toxic environment. They would have to go away from that dysfunctional home. *But where?*

After some serious thinking, I decided perhaps they should be sent to boarding schools. Although that would break all our hearts, but not for long. They would understand when they grew up and weighed my decision between growing up in an insecure and unsafe deviant environment versus breaking their hearts by sending them to a safe, secure place for their holistic development.

I broached the subject of boarding school with Vijay. They would have a structured curriculum all day and be nurtured in a disciplined, controlled environment.

But Vijay wouldn't listen. "You think all the successful people study in these elite schools? You think a child who studies in a government school cannot be a big man?"

He reeled off examples of the prime ministers and presidents of India who had gone to government schools. His concern was the exorbitant fees.

"You're talking of the exceptions," I said, then dropped the subject. I had no energy to argue with him.

I talked to my parents, who were in favor of sending the children to a boarding school. I arranged visits to Mayo in Jaipur and Gayatri Devi in Gwalior. Both schools were run by royal families. I would also need to visit Doon School and Welham in Dehradun for Nina, as I wanted her to be in a girls-only school.

Sending my children away was a brave decision, and I did not know where the money for the school fees would come from. I had to keep my faith. *The Universe has my back; I have to make this happen.*

I'd been searching for private boarding education for a year when Amrit gave me a surprise by calling me after five long years. I was excited to hear her exhilarating-but-poised voice. Her candor and strength was always encouraging.

When I mentioned my search for boarding schools, she said her son, Raj, was in boarding school in Shimla, up in the hills, at a British school run by a very capable principal, Ali Mustafa. Raj's dad had studied in the same school, which had been established in 1859 by Bishop George Edward Lynch Cotton when the British were in India.

Her phone call was exactly what I needed. A few minutes after her call, the phone rang again. Amrit had talked to her husband, Major Singh, who called the school and spoke with his batch mate from the army, who headed the administration. I should visit the school.

The next week, having traveled on an overnight train and then a taxi through the hills, Vijay and I sat in Principal Ali Mustafa's office at Bishop Cotton School (BCS). I loved the environment of the school: British architecture with a beautiful Catholic church; long stained-glass windows; clean dorms; well-equipped class-rooms; hygienic kitchen; dining rooms; gyms; an infirmary; and the surrounding area of the school. Ali seemed very capable and an intellectual, a good fit for a principal of this exceptional school. It was a boys-only school. We spent a few hours with Ali Mustafa and the decision was made.

Ali suggested Chelsea, an adjacent girls-only school, for Nina. We had a similar reaction when we saw Chelsea, also a British school at its inception with similar facilities, buildings, and a church.

The children took their admissions tests, and one month later they were ready to go. Nina was now thirteen, going to grade VIII, and the twins were turning ten soon, going to grade V. Long lists of uniforms and other clothing needed for winters and summers were provided to us. Twelve of each clothing item was needed, since the laundry took longer to dry during the winters and rains, in the hilly parts. We went on a shopping spree and shopped often after work to match the requirements of the lists. My parents sewed names to each item. Six large army trunks were bought from the army canteen, two for each child, and Dad wrote the names on each trunk in bold letters: NINA, KABIR, KUBER.

Vijay was involved in the preparations. We hired a big van to accommodate the trunks. Shimla is north of Delhi, in the southwestern range of the Himalayas, close to ten thousand feet above sea level. It took nine hours by car. From Kalka, at the base of the hills, elevation 2,152 feet, we wound up the mountain on a steep narrow road, the scenery lush, green, serene, and majestic. The deep valley on the other end of the road with no barricades was scary for someone with vertigo like me. We halted at a couple of places for lunch and tea. People here seemed uncomplicated and honest, as is often the way when not exposed to a city.

As the car ascended the hills, my anxiety to drop off the children gripped my gut. Their excitement of going to a new school and a new place had overshadowed the feeling of separation, if they had any.

Nina was to be dropped off first, as her school was on the way to the boys' school. Sister Rose was extremely kind as she welcomed Nina. We unloaded her trunks and carried them inside to her dormitory.

Nina seemed excited. I accompanied my daughter to the hostel, where everything looked neat and tidy. I settled her trunks, and, in the meantime, Nina struck up a conversation with her roommate. Nina had grown up to be an extremely affable and affectionate girl. Seeing her already making friends made it easier to say goodbye. We could not spend more time with her, as we had to go to the boys' school. The fact that Nina would now be miles away had not yet hit me.

As we drove to BCS, I felt as if somebody were grabbing my heart and ripping it out. The twins looked confused and a little lost after Nina was dropped off. However, they kept their smiles.

At the BCS complex, we headed for the admissions office. After the formalities, we went down the terraced hill to the boys' dorm. These were huge dorms, unlike Nina's. All the bunk beds sat in rows, keeping a reasonable distance. Older students who had been there earlier came forward to befriend them. Having twins in their dorm was an added attraction.

The afternoon was sunny, and several children were playing cricket on the grounds outside the dorm. We hugged the boys, hiding our emotions on leaving them. The twins joined the game with other dorm mates eagerly.

I came back to a barren house with a barren heart. All my babies were gone at the same time! My nest was suddenly empty. At the same time, a sudden sense of relief engulfed me. I was sad at one moment and calm at another for a few days. My children were safe now. They would miss my mothering, but now each would be brought up in a healthy, enlightened, and secure environment.

Triumph followed me.

I was now three steps ahead on the ramp taking us toward our freedom—the end goal.

Chapter 10

My Safe Haven

1995–1997

The house continued to feel empty and meaningless with the children gone. Their absence felt like someone poked under my skin, piercing my body with arrows and biting me. I would now get to see the children during summer vacations or our short visits during the school year but would no longer be holding them and mothering them. I'd been so excited before, telling myself this was a wise choice for the children to make their lives away from this troubled environment. They were thrilled at the idea and did not need any convincing. But now I was left by myself, alone, to feel the hurt.

Suzie, the children's dog, was my only solace. I wasn't particularly fond of pets then, but her unconditional love was therapeutic. Suzie, a black cocker spaniel and Great Dane mix, had become part of our family a year earlier. The children had grown attached to her, and she missed the children, too.

I had no indication of how Vijay felt about the kids gone away. Surely, he felt the children's absence, but if he felt sad, he didn't show it. We barely spoke. I would go to work and come home, and Vijay would ignore me to flirt with Crecy, our housekeeper. He had started to become freer with her, teasing me. He had a certain fondness for maids, before and after Crecy, since they took care of his basic needs, food, laundry, and morning tea, which was all that mattered to him. I had suspected inappropriateness between Vijay and the housekeepers but had only limited energy that I liked to spend on more important things. My focus was on the bigger picture, although I did confront him once when I observed unwelcome behavior with my own eyes.

"She does everything for me. What do you do?"

There was nothing to argue about. I didn't care, although it hurt me. I had more crucial things to worry about, like the fee for boarding schools which I sorted year after year with some financial juggling and unavoidable credit card debts.

My highlight for the week was when I received letters from the children.

The boys' first letter read, "Dear Mom and Papa, after the cricket game was over, it hit us that you had gone, that we have been left alone, our parents gone. God knows when you will come again. We were so lonely without you. We both try to console each other. Don't worry. Come soon. We miss you a lot!"

The letters grew increasingly emotional during the initial year or two until they got fully acclimated to the boarding school environment and the sad fact they would stay away and see us only occasionally for short durations. I anticipated the initial trauma of separating from their immediate family would be overcome when they made friends and got busy in activities. However, the trauma of seeing a father abuse their mother would never be overcome. It would always stick in their minds, damaging their psyche.

Vijay's dependency on drinking increased, and he turned his vicious attention to me like he always did. His verbal and physical abuse was back and more intense. I suspected he was punishing me for sending our children away.

My sadness turned into depression. I entered a dark dungeon alone, with no way out and no one to look out for me. My insomnia increased and my anxiety peaked. Vijay and I still shared a bedroom, where he would stay up late drinking most nights, making my insomnia worse. He would often black out and not remember things in the morning or maybe he didn't remember on purpose.

When the children were home, the house was a home filled with laughter and joy. I was also on full throttle, on a pursuit to nurture them. Their positive vibes brought energy to the environment. But when they went to boarding school, they took those vibes with them. The energy left, the positivity left, and there were no more soulful vibrations. The house was surrounded in a dark, deadly quiet.

With all three gone, I lost my life purpose. I identified myself with my children and now my "very being" was lost. I became neurotic and felt feeble and hollow. I took to pills to relax, pills to calm my nerves, and pills to sleep.

Vijay acted like I existed only to be abused by him. It was becoming too much to bear, my shoulders drooping from the burden and weight of living my pointless, wretched life. This man clearly didn't care about me. He ignored my presence, my very existence. He set his eyes on the maid servants in the same household. What did I live for? I decided to end it all, not realizing these thoughts were coming from a state of acute depression. I took a ridiculously large sum of sleeping pills. However, I woke up unaffected. My anxiety was so acute, the sleeping pills didn't faze me.

However, I had not given up the thought yet, so I called Crecy, gave her my prescription, and said, "Go get fifty more pills."

I swallowed them all. I don't remember anything after that, except Crecy and Vijay pulling and pushing my dangling legs onto the bed, perhaps in the middle of the night as I could hardly see them in the dark. I was on the bed and not fully conscious and, for some reason, they were tugging at my arms and legs. The first coherent thing I remember wasn't until the next day, when I opened my eyes to find my parents sitting by my bed. Dr. Wadhwa was there, and I had a drip in my arm. Crecy was there, too, but Vijay was missing.

Mr. Bose, my boss, and Abhinav Goswami, my colleague and friend at work, both came to visit. I was surprised to see them. Apparently, Neel's wife had mentioned my overdose to Abhinav Goswami's wife when they both dropped off their kids for school in the morning. She shouldn't have shared such sensitive information with anyone outside, especially a colleague's wife, knowing the news would reach my office. I did not want to show my weakness to the people I worked with.

I slept through the night and felt much better the next morning. The following morning, I returned to work, embarrassed. The secret I had hidden behind my constant smile at work was out.

Mr. Bose was extremely upset. "You could have shared some with us. Why did you not confide? We would have done something, like suggested a good lawyer for you. We could have helped you out."

I was ashamed, of course, when common sense flooded in, not thinking of the consequences for my kids and parents if I had succeeded in my selfish act.

Vijay continued to stare at me with anguish and hatred. The frequency of his mood cycles had worsened. His lows lasted longer, and his highs were shorter. He was completely oblivious of his roles and responsibilities toward the kids or me. Only if he understood the meaning of the word responsibility.

The only time we talked a little was while driving to Shimla to see the children. He always offered to drive, which meant he wanted to see them, too, and missed them.

The children longed to see us. They had made good friends. None of them had any complaints about the heavy school schedules, but they missed home.

Kabir once mentioned that he missed lying with his head in my lap. "We will be all grown up when we come back to you, Mom. We will miss our opportunity."

He was right. But was there any other option for my child? I wiped my wet nose with the tissue in my purse. I missed them as deeply and felt even worse that I didn't have a partner I could share these feelings with.

Later that night, I opened the front door to a limping and bleeding Vijay, reeking of alcohol. Next to him stood a tall, well-dressed man whom I recognized as a neighbor. Mr. Mahesh Puri worked as a senior manager for Vijay's organization. He told me Vijay's friend was driving him when the two had an accident. There were no laws against drunk driving then. Mr. Puri was driving by, so he brought Vijay home. I'm certain there was more to the story.

Vijay was bruised in a couple of places, with dried blood on some of them. His ribs hurt, but he refused to go to the hospital. I gave him a painkiller, and he lay down on the bed to sleep.

Vijay's ribs ached for weeks, but that didn't deter him from drinking. He said it made him forget the pain. A few days later, I suggested he should go to Alcoholics Anonymous.

He became furious. "Who is an alcoholic, and do you even know what that word means?" He refused to accept that he was an alcoholic. He had his own definition of an alcoholic, which was someone who starts drinking alcohol first thing in the morning. And since he drank tea in the morning, he did not qualify.

✻   ✻   ✻

Two weeks after the accident, Vijay's booze buddies came over on a Sunday morning to pick him up. We were in the bedroom, where he was shouting at me about something inane. He quickly left me, changed his clothes, and went out with them. For a moment, I felt a sense of relief, and then fear gripped me. What would happen when he would come home drunk?

At least now I didn't have children in the house to worry about.

When Vijay returned, he was in a foul mood, obviously drunk, eager to pick up the fight where he'd left off. He gripped my face and dug his fingers into my cheeks, saying, "You think you are so smart. Let me see how smart you are." Then he grabbed my hair and yanked until my head was bent so far back, I was looking right at him. He fixed me with his intimidating stare. I knew where this was going, so before he became more violent, I did what I could to protect myself and escape his wrath. I slapped him across his face as hard as he would to me. Then I ran into the other room, locked it from inside, threw some clothes in a bag, and rushed out.

"Get out of my house!" he shouted after me.

It was easy for me to walk out on him that night, not worrying about the children. But walking out of his life permanently still required more work and some more time, as the children were still minors. That was my compulsion and the dire reason that I had to keep going back to him. He would not have let me live by myself. If I did, he would either kill me or himself in a rage, putting the blame on me. Either way, I was in trouble. There were no restraining orders in play and no safety protection existed. A woman's plight in the world's largest democracy.

I would not go to my parents' house. I'd lost the trust they had in me by too often taking the refuge they provided and then going back to my husband.

I took a cab straight to Neel's house. He had recently moved from Gujarat to Delhi. I knocked on his door late at night and told him, "I need a roof for four or five days."

I planned on renting a small house. Rent would be an issue, but I was undeterred. I would cross the bridge when I get there. I needed to focus on my mission, the next steps toward our freedom.

I needed a roof over my head and a house I could call my own, where Vijay couldn't make me leave my own home. I couldn't avoid him moving in with me, but I would make the rules. Although in reality it would not make any difference if he got violent in my house and asked me to leave but it mentally gave me more confidence of living in my own house, where the roof belonged to me. It would provide me the courage to push him out of the house if he became violent. I vowed to myself that I would work toward buying a house of my own. While exhilarating, the thought was also challenging. I had become good at tackling challenges and continuously keeping the faith in that higher power who had my back.

I soon visited the new townhouses I had noticed on big billboards on the Gurgaon–Delhi highway. The complex looked almost exactly like the IT campus, a microcosm of where I'd grown up. The offices of the complex were closed, so I knocked on the door of one of the townhouses.

A lovely middle-aged Kashmiri couple opened the door and invited me in. They praised the complex, stating it was secure and well maintained. The house next door was vacant—#18/9. Nine was my lucky number. My three children were born in room nine, in bed nine, and this address was a double nine.

I visited the only mortgage company, Housing Development Corporation (HDC), the next day. A loan officer explained the terms and conditions and handed me a set of papers. The mortgage would be taken care of by my salary, but an equal value of guarantee was required.

Dad and Mom offered to put up their house as a guarantee against my loan. My eyes teared—only a parent could do that. This was a very bold step I was taking. I was going to buy the house, not just rent it. My house. My safe haven.

The house stood directly opposite the entrance to a three-acre park filled with lush green trees and beautiful red and yellow flowers. The streets were lined with big trees and well-lit. The community had its own strip market. I moved in November 1995, during the Diwali celebrations. Vijay moved in with me. I did not create any fuss at the moment, as the fear of his threats to kill himself always hung at the back of my mind. The twins were kept protected from this gory side of their father, and they were still too young to absorb it all.

I fell in love with the house. And while I didn't have much money to do the interiors, I went for a tasteful ethnic look. In search of cheaper material from local markets, I chose furniture and complementary colors for the curtains, rugs, and cushions. I visited local inside markets to buy decorative lights and chandeliers to make it a home. *My cozy home.*

The sprawling living room, kitchen, and one bedroom was on first floor, and a big balcony attached to the living room. When the children came home for their first winter vacation, they were thrilled to have their own rooms upstairs.

My favorite place was the balcony overlooking the trees and the park. I would sit outside watching the squirrels running on this big tree, with yellow hanging flowers at my entrance. I was excited to get up early in the morning to enjoy the fresh air and listen to the chirping of birds while flocks of them hopped in the green trees, resting on the way to their journey ahead. A pair or two of peacocks often strutted by and danced in the park, and the rabbits came out in the late evening. Since this was farmland bought by the builders, I was fortunate to see the wildlife.

❄ ❄ ❄

The children were thrilled with their well-furnished rooms upstairs. Both bedrooms had their own balconies. The twins' room was furnished with bunk beds, while Nina had a full bed to herself. They loved the look and location of the house, with a front park to play in.

Vijay was at his best with the children at home. He played cricket with the boys and liked cooking non-vegetarian dishes for them despite the cook there. I, being a pure vegetarian, had put no restrictions on the children. We dined, watched TV, played indoor games, joked, and laughed together.

By this time, I had a car of my own with a chauffeur, so I was more independent. I could take the children on excursions, picnics, shopping, and restaurants. Our vacations were full of love, fun, and laughter.

❄ ❄ ❄

By the end of the first year of boarding school, Nina expressed her dissatisfaction with living there. She could not fit into the groups with daughters of wealthy business families who identified with affluence and material things their parents owned. Nina found herself to be a misfit, as her values were not aligned with them, so she avoided being in her dorm after classes and spent her evenings in the church and with Sister Rose.

She wanted to come back home, and in my heart, I knew it was partly because of the school, but partly because she did not want to leave me alone with her father. Therefore, I decided to withdraw her from boarding school after completing one year of grade VIII, bring her home, and enroll her in a nearby high school in Gurgaon. As she grew into her teens, she understood me not just as a mother but also as a woman. She was blossoming into one, too.

At work, very disheartening news came. My boss, Mr. Bose—my mentor and friend—was diagnosed with lung cancer. It was hard to believe he would leave us. I could not fathom a smooth work life for me in his absence. He was a pure-spirited and compassionate human being. He passed on soon thereafter, despite undergoing treatments at Sloan in the United States and hospitals in India. I had a feeling of personal loss for a long time and never forgot his kindness.

I understood work life was going to be tougher for me with Mr. Bose gone. My reporting was made to Abhinav Goswami and the conducive culture under Bose's leadership tended to shift to a more autocratic culture. John Gordon, the Asia Pacific divisional president, intervened and moved Larry Young from the United States to take over the India division. Young saw my capabilities and took me under his wing, making me the country's HR head.

However, Mr. Bose remained my role model. He had provided me with direction and injected me with professional expertise that helped me build a solid foundation. I give a lot of credit to him for who I am today.

That summer, I flew to Hyderabad for three days to attend the Marshall Goldsmith seminar. It was rare for a coaching guru to offer a seminar in India to the CEOs of larger American companies.

At the end of the conference, when I flew back, Vijay surprised me at the airport to pick me up. Once in the car, I noticed too late his unsteady head and slurred voice. He gripped the wheel, put the car into gear, pressed the accelerator and took off, then suddenly swerved toward the footpath. I screamed when it looked like he was going to run over a cyclist.

I asked him to drive slowly. Perhaps that didn't agree with his bloated ego because he pressed the accelerator harder. To divert his attention from acting out, I asked how Nina was doing. He said he'd sent her to her grandmother's house to spend the weekend. I was surprised because we'd never done that before and, since I hadn't seen her for three days, I thought she would be home for my return.

At home, Vijay poured a glass of whiskey, then started in with his typical modus operandi.

"I could not find my brown shoes. Where did you hide them? And, by the way, why did your driver take off when you were gone? I know, you did it all on purpose." He came closer, dug his fingers into my cheeks, stared into my face, and snarled, "So who am I to you?"

I was quiet. He dug his fingers deeper. "Eyes down," he shouted.

I gave him a look. "Eyes down, I said!" He slapped me, twisted my arm, and punched me in my stomach. I screamed in pain.

A moment later, he picked on my dad, a known sensitive point. When I didn't react, he verbally abused my mom. I clenched my teeth and stared at him. He pushed me down on the floor and dragged me.

I shouted at him to leave me.

His grip loosened on me for a second and I got up. While I tried to break free, he pulled my hair, put his thumb inside my gullet, and pressed into the base of my throat, either to kill me or to create the fear of death in me. The more I pulled at his arm to make him let go, the harder he pressed. I struggled to breathe. I grabbed his arm with both of my hands and pulled with all my strength. But he was stronger than I was. I gagged and lost my breath, moving my arms in the air out of desperation to breathe, gasping for a few seconds which felt like minutes.

As quickly as he'd started, he let me free. I still could not get my breath back and then I ran into the hall, slipping and staggering out of fear—trying to shout for help through the closed doors. I was hoping for the servant boy of the Kashmiri couple next door would hear me, but no one did. Vijay opened the main door and tottered out of the house.

In the middle of the night, after I finally stopped crying and fell asleep, he returned and forced himself on me, as was his pattern. I shut my eyes tight. I did not have any energy to fight him off me.

I'd created a safe haven but with no safety for myself in it.

Nina came back the next day. She had already suspected what had happened. "Why would he send me to Grandma's house? He has never done that before."

She took me upstairs. We sat on her balcony, talking for hours. She wiped my tears, held my hands, and hugged me.

She was barely fourteen at the time, too young and tender to understand and digest all of it, but she was in the midst of it all. I knew this poisonous environment would impact her tender heart.

"Mom, you should tell Nanaji," she said.

"No, I can't. He has heart issues, and I cannot give him any worries. If something happens to him, I will feel guilty all my life. I would not pardon myself."

"But, Mom, think about it. Nanaji is sixty-plus years. He has lived his life. You are young. You have yet to live it."

I looked at her beautiful face, her logic, and her concern for me. She was right.

I held her hands, as I watched her sad eyes. "Things will be fine. You should not worry about me." And I embraced her tight to my bosom with all my compassion.

It was futile to tell her that. She heard the abuse from upstairs, sitting on the staircase, worried about me on a daily basis when he would press the doorbell late at night. While she shouldn't have been exposed to this acidic environment. She should not have been a part of this. But she was destined to become a part of my story. It was in her blueprint.

Out of my guilt for putting my child through this ordeal with me, I pampered her and went overboard, making up for the troubled times.

A couple years passed, and Vijay's situation worsened, just like Dr. Kothari, the psychiatrist, had diagnosed earlier. "Without medication, his behavior will become worse. You should divorce him now."

To protect Nina as much as possible, she spent much of her time after school at my parents. I needed to work on a solid plan, a permanent solution, and not solving one issue to create another one was precisely the reason that divorce could not be a solution yet, since the children were minors. I would solve the issue of setting myself free, but could I be free if Vijay got custody of even one of our three children?

My heart would skip a beat that it could be all three if he manufactured evidence that I was cheating on him. I could not let even one child go to him. That would be the end of their lives. My very existence would be in vain.

Getting far away from Vijay with my three children, somewhere across oceans and across borders where he could never find us, seemed the only viable solution. We needed to escape his wrath permanently.

All of these years of continuous struggle had brought a paradigm shift in my thought process. I was no longer seeking relief but facing challenges. I had made crucial decisions for our lives all by myself. I reminded myself, *I am bold and strong-willed and a fighter. I have the grit to handle hurdles.* Escaping the physical and emotional prison of Vijay was the biggest challenge I needed to tackle, my next step on the ramp toward our freedom. *The time has arrived!*

Mr. Bose had talked to me a about a divorce attorney, a friend of his, after my overdose incident. I had not yet met him, so I made an appointment to see him now.

Kartik Dubey was a bright professional who'd attended the top high school in Dehradun and then graduated from the University of London. He listened to me intently and finally said what I'd already heard twice before and didn't anticipate hearing from him, too.

"Since the children are minors, they would be divided between the two of you."

"But how could I let my children go to an alcoholic?" I asked in a choking voice. "A man who is violent, who does not know the meaning of the word 'responsibility,' and who refuses to take medication?"

His eyes locked on mine as he asked, "Were you born a martyr?"

"I don't understand," I said.

"Are you thinking of sacrificing yourself and your life? Look at yourself, you are so young. You need to be happy. Make yourself happy first to make your children happy. You wouldn't be there to see them if you continue being harsh on yourself. Remember always . . . 'Me first!'" He pulled out a blank paper from his printer and wrote in big, upper-case letters, ME FIRST, and underlined it before handing it to me.

"Be gentle to yourself, Kanchan" he said.

I came back disappointed about divorce not being an option, but Kartik was successful in opening my eyes. He was right. No one had ever said that to me during all these years of mayhem. Rather, society in general said, "Treat your husband like your fourth handicapped child. Where will he go? You are married to him. You need to look after him." My mind had become conditioned to that repetitive thought pattern in certain ways. However, living with Vijay had left me a wreck, hollowing me out, both mentally and emotionally.

His words kept echoing with me. *Make yourself happy first.* It made a lot of sense to me. That became my mantra from there on. He was my third angel. He gave me the resolve to look after myself first to make my children happy. My life took a sudden turn for the better. To be happy outside, I needed to be happy inside. And before that, I needed to feel happy in my skin. I needed to pamper myself more often. Putting myself first would not be an act of selfishness but self-preservation and self-compassion. I needed to be gentle to myself.

That weekend, I made an appointment at the spa close by for a body massage, then a salon for hair color, and then a manicure with bold red paint. I deserved this pampering. I pushed myself to start looking in the mirror again, just like before. I erected long mirrors around the house—this was my house, where I should have control—and started to like the petite, charming woman I saw in those mirrors.

I then unpacked the music system I'd bought in Singapore years before that had been neglected in a corner. I dusted it, set it up in the living room, and played the first CD of songs I loved, music of my choice. I also visited the Nath bookstore and bought a few novels instead of my usual management books to fulfill my desire to read. I picked the thickest novels by Aldous Huxley, *Roots* and *War and Peace* to indulge myself. I bought fashionable blouses to wear with my cotton and silk saris, and high heels I fancied.

I made a conscious habit of looking in the mirror each morning and saying, "I am the best." I repeated that each evening before going to bed. That became my tool. It boosted my self-esteem and began to change my own image of myself. I started to take in the compliments of my colleagues, which were plentiful each day, and enjoyed them.

Vijay had no issues with any of these changes. I figured he might take it out on me at some point, but the fear of reprisal didn't stop me.

My next action step on the ramp up-and-out was to move out of India with my children, far, far away, where Vijay couldn't find us. While a far-fetched thought, the pace to convert into reality would be slow, more like the speed of the tortoise in Aesop's *The Hare and the Tortoise*.

Mom used to tell us, "The moral of the story is that you can be more successful with no chance of failure by doing things slowly and steadily than by acting in haste. The tortoise raced at his own pace and was a sure winner at the end."

I will be that tortoise till I win the race.

Chapter *II*

Freedom Awaits,
Far, Far Away

1998–2003

I wasn't yet sure where we would go and was not ignorant of the fact that moving to a new country with three teenagers was going to be a herculean task. Instead of looking at the issues, I focused on the solution first. The first step was to tap the available resources for gathering information on easily accessible and developed countries with decent job markets and environments easy to merge into.

My dream since childhood was to move to the States, but it was extremely difficult to get a visa. So, I applied to other countries. There was no one to provide any information, but I finally found an agent to help me relocate to New Zealand. I paid him a massive fee, but after six months of following up, it turned out to be a fraud. I then put in my papers for immigration to Canada but was told it could take ten years. I then set my gaze on the United States. My desire was for my children to attend college there, a most liberal and powerful country, which embraced all religions and compatriots.

It seemed impossible, but there was no harm in dreaming big. I was not going to succumb to assumptions. After all, three of my big dreams had been realized. I'd landed an amazing job, enrolled the kids in good boarding schools, and managed to buy my own house. It was time to achieve my fourth dream: to move to the States.

My parents had moved to a house close to mine, where the three kids spent most of their time during vacations. It was Nina's second home, where she felt most safe and cared for, and where my dad imparted his worldly knowledge to her. Being a connoisseur of all subjects, he regaled the kids whenever they were around during vacation with stories from *Reader's Digest* and *National Geographic*. He reinforced table manners and general courtesies, as his dad had done with him in Iran, and as he had done with me. My mom was all smiles, plying her grandchildren with meals and snacks, and telling them moral stories, a teacher that she was. My children were also close with Leena's two children of the same age group, her son Adi and daughter Manna. They met quite often during summer vacations.

By this stage, Dad was getting seriously ill. In addition to his heart condition, he suffered from diabetes and kidney issues. I could not bear to leave him alone in that condition. *Once again*, I repeated, *I shall cross the river when I get there. God surely has his plans!*

The twins were doing extremely well in their studies as well as extracurricular activities. They earned medals in sports, debates, and drama, just as I had. The Moudgil twins, as they were known, were a famous pair in the school, liked for their dedication and fervor, their excellent attitude, and their willingness to participate in all school activities. They were humble and respectful of their teachers. As I heard teachers sing their praises, I congratulated myself for the resolve to send them away. The boys had realized it by then and were thankful for my tough decision.

Each year, as the twins prepared to return to school after vacation, their big military trunks filled to capacity, I would thoughtfully prepare a PowerPoint presentation for them. We would all sit in front of the computer, and I would go over the bullet points. We would discuss the preservation of their values, their strengths, their areas of improvement, and what was required to be a successful, wholesome individual, a good human being. I desired for them to be strong, well rounded, and ready to face the challenges of the world. The pace of social, technological, and economic change had picked up in the '80s, became faster in the '90s, and would surely continue. They needed to be prepared and keen.

One value never to be compromised was respect for women and the elderly. I loved it when my sons took responsibility to lock all the doors before stepping out and when they opened the car door and waited for me and Nina to slide in before they did. The ritual of PowerPoint presentations continued until they were admitted into business schools. The presentations evolved as they grew and matured. I saw their zeal and strong knowledge base in a myriad of subjects. Reading management books and professional magazines was made a habit in our household, as I had an interest in them, too. I remained friends with my children and in complete communication. They were always eager to listen to my feedback on their personality characteristics and behavior, since I was an HR professional.

They have told me then and now, how they appreciated those presentations, which helped them progress in their professions and personal lives.

Thankfully, the boys, for the most part, were oblivious to Vijay's behavior toward me. Nina and I, intentionally and collaboratively, didn't share much with them beyond his issues with anger, which were no secret. Their knowledge was limited to their own observations and perceptions. It was an unwritten code among us: they never mentioned it, and I never brought it up. Vijay played the role of a good father very well in front of his sons, and I wanted to keep it that way.

Back when the twins were eleven and on vacation from boarding school, Kabir had grabbed Vijay's wrist and held tight when he was about to hit me. Vijay, following through with the momentum he'd meant for me, hit the windowpane, shattering it. So, the boys had an inkling of how he treated me, but only to that extent. How long it would remain hidden, only time could tell.

Nina had become an accomplished Kathak dancer, a classical dance with both Hindu and Mogul elements where facial expressions were an essential part, along with arm and leg movements. She'd studied the art for years with top dance gurus. She danced gracefully, and the gurus appreciated her delicate movements.

Now she was in her first year of college and had grown even prettier—petite, sharp features, long hair, and an affectionate smile. She also had a cheerful demeanor. She brought home her daily challenges of the new college environment and the group dynamics she faced while making new friends. She was busy with studies and college activities, and by the end of the first semester, she'd made a lovely group of friends who sometimes came home with her and chatted with me. I granted her this newfound freedom after high school, just as my parents had granted it to me.

※   ※   ※

Dad's health had faded swiftly during the past year. It was consoling for me that Dad and Mom lived close. I was able to visit them after work almost every day. Dad looked comforted to see me in the evenings, and it was equally heartening for me to see that gratification in his eyes. Neel, his other favorite child, had already moved to the States, so I felt more responsible for my parents since I lived closer than my other siblings and had been the most pampered. I was also resourceful and more willing to be with him and to attend to his doctors in the hospitals. The frequency of his stays in the hospitals had increased.

Seeing my dad deteriorating each day, at the age of seventy, was killing me. Not only did I feel his pain, but also, I could not bear for him to die and leave us alone. Mom and Dad had been just like two birds on a branch, never losing sight of each other, always devoted.

In January 2000, we experienced the coldest winter days in Delhi, with foggy and misty mornings where flights were canceled or returned as they could not land due to the dense fog, the sun appearing rarely, and smog surrounding each mouth when it opened to talk. In every nook and cranny, little bonfires burned, and street workers or hawkers and shopkeepers sat around them. One had to keep heat convectors in each room to keep the temperature up. Then one morning Mom called and said Dad wanted to see me.

He asked me to sit close to him. He was sitting toward the end of the bed, so I tucked myself at the corner, next to his frail body.

He put his arm around me and said, "Allow me to go now. Your mother has."

I burst into tears and could not stop wailing as he held me tight. It ached me to realize how frail his once robust body had become. Then he kissed my forehead, raised my chin, and looked deeply into my eyes, full of affection, a compelling request in his eyes and a smile carrying his blessings.

He said, with all conviction, his last words to me. "Try going to America to realize your dreams."

I hugged his weak body softly. I quickly came to the kitchen where Mom was and howled, saying repeatedly, "He cannot go—I am not yet ready for him to go!"

Mom held my shoulders. "Kanchan, gather yourself, my baby. We need to let him free. He is in lots of pain. We will do fine." She did not wipe my tears and left me for a bit to cry. Then she held me tight.

"It's okay, Kanchan."

I stood there in her comforting hug for a while.

The next day, he was admitted to the ICU and slipped into a coma before I reached him after half a day at work. He lived on machines for three days and then passed over, calm and serene.

I was devastated. We all were. My mental and emotional support was gone. The one man who gave me and my children his unconditional love was gone. Our hero was gone.

My mother, Ravi, Leena, and I brought his body home from the hospital in an ambulance to dress him for cremation, the Hindu ritual. The attendants laid him on the floor. Neel was continuously on the phone from States where he had moved with his family in 1996.

I cried. "Put some blankets or something under him or he'll be cold." They ignored me, so I asked my mother, "Why aren't you putting his body on a bed? We need to move him to the bed."

She wrapped her arms around me and said, "No. It's okay. He's no more."

I was hysterical, completely out of control. Leena came and hugged me tight, and we cried in each other's arms.

My mom came into the room and said, "Baby, don't do that. It's okay. He had to go. We had to let him go."

She was the only strong one among us. Perhaps her spiritualism gave her the strength, and she understood his role on this creation was over—that his soul was set free and merged with the Source.

I came out of the room to look for the children. They were standing in one corner, crying and sobbing, wiping their tears, aggrieved over the death of their nanaji. In those moments none of us could think of a life without him. I embraced each one of them and calmed them.

The Indian custom was to bathe the body after death and before cremation. Ravi did that, performing the rituals, covering the body in a white sheet, and tying the sheet to a wooden ladder. My mom brought his favorite shawl and put it on his wrapped body. Four men then picked up the ladder, one holding each end of the two poles, and carried it to the cremation ground.

My father's death hit my children the hardest. Their father figure was no more. Fortunately, the twins were home for winter vacation, so they could be there for the cremation and see him pass on to his next journey.

Nina could not talk about him for years. The boys had him in their memories forever, remembering him at every significant milestone. Their Nanaji, granddad, would always remain their hero, their idol. I put a shutter to my memory for years, not consciously bringing him in front of my eyes. I could not see his picture for almost five years. Only remembering the richness of the life he lived helped me to live.

Although acceptance he was gone came to me within a week, the pain and grief remained for many years. Strangely, in one corner of my heart, I felt this weird sense of freedom. Freedom to move away from India. It was like my father had been holding me there. I had taken the responsibility of caring for my dad as my duty. While Mom would be left alone, but she would remain strong. I loved her dearly and she still had Ravi and Leena, but it was time to fully focus on my plans. Dad's last words to me brought strength and motivation. I gave myself the permission to get ready to build the rest of the unfinished ramp.

※   ※   ※

Within a week of my dad's passing in January 2000, I called Mike Joshua, Global Technologies worldwide vice president of human resources, who was in India to visit our plant for a couple of days. He worked at the company's headquarters in Syracuse, New York. Mike had always appreciated me as a person and as a professional. Although I was on bereavement leave, I requested a thirty-minute meeting.

The next morning, I met him in the Maurya Sheraton lobby, where he was staying. Mike was a towering personality in a lean frame, always well-groomed, soft-spoken, an accomplished professional, and a great leader. He expressed his condolences.

"I would like to move to one of the divisions of Global Technologies in the States with my children. I want them to continue their education there." I discreetly added, "I have been in an abusive marriage for years and I need to leave India to protect my children and myself."

He did not seem surprised. I wondered if Mr. Bose had shared some information with him.

He listened carefully and empathetically. "Kanchan, I have always appreciated you professionally and liked you as a person. I will do all in my capacity to see if I can make this happen, but I cannot promise you."

I extended my hand to thank him. "It's a fair response. I don't want you to promise me. I am confident if there is a possibility, you shall manage it."

He smiled as we shook hands and parted.

I then wrote a personal note to the president of Paramount division, John Gordon, about my desire to move to the United States, knowing his approval was a requirement when Mike presented my case. Although I had never worked directly for John, I trusted he would not mind me writing to him. I was greatly influenced by John and his leadership style. His personality was unmatched as was his humility. All executives replicated his immaculate dressing sense. He had an aura about him, and his charisma drew followers from all round the organization and beyond.

I knew John valued loyalty and had a soft spot for India. Whenever he visited, he had made sure to talk to me about my work, and I was always a part of the team, the only female manager invited for official dinners with him. John was close to Mr. Bose, despite having a boss-subordinate relationship. They had respected each other, and John had a special place for Mr. Bose for his loyalty and friendship.

A few days later, I received an unexpected call from Abhinav Goswami. He said he was calling in response to my letter to John and my conversation with Mike. The task of looking at possibilities for my relocation was given to Abhinav, my ex-boss and friend, who had moved to the United States along with John and Mike. For the next few weeks, I was interviewed by phone by various divisional HR heads from Global Technologies, which went well, as I was invited for face-to-face interviews in the United States during April 2000.

I flew to the United States. I had several interviews at the Syracuse headquarters and in Connecticut. I was made an offer at the end of the second day. I was excited for myself and children. My longtime dream was coming true. John was another angel in my life who had changed the course of our lives, supporting me in my ramp building.

On arriving home, I headed to Nina's room. She saw me smiling and she jumped. She knew, and then we both called the twins, informing them of the good news. They were super-thrilled, and the boys nicknamed me Jhansi Ki Rani and Indira Gandhi, two strong women in Indian history who won battles and political wars.

There was a lot to be done. Winding up a life of forty-two years and moving to a foreign country required serious planning. However, it was exhilarating, liberating, and encouraging. I was filled with adoration and gratitude for that higher power who was giving me the strength to keep moving forward and bringing me angels like Kiran, the UK lady, Kartik, and John to make this happen. I told Vijay, about the offer. He was out of a job again and was now talking about starting his own consulting firm with another ex-colleague of his. I told him he could keep working from home since I didn't need to sell the house immediately.

During one of his sober moments, while we were planning our move, he said, "I want to set you free."

I think somewhere inside, he'd started to feel how much he'd wronged me and the children. In nicer moments, he told me he was looking inward and trying to improve. While I felt empathy for him, I wasn't at all certain if he truly meant those words, or if he was creating a soft corner in my heart before leaving, or if he was manipulating me to allow him to move to the United States with us.

The preparations to leave for the States were now in full swing: passports and visas, wrapping up work and the household, and buying clothes and suitcases. Vijay grew increasingly anxious, though he still helped us with all the preparations. His extra graciousness toward me was pinching me. I did not want my sympathy for him to overpower my decision or my compassion on humanitarian grounds to awaken. But somewhere deep inside, I never stopped being empathetic to him for the good times we'd had.

It was time to book the tickets. The US branch of the company paid our moving costs, plane tickets, food, and lodging for the first six-to-eight weeks. Vijay asked if he could join us and stay for a couple of weeks, then return to India to continue his consulting business. I couldn't be as cruel to him as he was to me. He wasn't a good husband, but in the small amount of time he spent with the kids, he wasn't a bad father. After lot of brainstorming, I decided Vijay could come with us for a few weeks, just to see where his kids were going to be living. He was their father, and I didn't want to keep that from him.

I also did not want the boys, who had not much knowledge of his dreadful behavior toward me, to feel I had abandoned him. I had to take that step of leaving him behind with a buy-in from all the three.

In addition, I was apprehensive about going to a foreign land by myself with my children. Fear and anxiety gripped me about the unknown—a new place, a new job, new people. I couldn't even drive on my own. Having another adult with me might make the transition a little easier. I knew I was almost free from his clutches—so close—so what harm could he really do me now? Besides, we'd all heard stories of people calling 911 and how domestic abuse wasn't tolerated in the States. Vijay wouldn't risk being thrown in a US jail. And just to be sure his stay was temporary, I bought a return ticket for him.

My mother supported me in my decision to take Vijay. I did not have the heart to leave Mom alone within six months of my dad's passing. I called Neel and we decided that we would fly through Chicago's O'Hare Airport to drop Mom off to visit Neel for a while in Bloomington before visiting me in New York once we had settled.

The day of our departure arrived. We packed the belongings we could fit into our suitcases—mostly clothes and shoes—and left a fully furnished house behind for Vijay to come back to and live his life. It was the first time my mom and the twins had flown on an international flight. Nina had flown to Singapore with me at the age of fourteen. I felt peace in my heart that I'd convinced Mom to come with us, although I did miss Dad.

When we landed at O'Hare, Neel and his wife waited to take Mom with them, and we proceeded to the domestic airport. There, we boarded a thirty-two-seater to Syracuse, New York, flying low as we rattled along. All the nuts and bolts of the plane felt loose as if the plane would give out at any time. It was a scary flight—little did I realize that all the small, low-flying planes made the same rattling sound.

The children were so excited. It would take us a few days to recognize the reality of a new, different world and the challenges it would bring. I always felt we were pretty westernized by India's standards, but in the States, the most powerful and affluent nation, with vastness and diversity all around, everything was so different and new.

We enjoyed the first two days just staying in the hotel. It was raining in July, and we needed to recover from our jet lag.

On the third day, I reported to work. Lynn Durocher, my team manager, met me at the reception desk to usher me in. I walked into an open-office environment where there were no walls—just individual cubicles, each containing a desk and a computer. Most desks held pictures of what I assumed were the employees' families. Everyone stared at their computer screens with their hands on the computer, fingers typing mechanically and fast. No heads turned. All this was new to me.

Lynn walked me to her office, a room with a desk and a large table. Lynn was extremely polite and had a melodious tone to her voice, which made me like her from the moment we met.

I felt nervous in this new and different work environment, yet confident I would soon adapt. Lynn explained the job, then took me around, introducing me to the team.

She showed me to my cubicle, then left me alone. This six-by-six cubicle was a huge change from my large office in Gurgaon. Sitting at my new desk in my new office, in a country I had visited only once for four days, it hit me what a stranger I was here.

I'd left an office of six hundred blue-collar workers and seven hundred white-collar staff, where I'd been liked and respected. In Gurgaon, each morning, my driver would drive through the office gate, where two security guards would salute and two more would salute at the entrance to the building. By the time I'd reach my own office, I'd exchange greetings and smiles with several people in the halls. Then the gardener would come with a vase of fresh roses, while another helper would bring a bottle of chilled water with a glass on a tray. And finally, my secretary would enter with his steno pad.

And here I was in my new office, setting up my own computer and phone—which I had no clue how to do—crawling under the desk, fidgeting with the cords, red, blue, and yellow, and plugging them into the power sockets. I was expected to do my own photocopying and faxing, and even make my own coffee. In India, we had peons or helpers for "non-value-add jobs," such as photo-copying and faxing, and bringing coffee, which perhaps increased productivity, or maybe not.

This place was full of trials and required a rapid adoption of new habits. I soon became aware that, to fit in, I had to change my communication style, body language, and managing style. What was considered a sign of respect in India, such as standing up when my boss entered the room, was considered a sign of submissiveness here. Calling my boss or senior management by their first name was disgraceful to the person by Indian standards. Understanding the people and adapting would take time. The people outwardly seemed to be dry and unwelcoming, keeping to themselves.

The first couple of weeks, we drove the streets, trying to sense the new city, the marketplaces, and the malls. The roads were wide, some of them with five lanes. The strangest thing was that no one honked. Vijay practiced left-handed driving, which is opposite from India. In the passenger seat would be Kabir with printed Yahoo maps for navigation. Nina was our person for studying the menus and ordering in the fast-food joints or coffee places. Starbucks had huge lines in the drive-in lane. People buying coffee for work through these fast lanes was a new experience again. It was all a mixture of fun, surprises, and anxiety.

Within three weeks, we had moved into a two-bedroom apartment in Manlius, a suburb of Syracuse, and the boys were admitted to eleventh grade at Manlius High School, a reputable school where John and Abhinav's children also studied. The Man-lius school bus came right to our door.

Nina was admitted to Syracuse University, an expensive pri-vate school. She took the public bus, and later her friends picked her up and brought her home. She and I engaged a driving instruc-tor to train us so we could get our driver's licenses. It was odd for me and my young daughter to be sitting next to a big stranger. Tom wore tight shorts, which showed his thighs, but he was par-doned since he turned out to be a good-hearted man.

Vijay seemed involved and enthusiastic about settling us in. We furnished the house quickly with basics, leased a family-sized van, filled the kitchen with groceries, and were all settled to start a new life. But I was realistic in my expectations. Life wouldn't be a bed of roses from that point on. It hadn't been so far. Life just isn't.

Vijay surprised me. After six weeks, he was still on good behavior. But six weeks was long enough, so I reminded him that he needed to go back and continue his consulting project. His consulting partner called, suggesting the same. And since I had bought him a return ticket, he flew back without causing any problems.

I also had to adjust to having no domestic help. I started family meetings around the dining table, assigning the kids household chores. I discussed our monthly budget to make them aware of what we could afford to spend on groceries, gas, and other expenses. We were all involved.

The peer pressure was huge for the kids. I'd never heard the use of the term "peer pressure" before coming to the States. The boys didn't tell me about the pressures at school for a long time because they didn't want to stress me any further, and Nina was the same. The twins had each other's company, at least. They started to write in their journals and, fighters that they were, they kept going on their own. They could see I needed to be left alone to face my own daily challenges at work. Nina struggled to adjust to the college environment, though, being very personable and outgoing, she seemed okay on the outside.

❄ ❄ ❄

On weekends, we made a point to see the new world around us and also have some fun. We visited malls, went to lakes for picnics, and drove on Albany Road to watch the amazing, breathtaking spring trees bear leaves of all colors imaginable—purple, magenta, maroon, red—in spectacular bloom.

For our first winter, when the first snow flurry came, the children and I piled into the van and drove through the streets, watching the snow fall around us, on the car windshield, and the green grass slowly turning white. I loved the whiteness on the branches of the trees and on the sidewalks the next morning, as if an artist had painted everything in white strokes.

And then, after about five months, I opened the door to find Vijay standing there with his luggage. I was shocked.

"I can't live alone," he said.

I suspected he had failed in his consulting venture. I did not know what else to do except let him in.

The next day, I asked him to look for work since, under the L-1A visa he'd been issued, he had a work permit.

Eight months later, when we were more settled, I began working toward my MBA at Syracuse University, attending evening classes. I sure had a career path in my head; I had to elevate up from a manager level.

Life seemed normal enough. We were happy. Nina's friends from college started coming home. The twins took summer jobs at Pizza Hut and worked for a doctor. They had picked up this wonderful trait of value for money from the boarding school, where the money was limited for eating out on weekend breaks on the Shimla Mall road. They bought me a watch out of the money they earned from their first summer job. *The payback had begun!*

But every night when I came home, Vijay would have a drink in his hand. He would pour the drink into a steel cup to camouflage the contents, but we all knew.

I did not want the boys to see him drinking every day, so one evening I sat Vijay down and said, "I'll take care of everything—the kids, the finances, their studies, and even their marriages. In return, I only want you to not drink and give me the respect I deserve."

He stared at me for a good thirty seconds with a completely indifferent expression. Then, without a word, he stood up and walked away.

His drinking and anger issues continued. He didn't help with household chores or with school and college admissions for the kids. I was also stressed about acquiring green cards—our pass to continue our stay. However, he never raised his hand to me. He was intelligent enough to understand American laws, and he was afraid of the kids or me dialing 911.

Instead of Vijay, Nina and the boys helped around the house and continued to do well with their studies. The boys were on the dean's honor list. They both were writing their journals every evening and spent late evenings and weekends prepping for their SATs. Both the boys, the Underdogs as they called themselves, scored well-above average scores to get them into good schools, but I could not afford fancy schools. The closest was State University of New York-Binghamton where they would live in dorms. Nina also transferred to Binghamton from Syracuse University and chose to live in a single room shared with a roommate. Nina was already feeling aloof and a little withdrawn, but her face didn't show it.

Two years had passed since we'd moved to the States. In June 2002, just before the kids had to begin university, Mike moved me to Global Engines, Inc., another subsidiary of Global Technologies in Connecticut, for a new assignment. He had also moved to Global Engines to Connecticut. Therefore, we had to keep two households—one in Syracuse, as the children were close to completing their semester, and another in Connecticut, where I lived—but, fortunately, the company agreed to pay the rent. By now, Vijay had started night jobs in motels run by Indian Gujarati families. As soon as the children went to university, Vijay moved to a smaller apartment close to his work.

In Connecticut, I lived in Manchester and took surface streets to go to work, as I had not gotten over the fear of driving on highways yet. While I'd grown used to the American ways of work, I had no friends. Home felt very desolate. With no neighborhood acquaintances, I often was lonesome and longed to talk to people around me. But this was not India.

❋   ❋   ❋

One night, I woke up to the phone ringing at 2:00 a.m., in the middle of the semester. It was Nina, sobbing. She sounded depressed. She wanted to come home to me. She could not make herself get up and go to classes. This was concerning. I consoled her and told her I would be on my way as soon as the darkness outside subsided. By 4:00 a.m. I was on highway 90E driving toward Binghamton.

When I met her, she looked withdrawn, her eyes distant, stiff as a stone. My heart stopped. I brought her home to Connecticut. She was not talking, withdrawn into her shell. I started to look for doctors and therapists. I knew in my heart that she was going through the cumulative deep-set sadness from over the years and now the massive changes in her life in the previous couple of years, which she had not been sharing with anyone.

She said she missed her grandfather. She had not had closure with him. She was melancholic at parting with her loving companion, her golden Lab, Poochee, whom she had reared from three weeks old, feeding him milk with bottles. She had needed to leave him back with another family. She also had to part with her childhood and college friends.

Added to all that was the pressure of integrating into a new country, feeling peer pressure, and being inclusive with all races and religions in the classroom. All this snowballing affected her, emotionally and mentally. She expressed that she might be suffering through the trauma of this move—which left her with no desire to live. I figured she had to be brought home to be with me, as I knew that she was struggling with her demons by herself. Little did I realize the extent of her condition.

She went into therapy and was prescribed heavy medication. Luckily, we found a great therapist in Connecticut, after going through several for a good fit. I thought I knew how to take care of her by cajoling and paying attention, but that was not what she needed in her depressive state. Inside, she was broken and needed mending, but she kept this truth from me. Her memories of trauma from her earlier years started to surface. I tried to understand her condition by reading material online and in books. It took me a long time to understand her plight. I still remained in denial. How could she not love life?

One man's wrongdoing, and not accepting help, could ruin so many lives. I was angry at Vijay.

The boys were doing well. Peer pressure was prevalent for them, too. They were fighters, focused and forward-thinking, so the everyday stress did not deter them. I had seen their boxing bout against each other in the finals at BCS. I had not seen such determined faces, expressions of grit, and knife-like focus as on them. I was amazed at their strategy. They were not looking at the fists but in the eyes of their opponent. What a match it was, with the whole school of five hundred students in the arena, wooing, cheering, and applauding equally for both, as they all belonged to both. Kabir was going to win, but in the last round, he let Kuber win. Kabir, being the older twin, always showed his graciousness to his very-competitive-but-equally-loving younger brother.

He later told me, "Ma, it was good enough to know I was winning, so I let him take the trophy. Now we are both happy." I would tell Kabir that he was the older brother, although only fifteen minutes apart, and that he should take care of Kuber. Kabir, being a compassionate human being, took that responsibility seriously while growing up. I quietly prayed that none of my children would get their father's genes. From a very early age, all three have consciously worked toward defying their father's dominant genes.

My grave concern was what if Nina got them? I was fearful of leaving her alone at home when I went to work, having all kinds of scary thoughts, as she had mentioned more than once that life was not worth living. This stress kept accumulating, and I decided it was now time for me to see a therapist to ease my own nerves.

I opened my heart to Susan, a very competent and apt therapist. I discussed Nina's state and mine. Susan helped me dig deeper.

After several sittings, she concluded, "Nina feels betrayed by you, Kanchan. You had your encounters with your husband, then you would go to Nina, take her counsel, and share your sorrows with her. She held your hand. She hated her father for doing this to you. However, a few days later, she saw you making up with the same man. She felt hurt and betrayed by you. Even if you are now separated and don't live together, she needs to see a paper that says you are divorced."

Susan came as an angel in my journey. She helped me change my beliefs.

I had always given myself credit for providing everything to Nina, maybe more than for a normal child. Listening to Susan, I knew Nina got everything as per my perception but did not get what she really needed, what was truly hers.

Although I found Susan's words unsettling, they were a huge validation of what I knew to be true. During this time, in moments of helplessness, grief, and agony, I would stand in front of my guru's picture, shedding tears of grief, and talk to him as a daughter talking to her father. "Why are you still annoyed with me?" I'd ask. "Show me the direction. Give me the signal. How can I help Nina, my desolate child?"

Around this time, out of desperation, I was able to break the ice with three ladies at work—Diane, Nancy, and Elaine—who were friends with each other. The four of us soon became a tight-knit group. I shared my story with them and, slowly, they opened up, too. They were very supportive. They would come home and pray with us and get flowers and nicely worded cards for Nina.

Diane mentioned a church near my house that she felt would give me a feeling of community, so I started going regularly in search of greater peace. The pastor was a very learned person, so I listened to his sermons intently. The hymns and the explanation of Bible verses comforted me immensely. I became acquainted with fellow churchgoers. I was particularly impressed by the community feeling in the church, supporting and helping fellow churchmen and churchwomen in all different ways. I was much moved.

I approached the pastor, a tall, lean man with bright, shining, crinkly eyes, wearing a Duchenne smile, his cheeks lifted. His face looked as if he was immersed in the Lord's blessings and enjoying them. Something about him made it easy to trust him. I found myself compelled to talk to him about my problem and ask for his advice. He had seen me a few times and acknowledged my regular visits to the church by nodding when I entered on Sunday mornings.

I requested some time with him. "My daughter has been depressed and withdrawn," I said. "I suspect it's because of my troubled relationship with my husband, which she has witnessed since she was a young child."

The pastor listened quietly. Then, in six clear, concise sentences, he gave me the advice that left a deep impression on my mind and touched my heart.

"That man is not your responsibility. He used you as his crutch. He needed to get medical help, which he did not. You and the children are his responsibility, which he has obviously and conveniently neglected. You are not his guardian. Divorcing such a man and seeking a happy life is your right as a human being."

The pastor was certainly a mediator of God and an angel. He said what I needed to hear at this time in my life. As they say, everything has its own time. The blueprint of my life was in His hands, He knew better.

I called Vijay, who had now acquired a green card. I shared with him Nina's acute state, as well as Susan's and the pastor's advice, along with my thoughts about getting a divorce. I told him we could apply for a mutual, uncontested divorce since I didn't want any money from him.

Vijay responded without any anger or sadness—only a deep sigh of relief. In his heart, he knew what a terrible role he'd played as a husband and father and with Nina's condition, I didn't have to convince him. Or maybe he never thought of himself as a bad husband or father—a narcissist would not—and he was better off by himself with his own freedom away from any household responsibilities. He agreed to proceed with the paperwork. The divorce was to be mutual, with me agreeing on $1.00 in a settlement. It came as a big relief to me as well. The children, who'd already said, "Mom, you need and deserve a better life away from him," were equally relieved.

My friend Diane referred me to her lawyer. The separation time was three months in Connecticut before getting a decree, which we received on October 14, 2003.

We walked out of the courtroom together, along with the attorney. As the attorney stepped away, Vijay looked at me with some contempt in his eyes, as if he had lost the match that he planned on winning. "Are you happy now?"

"Yes," I said, observing him for a few seconds before walking away. *You have played enough games with me. You thought you won in your game every time I returned to you, but each time I was back, I became stronger.* I was making myself ready, with a strategy for making the final goal of victory for my players, my children.

We drove away in opposite directions—he went south, and I went north. I felt liberated in both my body and mind.

Chapter 12

Cost of Freedom

2003–2008

I felt like a free bird, seeing myself as a white swan gliding high in the infinite sky—who had no boundaries, no limits, no shackles, no fear, no apprehensions—just soaring higher and higher. For a few moments, I set everything aside, emptied my brain, and sat with a glass of wine to celebrate my newfound freedom.

Nina's condition improved slowly. She drove fifty miles to attend Kathak dance classes, to divert her attention and get back some focus and drive.

Again, unexpectedly, I received a call from my good friend Amrit. She was in New York, visiting her sister, and said she planned on coming to see us in Connecticut.

I shared Nina's situation with her, and she said, "Wait, I will come and make her laugh."

As usual, she was full of humor and lightheartedness.

At least five years had passed since I'd last seen her. I waited eagerly to hear the bell ring. I opened the door and there she stood, the same charm and a tall elegance. Behind her stood a good-looking boy, at least six feet. Raj! Her son, all grown up.

Nina had just walked out of the shower, with her long hair still wrapped in a towel. The bathroom door opened to the living room when she saw Amrit and her son. I saw Raj eyeing Nina. They'd played together as kids when I used to visit Amrit. I even had that unforgettable, cute picture of them innocently kissing each other, when they were three years old, with Coke bottles in their hands.

We had a fun time catching up—some nostalgia, some talk of what was going on in our lives, and some future plans, remembering good times and laughing. Amrit's sense of humor and her typical jokes made the environment light and hilarious. Nina and Raj hung out together. Those moments brought a new life to both Nina and me.

Raj called me a week later to ask if he could take Nina out. Of course, I agreed. It took some convincing for Nina to step out of the house.

Raj visited Nina at her Kathak classes, driving all the way from New York City. Nina said he seemed keen on dating her, but she wasn't ready for a relationship. I liked the idea of her being with someone, and if that someone was Raj, it would be even better.

By way of encouragement, I reminded her, "He's a good boy from a family we know well. He's a Berkeley graduate, and he works in New York City. The family knows our entire background. Go ahead and go on a date. You don't have to marry him."

So, they started dating. Soon they fell in love, and Raj became the love of her life. Raj knew from his mother she had not been doing well. He took loving care of her. She told me after a few months that they would like to move in together. I had no objection, seeing how happy he made her. She seemed cheery and looked forward to living with Raj in New York.

It was my mindset that all my children should live with their partners before marrying. Although those were not my original values, my own troubled marriage had changed my belief.

Life looked brighter for Nina. She left her depressive feelings behind and gave herself the permission to be happy again.

I sensed respite, with Nina feeling better and moving out, the boys in college, my job at hand, and a few affiliations at work. It was true liberation!

❋ ❋ ❋

One morning in June 2004, I was called into a meeting with my new manager, Cicely.

"Kanchan, as you know, the division hasn't done well this year and we are forced to restructure. Unfortunately, your position is part of that restructuring, and it will be eliminated," she said.

"Sorry, I don't understand."

"Kanchan, it's not a reflection on your capabilities, but we have no option."

"So, you are not repositioning me in any other department or division?"

"No."

"You are telling me that you are terminating my services from today." My voice had started to quiver, my throat had a big lump while I spoke, and my chest was going up and down with each breath, which felt so heavy. Hell broke on me, and all my plans shattered in that one moment.

Cicely was trying to be nice, informing me a severance would be offered to me and COBRA would cover my medical insurance needs. But my brain had already shut down. I kept gazing at her and then got up and walked out before breaking down in tears.

I walked hastily into the restroom, howled, and pressed both hands on my mouth to smother my voice. Then I gathered myself, washed my face, went to my desk, and quietly collected my personal stuff in a box, exactly how I had seen in western movies and TV shows. I held the box to my chest and walked out. I managed to drive home, confused, shocked, and helpless.

The newly appointed HR director wanted to present cost reductions to upper management to better position herself within the company, and my well-paid manager position had caught her eye. My heart wanted to contest this involuntary termination—it was pure discrimination of my age, ethnicity, and gender. But my mind and wisdom told me otherwise. I would not be ungrateful to my mentors who sat on the company's board of directors, who gave me this opportunity of moving to the States and changing my children's lives forever. I would not offend them by suing the company or the company manager for wrongful termination. I felt disheartened but not broken. I carried close to five years of rich experience of working in a Fortune 100 company. I was ready to explore the job market on my own. I was a permanent resident of the United States by now, which was an added parameter for being hired.

I took up a contract job offered by Mike for six months in the same company, a low-paid hourly job, while I searched for full-time work. Unfortunately, the employment market at the time was at its lowest. To add to the crisis, outsourcing to India was at its peak, and lobbyists protested outsourcing at every turn, so employers had their reservations about hiring non-US citizens. The contract job, which was barely able to cover my rent and groceries, was over by December 2004.

I applied for several jobs each day. I would get interview calls, giving me some hope. I would get excellent reviews in the first two rounds, building my hopes, but faced rejection by the third round.

I held out hope, month after month for twelve months, living in Connecticut running a household, paying bills—rent, car payment, partial parent loan installments, and pocket money to the children. I was in the doldrums as to what should be my course of action. I took down the picture of my guru on the refrigerator, as I got frustrated and agonized with time passing by. Why was he not giving me any direction? Why was my path not visible? Why was I stuck at a point of no return?

By the end of fourteen months out of a job, I was broke, alone, and lost. I had eaten away 401(k) savings of four or so years and left with no money to pay the rent. I was nervous and full of anxiety and had no one to talk to and no support. My friend Abhinav had moved to another company with John Gordon. He was aware of my situation, and it seemed was not in a position to help me at the time.

I did not tell the children about any of this. I handled it alone. Their studies were important and giving them any worries would demolish the ramp that I had built so far. Nina had barely gained some happiness in life and was getting settled with Raj, so it was out of the question to talk to her.

I felt cornered. I was going insane keeping all the stress within me, with no one to talk to or share my strain. To add to the misery, I developed pains in my stomach and had difficulty walking, but in the absence of any medical insurance, I could not see a doctor. With nowhere to turn, I quietly bought a ticket to India in October 2005.

❋ ❋ ❋

I never wanted to leave the children alone in this vast country but taking them out of their studies was not an option. They were studying abroad at the time on a student exchange program, Kabir in Australia and Kuber in Spain. Nina was with Raj.

I made an excuse to the children that I was feeling very lonely in the States and needed to return and also look after Mom. I left my return date open, as I had no long-term plans for how to move ahead in life.

I intended to look for a job in a global company in New Delhi, which was the hub of all foreign companies opening their offices. I could take a job at a senior level that paid well and would help with my children's expenses in the States. They were taking care of their tuition fees through the student loans they had taken which was a huge support. I instructed the twins to continue with their studies. Nina was safe in New York. My move wouldn't disrupt their lives. Then I packed my suitcases, sold my stuff in a garage sale for pennies, settled any account balances, and boarded a plane for India with my two suitcases.

❋ ❋ ❋

My mom was super excited to see me, as was I to see her. Obviously, no one in India needed to know I had lost my job and was penniless, exhausted, sad, and uncertain of the future. I firmed up my decision to stay in India for a few years until the boys graduated. I also decided that I wouldn't look for a job for at least a month or two. After fourteen months of turmoil, I was going to relax my mind and recoup my energy in my mother's house. Seventeen years of working had left me no money from either country. But I still held three life insurance policies, which I'd bought to save taxes while working in India for thirteen years. I cashed them out so I wouldn't be a burden to my mother.

I felt safe and free in my mom's house, where I wasn't responsible for anyone or anything, accountable to no one. Mom pampered me as she would a child. She granted me total independence, no questions asked. Although in my late forties, I was back to living the life I'd left at twenty-two, a life I'd thought I'd live with Vijay—no stress, no job, maids to do the housework, a chauffeur to drive me anywhere I wanted to go. It was a lifestyle I could never afford in the United States, where domestic help was far more expensive. Although this could go on for only so long, I just wanted to live the life of my dreams for a few weeks.

But before I could really enjoy it, I still had one task to finish. I had to pay a visit to my in-laws to inform them of the divorce, in case Vijay had not done so. They needed to know I was no longer their son's caretaker. He was their responsibility going forward.

This time when I entered the house, my shoulders were straight up, and my chin was high. I didn't so much as cover my head since I was no longer the daughter-in-law. They were not expecting me, so they were surprised to see me at their door. They were cordial and let me in. I was upfront in telling them I was there to share something important of their concern. "Vijay and I have signed the divorce papers," I said. Then I briefly recapped my troubled and broken relationship with their son and my struggle and hard work for twenty-three long years. My younger brother-in-law tried to interrupt, but I stopped him, showing him my hand, my palm facing him. He was not in a place to utter a word. He was known for his temper, the one who had thrown red chilies into the eyes of my brother's friend.

I looked at my father-in-law and said, "All you can do at this moment is give me a pat on the back for what I have made of your grandchildren. They are in the United States right now, being educated. They have great values, and they have respect for women. From now on, your son is your responsibility."

I was quite taken aback when no surprise showed on Dev's or Shiela's faces. In fact, all of them were quiet, just looking at me. I didn't see any expressions of anguish or embarrassment, either. Perhaps time had changed them. It was twenty-five years since their son's marriage and almost twenty years since I had seen them last. I got the impression they were almost pleased with what I'd achieved over the years, immigrating to the United States, my children studying there, and their own son a US citizen living there, which was a dream of every Indian. They had known what Vijay was doing to me and never intervened, never talked to him about mending his ways, never came to me to show their concern or compassion, never made an attempt to see their grandchildren, and, except for the one time his brother had visited, never advised Vijay to take medication. They had known him for thirty-two years before he married me. They knew who he was, yet they'd been cruel and negligent, not only in arranging his marriage to a naive young girl—brought up in an enlightened family—in the first place, but also in condemning my children to a life filled with violence and torment.

I took care of their broken son for years, which was actually their responsibility, one they had shirked. It was a good thing they were nice to me during that visit. Otherwise, I was completely prepared to unleash my pent-up emotions, telling them everything Vijay had done to me and my children, for which I felt they, his family, were somewhat liable. It may not seem relevant in Western countries, but in India, a son's natal family takes liability for the son's married family, especially if he isn't capable of caring for them. They could have saved five lives from being broken, five people from living in chaos, five people from getting stuck in their past, paralyzing their lives.

I came home light and relieved. That chapter of my life was closed forever.

189

With that task out of the way, I picked up my life where I'd left off at twenty-two. Covering my arms with colorful bangles and henna, I was back to being a free spirit in a free bird. I smiled and laughed and dressed up and joked. I traveled to Mumbai beaches and Kerala backwaters all by myself, as the fearless and stronger person I had become. Nothing was not doable, and nothing was impossible anymore. It was a great time of freedom, with no children to look after and no boundaries or obligations—just me and a long-missed infinite, star-studded sky, the luminous moon changing shape every night.

After a few weeks, I approached a couple of recruiters and soon landed a good job as an HR director in one of the Global companies. I moved back to my own house after giving notice to the tenant. There I was, in an empty house with bare walls, no furniture, and no possessions except for my two suitcases and a few utensils Mom had given to me from her kitchen. For weeks, I slept on the floor on a carpet until I could buy furniture, furnishings, and everything else I needed to set up the house.

Mom worried about me being alone. "When will you settle down with a man in your life?" she often asked. "How will you spend it alone? Look for someone for yourself."

I had no such plans. I wasn't going to jeopardize my new-found freedom.

Surely, it was not easy to live as a divorced woman in India. The society was still stuck where I had left it. No compassion for a single woman. Surely, I had brought it on myself, people reasoned, the abuse and violence. Society, no matter what class, didn't respect a separated woman. They only respected a woman with a husband standing beside her, even if he was useless or a wife beater. And irrespective of class, men felt they had the right to harass a divorcée, to go up and ask for her phone number or to X-ray her with their eyes when she passed by on the street. My blood boiled when this happened. It was everything I'd come to realize with Dr. Sarkar, my boss from my first job. Only now I was fully living it.

I'd even noticed married women shying away from me in a gathering of couples or looking above my head as if I didn't exist.

Instead of welcoming me, they would quickly find their husbands and cling to them, holding their arms in a gesture that declared, "He is mine. Stay away." It was as if these women thought I was out to steal their husbands. Because I defied tradition, in their eyes, anything was possible! The result was that I had no female friends. And since I had to also watch out for men, this meant I couldn't make any male friends either. It would always be a quid pro quo, if I made one. After a few months, I figured out that this would be my way of life. I chose to become aloof rather than the center of gossip. There was no point in trying to make friends. I had no emotional support during my days of stress. It was a very disturbing time.

Around 2008, one of Vijay's close booze buddies started stalking me, in connivance with and encouraged by Vijay to harass me. He first called me several times a day and then began sending nasty emails to all the people around me. I approached cyber privacy experts, but they said they couldn't help. There were no cyber privacy laws in India. "You mentioned you were in the States," the officer said. "You should go back. You will get protection there."

Vijay called, to my surprise. Perhaps the two buddies had colluded to not let me live. The first call from Vijay was congenial, so I was open to talking to him. He called the next day and then the next. Within a week, he graduated to his old tactics of verbal abuse, shouting and bullying over the phone. How miserable was that! I understood that he was getting drunk and then calling me. I could not switch off the phone at night because of my children alone in the States. What if they called? By now, tired of harassment and bullying, I felt ready to detonate. My body and mind couldn't take the frustration and anger of dealing with the stalker and my ex-husband, added to it the victimization by society as a single, divorced woman, especially when I didn't behave as a victim. I needed to help myself because, clearly, no one was going to help me. I had to refocus. Get back on the track. I could not waste another day of my life for these incorrigibles and criminals. I had to do something different to move forward.

When I felt aggravated beyond belief, I shared the stalking with the boys over the phone. They immediately called their father and said, "We know you've given Mom's details to your friend. If you don't call him and stop him, we will never, ever talk to you again."

The twins then called and asked me to return to the States. I wasn't expecting this. "Why are you alone in India?" they asked. "We're here. We're working now. You have to come back to us, live in a safer place, where we can be there for you when you need us."

They're fully grown men now, I thought with a grin. It had been close to five years since I'd left for India. They were now twenty-four. They called me again the next day. "Mom, sell the house before coming so you're not left with an option to go back."

I liked what they said. I was ready to go back to the States to my grown-up sons, where I could feel protected rather than vulnerable, where there were laws to protect me, where women had freedom to walk alone without being judged.

Nina and Raj had their own plans. They were going to live in London. I'd go back to my sons, my cubs, my heroes, my rocks. I put the house up for sale immediately and didn't give in to the chauvinist real estate agents who came around trying to bring the price down. I had my secret in the Universe. I trusted my instincts and the patterns of my life so far, bolstered through faith and trust in the higher power, my guru, and in myself. Although the real estate agents—all male, mostly from nearby villages at that time—were offering me a much lower price, finally—two days before my departure, as God would have it—a private party came to see the house. "Auntie we love your house."

It sold at my asking price.

Chapter 13

A New Life of Redemption

2009–2012

I flew to Newark's Liberty Airport in April 2009 to live with the twins. I arrived with the same two suitcases I'd taken to India five years earlier, the same two suitcases that had carried my only possessions when I'd first come to the United States in 2000. For the third time in the last nine years, I'd left behind a household of furnishings: antique furniture, crystal, artifacts, wall paintings, and silk curtains. When I would find my own place again, I'd have to rebuild another household from scratch. Did I have any regrets? None whatsoever. That's what life is about.

My only remorse was leaving behind my collection of books I'd accumulated over the years, the books I'd dated, marked, and highlighted, the collection that I considered my legacy. Nevertheless, I felt relieved to be back with my two boys. It gave me peace and strength. I was going to start afresh, begin a new life, focus on my present, and plan for the immediate future. However, I had to do something different to get different results this time.

On the fourteen-hour flight from New Delhi, I resolved to put my unforgettable and agonizing past behind me. All that I had suppressed wrapped in patterns and false beliefs, haunting me in my dreams, played repeatedly like film clips. Every morning, I would wake up, startled by the nightmares, by those gruesome episodes that resurfaced each day. The trauma had not left me. The compulsive thoughts possessed me. I carried that pain and hurt for most of my mornings until I'd push myself and get busy. There had to be a way to end this.

My determination assured me I was not beyond redemption, that reclamation of my normal, healthy life was a possibility. I had to let go of these crippling thoughts that prolonged my pain and its effects. I needed to tame my mind and feed it good thoughts, identifying with myself, who I truly was!

I reminded myself of Norman Doidge, *The Brain That Changes Itself*, a book I had read on an innovative, growing discovery by neuroscientists about a new concept of neuroplasticity and rewiring. What stuck with me, in layperson's terms, was the idea that a new, clean path was formed when someone tread on a path covered with weeds and wild grass in the wilderness. Everyday walking crushed the weeds and wild grass. According to neuroscience, my brain could build new neural pathways and let go of my old, hurtful memories, if I replaced them with new wholesome thoughts. I came off the flight in Newark with a new resolve to rewire my brain.

The boys now lived on Washington Street in a newly constructed, gated, high-rise with all the conveniences within walking distance: the train station, bars, restaurants, a mall, grocery stores, and the long boardwalk by the Hudson River. Their building contained a library, business center, and a sprawling outdoor sitting area on the fifth floor. I took complete advantage of the facilities.

When the boys left for work, I'd stride along the boardwalk, the sun shining on the river showing silver ripples. I smiled at the sight of the familiar mama duck and her ducklings crossing, all in a line, to the bank of the river. I could not believe how every dog was accompanied by a walker or owner—on a leash, several different breeds—and how well-bred and trained they were. In India, no one kept dogs as pets. They were mostly underfed strays that lived on the streets.

To enjoy this new world, I had to overwrite my depressing thoughts with happy thoughts. I had to push away the unworthy emotions I was carrying. But how exactly would I do that? I decided to try chanting a mantra in praise of God while I walked. Most evenings, when we were young, my parents would chant—*binati*—like a prayer or hymn. My siblings and I would sit with them. Hands folded in front of us, and eyes closed, we would chant with them, finishing by bowing our heads in gratitude for all He had blessed us with. I never knew the meaning of that prayer at the time, but I remembered the words:

Thwameva matha cha pitha thwameva, Thwameva bhandusha, sakha thwameva, Thwameva vidhya, dravinam thwameva, Thwameva sarvam mama deva.

Now I knew their meaning:

You truly are my Mother, and you truly are my Father; you truly are my Relations, and you truly are my Friend; you truly are my Knowledge, and you truly are my Wealth; you truly are my All, my God of Gods, the Higher Power.

For the first few days of chanting on my early morning walks, I could not focus. While I chanted, my mind wandered to thoughts of the past. However, I did not succumb to my mind. I let it chatter at the back while I chanted the words. Soon, I was repeating the words mindfully. I would look at the green trees, flowers, and squirrels, and I'd keep chanting. I wouldn't let my mind rest or give myself time to think about anything else. I wouldn't let my thoughts stray from the words I chanted because those words had meaning.

I'd have my coffee at Starbucks, return home, shower, and again head toward the boardwalk, this time with my backpack, a water bottle, a book, pen, pad, and something to munch on. It was a perfect place for thinking and planning. I sat on a bench and read several books on women leaders, women's empowerment, women bringing change, women in space, women on K2, and women leaders in the corporate world. Then I read the new genre of day-to-day women just like me in *Eat, Pray, Love*; *Under the Tuscan Sun*; and *Good Harbor*. I loved watching the red-and-white lighthouse anchored in the Hudson River by the boardwalk and the big white-and-blue yacht with a restaurant on its deck.

During one of my morning walks, my neighbor Rita, whom I had seen a couple of times in the elevator of our building, was coming from the opposite side. We smiled and exchanged a hello. Coincidentally, after that we saw each other every other day at the boardwalk. Our familiarity progressed into sitting on the bench and talking about life.

Rita said, "I noticed you live with your sons. Where is your husband?"

"I don't have a husband."

"Are you divorced, or did your husband pass away?"

"I had a troubled marriage. I survived the trap of a violent husband. I have three grown-up children but have been carrying the baggage of the past and have not been able to settle down in one place."

"Why haven't you let go of him and unburdened yourself?"

"I don't have an answer," I said. "I don't know how to let go of the pain and hurt. It keeps coming back."

"He was brought into your life to give you the three lovely children you just told me about," she said. "His role was over after that. Get over him and move on."

She was so right. Her words resonated in my head and, over the next few days, brought clarity to me. Yes, that was his only role in my life. End of story!

It was only a few words Rita, another angel in my life, had said, but they were therapeutic. Those words changed another belief of mine. After that, the "rewiring" occurred on its own. I was aware of the clutter and waste I was carrying. It had no room in my brain. My brain needed cleansing. I continued chanting each morning, overlaying agitation with stillness, terror with peace, hatefulness with love. Slowly but steadily, the clutter in my mind started to fade. I experienced a shift in the thoughts I identified with.

A few weeks later, the compulsive thinking disappeared. The neural pathways had changed their course and rewired to a new thinking. I was a new person with no past or at least not a past that had imprisoned me. Now living in the present, there was a sudden influx of joy and inner peace. My drained energy shifted to vigor and a newfound enthusiasm.

Rita was God-sent, and the few moments He provided me with her set me free!

※　　※　　※

I could not stop singing Dana Winner's song, "One Moment in Time," as I raced against destiny, fighting for my own eternal moment. My rewiring brought me infinite peace.

Mitch Albom stated in *The Five People You Meet in Heaven* that we come across people every day who play a role in our lives. When the time together is complete, they're gone. My marriage was a tragedy. However, the result was my three wonderful children, my cubs!

I was in a better place, yet as the days passed, I sensed pain within the boys. They seemed to have grown distant. In our family, we'd always been open, expressing our emotions and love for each other, but now our communication seemed superficial. I craved tight hugs after having gone through the tumultuous times in my life. I initially gave the boys the benefit of the doubt since both had ridiculously long work hours in the financial institutions they worked. They were also not oblivious of my anxiety.

Kuber said to me one evening, "Let me take you to dinner to talk and clear the air."

I was so ready for this.

"Mom, you don't deserve this silence from us. We felt very lonely and abandoned when you went so far away. We could not even reach you, see you, or share our wins and our lows."

I was quietly listening without interrupting. I let him vent.

He said, "I was depressed in the last semester of college and could not get out of bed to attend classes, which affected my grades. We were caught in situations where we had to call our dad since he was the only connecting link here."

I held his hand and expressed my feelings of hurt listening to this sad story. "But why didn't you ever talk to me about your depression? That was not fair to you or me. Our communication had always been so strong, so what happened? What made you think I abandoned you?"

Maybe he was right. We had not lived together under one roof since they went to boarding schools, except for the two years in Syracuse, which were the most stressful years, too, as we were new to the States. Acclimatizing to a new country, a new culture had taken our toll.

I gave him comfort and briefly shared my reason for moving to India. I wanted Kabir and Kuber together when I gave the details.

A few days later Kabir and I went out for dinner with the same purpose of talking and listening. He seemed agonized that I'd decided to go to India when he and his brother had needed me most. It hurt, but I needed to listen. Based on our conversations, I learned how they'd felt about being left alone. "There was no one to share our everyday life. You were so far away that we could not bother you to comfort us during our sad days. Mom, you should not have gone." They had similar feelings when they'd been left in the boarding school at the tender age of ten. I also couldn't attend their college graduation, a significant milestone in their lives. An added sore point. While we had, of course, spoken on the phone, it wasn't the same. International calls cost a lot, so we could not talk every day. They held me responsible for making the decision to go back to India, and rightly so, although they knew in their heart there had to be a bigger reason for Mom to have made that decision, leaving them behind.

It was time for me to share my compelling reasons for going back to India, as it was proving detrimental to hide it from them. I called them both and sat them together in front of me.

"I am extremely sorry that you felt lonely and abandoned.

"My reasons and intentions had been so different from what you have perceived. I am responsible for you feeling the way you both have expressed separately, and I'm sorry. I didn't want you to leave school and come with me to India."

I gave them the details of having no job for the longest time, left with no money. "I had to go to India to survive. Get a job which could enable me to send some pocket money for all three of you, besides the massive student loans you all had taken. I also had a compulsion to go back to keep my sanity and take care of my health. I was having weird pains in my stomach and had no insurance. I was also quite depressed for which I needed to visit a doctor. I could not see any solution coming for months ahead. I was left with no option."

My eyes started to tear. They both held my hand. I continued. "I didn't make a big deal to you both because I knew you wouldn't want me to face this alone and you would have made a wrong decision in haste, from your heart and not your mind to leave your studies and come with me to India. It would have destroyed it all. We all collectively had to make that sacrifice to keep moving forward." Their grip on my hands tightened. Then they got up and hugged me. We all hugged each other firmly.

"How's your health now, Mom?" Kabir asked.

Before I could reply, Kuber said, "Mom are you still depressed?"

I held their hands and gave them the assurance, "I am fine. The pain in the stomach was a hernia."

After listening, they softened and understood my reasons. Kabir said, "Mom, we are adults, so you need to share your struggles with us and not keep protecting us."

Kuber immediately took over, "We are one family, and we need to know what you are going through."

I concurred. I had to stop treating them as young and vulnerable. We hugged again and we were back where we'd left off—one solid unit. We came up with the name for the four of us: *Ek muthi*, one strong fist.

My walks continued, as did my reading by the river. And as sun brought warmth, I would move to Starbucks on the river to sit for hours. It was *Eat, Pray, Love* that changed my direction and reinforced my spiritual path. I was influenced by Elizabeth Gilbert's journey. The thought of the author in an ashram in India was appealing, and her visits to Italy and Bali felt absolutely liberating. The book haunted me in a good way.

I was amazed that the author traveled all the way to India in search of balance in life and peace. I lived in the country for forty-seven years of my life! Why could I have not yielded to a place like that during my struggle and found peace? Of course, I knew the answer. *Everything has its own time and place. For me, the time was now.*

I called my mom in India and shared Gilbert's story with her, as well as my innate desire to rekindle my spiritual path. I wanted to be back on the journey, in love with the teachings and philosophy of my guru.

"Mom, I am getting an inner calling. The feeling is intense. I want to visit his ashram as we visited during our childhood. That is what has given me my faith."

The memories of the ashram came alive, and I became very passionate. My whole heart, my body, my soul, and every part of me was immersed in that passion.

Mom listened and said, "If you have so much desire to see him, you will certainly have his *darshan*, his appearance, where you are."

"But how?"

I stayed on the phone and Googled it. No sooner had I pressed enter than I found congregations of followers in New Jersey and New York.

Raghu, the secretary of the *satsang ghar*, the Indian church, answered my call.

"Yes, you have called the right number. We have a congregation of about four hundred people in New Jersey, but New York may be closer to you, which has about two hundred people attending the satsang. I'll give you Rani's number, who is in charge there."

Raghu called me an hour later and said the guru was visiting Malaga, Spain, in August.

"You should go!" he said.

I shared the whole incident with the boys in the evening. They were equally excited about it. They both said in unison, "Mom you should definitely go."

Come August, I was at JFK airport, at the gate, surrounded by Indian faces. There was talk of flights rerouted or canceled because of ash in the air over Italy due to the Mount Etna eruption. His blessings were with me, however, and there I was sitting in the flight to Heathrow.

The hotel in Malaga was mostly booked by people going to the satsang. A lady in white with noticeable red nail polish came up to me to say she'd booked a cab in the morning, and she could give me a ride. I was not sure what drew her to me, but we soon became friends. Lots of the satsangis carried meals and snacks with them. A group invited me to share their food, and I happily joined them. I felt such a connection, a feeling of community.

The entrance gates to the satsang compound opened at 7:00 a.m., but since there was a large following, I would need to arrive early to get a seat closer to the dais. I got up at 4:00 a.m. Jyotsna, the lady with the red nail polish, met me at the reception hall and we arrived at the location by 5:30 a.m.

The lines were already long. I was amazed at the organization and the efficient management of thousands of people, from the courteous welcome by the *sevadars* (the service volunteers) to the spick-and-span surroundings and the shining restrooms. I had gotten a seat in the third row, which was still far from the dais where the guru would preside. As we filed in and waited, singers sang *bhajans* (devotional songs), the only sounds while the congregation waited and longed to see the guru.

At exactly 9:00 a.m., the guru stepped onto the dais, clad in a white *kurta* (a long shirt), white pajama pants, and a black waist jacket. He glowed. His radiant face had a magnetic attraction. His discourse was about spiritualism versus the path of the world and why we had to be mindful and still, continually seeking a spiritual path to get in touch with our inner conscious. He quoted Jesus, Krishna, Muhammad, Buddha, Guru Nanak, Kabir, and other saints.

My attention was singularly on the guru. Although he was far, with hundreds of people between us, it was like we were the only two there. Nothing else existed—only my guru and me.

His aura surrounded me. I never wanted it to end. Tears of love streamed down my cheeks, and they continued to fall during the entire discourse.

If I could connect with the higher conscious, then all my fear and stress would dissolve. I may be able to find the essence of our existence, this life that was an illusion, with no basis in reality, and no truth.

Peace and stability filled my body and spirit. I captured those precious moments and came back serene and calm. I bathed in the beauty for several days and bought books on spiritualism—a range of authors, periods, and philosophies—and started to attend the satsang (discourse) in the New York center on Sundays.

❄ ❄ ❄

In April 2010, almost a year later, the boys moved to Manhattan. The intense energy, vibrancy, and diversity fascinated and invigorated me. I went for my walks to Madison Park and spent my days in Barnes & Noble on Seventeenth Street and Park Avenue. It was fascinating to watch a thousand heads and two thousand legs walking ahead of me and behind me in the mornings going to work. Women typically in flat shoes, with a purse and a bag hanging on their shoulders, perhaps carrying their change of heels, I assumed. After dinner, I'd walk to Union Park, a few blocks away. People were out in droves, sitting on the stairs, playing music, and enjoying the breeze. What a life!

My search for an opportunity to become financially independent continued. I tried several options, but in vain, as they were not a good fit.

Abhinav was now well established in a global company headquartered in Chicago. He called me about a position as a training and organization development manager in Southern California, a division of Precision Edge Tools, the same company I worked for in India. Several rounds of interviews resulted in an offer. California was one of my dream places. I moved there in August 2010.

At Precision Edge Tools, I was reminded that the American corporate environment was not as easy to adjust to as the corporate environment in India. My boss was kind but unpredictable and erratic. It took time to get acclimated to the work environment, get familiar with my boss's idiosyncrasies, and get along with the rest of the employees. It did not feel good initially. I felt chronically stressed and needed to stop any accumulation of the stress turning into anxiety. So, I designed a tool. I strategically taught myself to compartmentalize issues, to create separate boxes for each stressful situation, place it in its own assigned box, lock the box, and keep it away, just as a computer does. Everything related to one subject was stored in one folder. I had several folders, but I opened only one at a time to retrieve the specific file and work on it. This kept me from stressing about everything at once.

I did the same thing with my personal life. I locked away any issues concerning children in separate boxes and opened the one which needed attention, keeping the others locked till I was relaxed and fresh to open the other one. I had boxes for my siblings in India too. This strategy worked well. By this time, I well understood, being healthy physically and mentally was crucial for me. I needed to take care of myself and remove any mental stress and fatigue. Besides, if I loved my children, then the best gift I could offer them was to stay healthy. Self-preservation became my mantra.

I started with a ritual of Friday evenings after work devoted to relaxation, de-stressing, and self-entertainment. It was my space to unwind and be with myself. A glass of wine and music that touched my soul did wonders to soothe my nerves. I'd set the patio table with a glass of red wine, whichever cheese appealed to me from the three hundred kinds of cheese the store carried, and some pitted Kalamata olives. I turned on my favorite Bollywood, Sufi, or classic rock from the '70s and '80s and let the music wash over me. I relaxed for hours in the cool breeze, under the clear sky, the moon peeking behind one palm tree and then another as it rose high in the sky by the time my beautiful evening ended.

However, every Saturday, I'd wake up anxious and full of guilt for drinking wine, which was against my guru's teachings. Still, I continued the ritual. It was important for my sanity. And though I sipped a glass of wine, I would not give up my spiritual path, as both brought inner peace and an abundance of pure love and joy.

The boys visited whenever they could, which wasn't as often as we'd like, given their jobs. They had finished their chartered financial analyst (CFA) certifications and were now preparing for the GMATs to apply to business schools for their MBAs. Their vision was to be in the top schools. They were strong-willed boys and, like me, had a singular goal. If they wanted something, they worked hard toward it until they got it.

They were accepted into schools ranked in the top ten: Northwestern University's Kellogg School of Management, and the University of Pennsylvania's Wharton School. My pride in them skyrocketed. It was a surreal moment when they received their congratulatory packages. *Is it even true I have come this far with them?*

During one of their visits, they asked if I desired for them to marry Indian girls. Humbled that they asked me, I told them to find women who loved them and whom they loved in return, women to whom they'd be good partners—respectful, sharing the household chores, and valuing their input—even better if they chose to have large families—the more the merrier! Color, caste, creed—none of that mattered to me. Equality had been the foundation of my upbringing, which I instilled strongly in my children.

Before they left, they asked if I had a PowerPoint presentation for them. They wanted to know if there was anything they needed to work on improving.

"You do not need any more presentations from me," I said. "You have reached a point far beyond my dreams!"

As our eyes welled with tears of joy, they both held me in a tight bear hug.

Chapter 14

Taking New Vows

2011–2014

My curiosity and love for the spiritual path brought me to a new satsang congregation, located in Anaheim, not far from Yorba Linda. I trusted following my guru's teachings was the road to lead me to tranquility and centeredness. I had enough clarity that it was a path leading to "God realization" by means of contemplation and surrender. It was not a cult. The choice to follow or not lay with the disciple. The discourses every Sunday were profound and carried a dimension of depth touching the soul.

In search of seeking explanation to my trepidation of committing to the five vows on the path, I met Vince, the head of the California region.

"Vince, the one question that has bothered me is the prohibition of wine, even one glass. Why is it considered a hindrance to the progress on the path?"

Vince looked at me with affection and compassion, just like a father looks at the naivety of his child. With a smile on his lips, his eyes bright and nonjudgmental, he listened to me keenly without answering.

"Why is this a part of the five vows, which are a must to take *naam* (the five secret words used for chanting during meditation) and be truly on the spiritual path recommended by our guru?" I took a deep breath while he sat still, knowing I had more to say. "I understood hard liquor to be prohibited, given everything I'd endured with my ex-husband, but a glass of wine could hardly have any effect on a person's mind. Does that make someone a bad person?"

His smile continued, and so did his gaze. There was no change in his expression as he spoke.

"It is to instigate the discipline of resisting temptation, right from the beginning," he answered.

His demeanor and soft but authentic voice made sense. But was I convinced? I wasn't sure. However, I agreed to give abstinence a chance.

Serious but not blindly committed to the path yet, I attended the satsang every Sunday and read spiritual books in the evenings after work. I called Mom regularly and talked with her about the path, seeking clarification about any questions that bothered me. However, I didn't bring up my question about wine since she never had any. I wasn't sure she'd understand or like the idea of me having wine.

I volunteered for several services available for *satsangis*, called *seva*: book seva, kitchen seva, ushering seva, sewing seva. The purpose was to bring the human souls together irrespective of their cast and creed and create tolerance and love for each other.

After the first year at work, I had acclimated to the environment and developed a good rapport with the employees. However, I clearly saw the glass ceilings: the acceptance of a woman doing jobs as successfully as men, didn't exist. The organizational dynamics of a corporate world remained the same whether in India or America, as both consisted of human beings.

But I had faith things would change when the right time came. Meanwhile, recognizing my potential for counseling and coaching, I enrolled in a business coaching course, which kept me mentally engaged and fulfilled when the job didn't.

As the Universe would have it, by the third year in my job, an unexpected opportunity fell into my lap. One afternoon, I was invited into the boardroom. I made my way there, hesitant, nervous, and unsure. I pushed open the heavy, high intimidating doors to the boardroom to find the division president and three senior VPs visiting from headquarters waiting for me. Butterflies filled my stomach and my breathing slowed with a muffled panting of breath. Then my grit spoke to me, *You have put in hard work and made several head wins in the last three years. The company sees it all, so calm down.*

"Take a seat."

I looked at the long, plush table and saw all four huddled at the far end, their attention on me.

Mr. Woodland, the division president, spoke first. "We had to let go of the facility HR manager, your boss, today and we would like to make this offer to you. Do you need time to think about it?"

My panting subsided. "I am happy to take the offer," I said, in a second, excitement filling my voice. Mr. Young, my division VP, handed me a letter of promotion, which stated the terms of the new job. I accepted the much awaited and challenging job offer with a smile, shook hands, and turned to get out of the room as fast as I could to breathe a sigh of relief and celebrate my victory.

This was the job of my choice and desire. It was an added enrichment and a broader extension of my current job as an organization development manager. This was the beginning of things looking up. I had no doubt that I would shine with my pure tenacity and hard work. Gradually, my work life changed, and so did my disposition and confidence.

In 2012, on my annual vacation to see my mom in India, I visited the ashram, Dera, where I'd desired living with my young children many years ago. I planned to stay in the Dera for a few days, situated in East Punjab, about a six-hour train ride from Delhi.

I had been inside the Dera a few times as a child with my family. Those memories flashed back to me as if they had never left me.

Nothing had changed after forty long years as far as the soul of the Dera was concerned. But it had grown miles all around. Only because the followers had increased manifold, more structures sprang up. There were acres of fields and farmland with old trees and greenery surrounding the area, everything fresh and clean. Not even the smallest pebble could be found on the clean roads or a dead leaf under a tree. The sevadars kept the place immaculate. There were hostels for foreigners and non-resident Indians, rooms for satsangis (seekers of truth) from within other states of India, and temporary sheds for lodging the locals.

For meals, crops were organic, grown at the Dera and prepared in big, well-equipped kitchens with love and devotion of the sevadars. Men and women sorted and cut vegetables, kneaded dough, and rolled tortillas called *rotis*. Men moved big ladles in large copper pots, cooking lentils on huge hearths made of clay. They sang *shabad* (spiritual songs) in unison, spreading pure vibes to the environment, where meals in the form of *prasad*, with blessings from the guru, were being prepared. Utensils shone like new, dedicatedly cleaned and passed on from the first step of rinsing to the next step of applying dish soap, and then washed and wiped by the engaged sevadars, as organized and efficient as an assembly line in a manufacturing plant.

In addition to meals, religious feasts called langar services were served around the clock. The food was consumed in worship, with an understanding that it had sanctification of the higher power. The place was an oasis of extreme calm and harmony in stark opposition to the life outside the Dera.

There was no chaos, only regulation, efficiency, and devotion to service. Visitors could volunteer for seva each day in the Dera, hospital, library, or book stall, labor seva in the new construction area, or prune plants. Anything and everything one was willing to do could be done.

Every day, the 3:30 a.m. bell for morning meditation echoed throughout the Dera. This time was believed to be sacred. The satsangis were to get up and sit for meditation. The shabad started at 6:00 a.m. and reverberated through the campus, making the atmosphere divine.

On weekends, the guru gave his discourse. Thousands of people from surrounding areas and temporary residents from all over the world gathered to listen to the satsang. Foreigners were given special passes to sit in the front section during discourses, a practice not meant to discriminate but to acknowledge the special guests who had traveled long distances.

I hired a local rickshaw pulled by sevadars inside the Dera to take me to the Punjab River, which flowed through the ashram. This wide river was a sight to behold, especially at sunset, when hues of orange painted the entire sky. As late evening fell, the light-bluish-gray water and light-bluish-gray sky merged as one. A cool gentle breeze arose. It was a serene place to sit and meditate, a time to search my soul and be a part of the stillness. The divinity of the place made me feel connected and purified. This was also the river where my dad's ashes were immersed, making the connection even deeper. I sat on the bank with my eyes closed while tears of love for my beloved fell on my cold cheeks. It was love . . . and more. It was love at first sight!

I always felt sad to leave the Dera, even as a child, as if I were leaving my spirit behind. But my body was energized, my mind peaceful, and my faith stronger and steadfast.

❋　❋　❋

My practice deepened over the next few months. Meditation became an evening ritual. I listened to spiritual tapes. My spiritual path and work became my life.

Three of my guru's teachings were closest to my heart: acceptance, forgiveness, and gratitude. Acceptance, the guru preached, was to remain in God's will and not resist it because He knew better. Resistance would only bring anger and disappointment.

Forgiveness was a virtue, which dissolved pain and hurt. It was the foundation of emotional and spiritual healing. For spiritual progress, I had to address and resolve those aspects of my past not in accordance with my divine nature. Pondering forgiveness took me back to my past. *Have I really moved on in my life? Am I still carrying the burden of my past? Have I forgiven Vijay?*

Gratitude was to be in His grace, thanking Him for this life, this Universe, and the Divine.

These teachings changed my way of thinking and my beliefs. Until then, I'd always believed we wrote our own life stories, designed our own destinies while holding the pen firmly in our own hands. We then put in an effort to live that story we'd outlined. *Wasn't that what I'd done to get here in my life?* I certainly believed I had made my own path. My unwavering faith in the higher power blessed me with various ways to make it happen.

On this journey, my mental model shifted. It was not me, but Him who held the blueprint designed for me. Everything happened per that blueprint in collusion with the Universe. We were the puppets on this planet, our strings in the hands of that higher power we call God. He decided when to move from point A to B. Every moment of my life was a result of that design called *destiny*.

I recalled how I repeatedly hid the letter Vijay's father had written when my family searched for suitors for me. My dad kept pulling it out from under the box and convinced me to reply. How often I thought my parents shouldn't have placed blind faith in a faraway neighbor who suggested my match. Dad had made a terrible mistake in trusting him when it came to the selection of a groom, a life partner for his most beloved child, that he should have done the due diligence of my match. Mom's added approval of my future husband further muddled my judgment. But these were all afterthoughts. Destiny was playing its part. I have questioned in the past, *Did my instinctual apprehension to reject his proposal ever stand a chance? Could Dad's explicit response to Dev's comment change our decision? Was I destined to marry Vijay?*

My response now, since my paradigm shift, was, "Yes, I was destined to marry Vijay." The Universe had chosen him to come into my life and give me three lovely kids and perhaps also to make me stronger, to make me who I am today. The rest of it was my karma. That was the best way to accept my past.

In 2014, while I was at the Dera, during my annual trip to India, I stood in the cafeteria by one of the tables, sipping masala chai made with goat's milk and nibbling on a glucose biscuit, when a middle-aged man came up and stood next to me. He had an aura about him, his face shining and an affectionate smile lighting his face. We made small talk to get acquainted.

"Are you initiated?" he asked, meaning had I taken the secret mantra from the guru himself for chanting during contemplation leading to God realization.

"No," I said.

"So, what are you waiting for? Is there a definitive time or date in your mind?"

I remained quiet, out of embarrassment. It was true I struggled with taking the naam and the timing of it.

"If you keep waiting," he said, "the moment will come and go, and you won't even know it. The time is now." Then he walked away, leaving me dazed and a little shaken.

Who was this man? Where did he come from? He just appeared out of nowhere, passed on his message, and then disappeared. I left the porch feeling a bit different, changed.

I had no idea who he was. His words kept playing in my mind. When I got up from the evening meditation, my mind was made up. I was going to take the vows—the naam—officially. I wanted to be initiated.

After morning meditation at 3:30 a.m., I showered and walked swiftly toward the tents, where the lines of seekers swelled. At the registration table outside, I gave my name for going through the filtering process of who was ready to be initiated—the ones who did not consume alcohol, eat meat, had honest living. The computer had my details on file. After the check-in, I was sent for an interview. The fact that my family had followed these teachings since 1948 was a big plus. I ate no meat or eggs was another. I was selected to stand in the line to be sent inside the tent, where the guru would come and give us naam to be chanted and repeated during *dhyan* (meditation). We stood in lines parallel to each other, waiting for his *darshna* (his appearance). The five vows which were to be followed as a way of life for satsangi's were different from the five words, called naam, which were to be chanted to focus when sitting for meditation.

When the guru arrived, he walked past every individual, looking deeply into the eyes of each person. I was humbled to see my guru so close. He had an aura about him, he was only thirty-two when he was given this huge responsibility of being the spiritual guru for millions of people not only in India but all over the world. He was married with two children before he became the Master. At the time of my initiation, he was sixty.

About ten thousand satsangis were to be initiated each day, three days in a row. We sat in the tents for him to give us the discourse about how to sit for two-and-a-half hours of meditation.

One begins with *simran*, which is repetition of naam. This is done to bring the thoughts to the eye center, between and behind the two eyes, called dhyan (focus). Dhyan is followed by *bhajan* (contemplation which is a form of meditation), listening to the sound current. Dhyan itself is not the goal; it is the means to become one with the sound, which happens by practicing bhajan. Both are equally important. Dhyan centers us at a point where super consciousness begins. It releases us from other mental activities, gives us a break from the ego-full self, anchors us in the present, and delivers us to the quiet place where we begin our real work of bhajan. What really matters is that repetition habituates us to the eye center, where bhajan will hold us and take us inward and upward. We keep our eyes closed and listen to the sound current because that sound will connect us to the higher power: take us to our true home.

Chanting that day in the tent changed the course of my life. All this while, I was searching for happiness, not yet realizing happiness was within me, not outside.

I returned home, determined to be a serious satsangi. I set up a corner of my bedroom in Brea, California, as a meditation area. I bought three new cushions: one to sit on and one to place under each of my folded legs in the lotus pose. I draped a scarf over my head to cover half my face and closed my eyes, which helped tune out the world, although none of this was a requirement. I had seen my grandmother and parents sit like that, so I had a natural instinct to follow their practice.

I sat for simran and bhajan every day, building up to added time with each sitting, but I could never make it to two-and-a-half hours.

I would begin by chanting and slowly turn my attention to the center of the forehead, the third eye. For the first fifteen minutes, I found it difficult to concentrate, but then I settled and could focus inside that darkness. One time, after about two weeks, as I meditated, my body started to feel numb—my legs, fingers, and arms. I felt as if my body rose above the floor. It was a euphoric, blissful stillness surrounding me, as if I were floating in space.

I remained like this for a few minutes and then suddenly opened my eyes, coming out of this strange sensation. When I looked at the clock, forty-five minutes had passed! I felt calm and happy but also out of the ordinary. That was the only time I had felt that sensation. I did feel the numbness in my body a few other times but not the euphoria that accompanied the sensation of rising above the ground. That soothing and mystifying experience remained with me for a few days. I longed to repeat the experience, to feel the stillness it brought to me. I tried every day.

After over two years of continued and consistent practice, I felt composed and tranquil. I also felt more centered in my body and mind. But then the initial enthusiasm of taking the vows and following the path began to wane. By the third year on the spiritual path, I felt gloomy and depressed. I had no life outside work. I came home, read spiritual books, listened to devotional music, and sat chanting in meditation or doing bhajan. I was becoming saint-like. *This is not who I am*, I thought. *This is not what I want.*

But this was what the intellectual mind did: it started to play games. Questioned and debated. That's why the uneducated, simple people from the hills and rural areas who didn't question and just followed what was told to them, could contemplate sooner and easier. *But I was educated with a mind of my own—right or wrong.*

As my internal struggles continued, I thought and deliberated on the five vows. I was okay with three of the five. But the "no alcohol" vow and the two-and-a-half hours of meditation were difficult and started to sound unreasonable. Out of my sixteen waking hours, I barely had two-and-a-half hours left after work for everything I needed to accomplish before going to bed. I was left with no time for myself. I would try to meditate for half an hour after coming home from work and then for half an hour before sleeping. But I would end up thinking about the day's activities, which then made it hard to sleep. Or I would fall asleep while meditating. Either way, I felt guilty.

I was trying my best, but all weekdays became alike—meditating or feeling guilty about not meditating, reading spiritual books, and listening to devotional music. I relinquished my Friday evening ritual. I even stopped listening to music on Fridays, the love of my life. If I put on music of my choice, which was romantic rather than devotional, I felt guilty, and my mind poked and prodded me to spend the time reading a spiritual book or meditating. I tried making a nonalcoholic cocktail and drinking it from a wine glass to recapture my Friday night ritual, but it was never the same. And missing the wine, even thinking about missing it, just added to my guilt.

Sundays spent in bookstores or Starbucks reading, drinking coffee, and people-watching were now spent at the Indian church, either at the satsang or volunteering. I felt suffocated inside the closed boundaries around me.

Why am I doing this to myself? I want to live life and enjoy this creation in the short time that I have.

❋   ❋   ❋

After some pondering and talking to the heads of the congregation, I made up my mind to follow the path and all the teachings of my guru, which are similar to those of Christ, Muhammad, and

Buddha, as I had always done, but on my own terms. I was sent by the higher power to be happy in his creation and enjoy it. I wanted to be spiritual but in moderation. I could follow the path and still relish my life with the pleasantries of the world. Spirituality for me also meant my personal growth: getting rid of five inner vices: Desire, anger, greed, attachments, and ego. Working on these so-called five thieves will simplify life and bring me closer to my soul, which was the basis for spirituality. This would bring a good balance for me. A life of guilt was no free life, and I was free now. Living life on my own terms.

The children were concerned about me living in California alone. They could not make trips often due to their busy schedules.

Kuber was on the phone, "Mom, you definitely need a companion in life."

I wasn't sure about this. He conferenced Kabir on the phone to try convincing me. "We have thrown hints to you earlier about going on the dating sites and you have ignored us. It's high time mom," Kabir said.

"We have a credit card ready. And you're going to set up your profile on eHarmony or matrimony.com, right now while we are on the phone."

This did seem in keeping with my newfound decision to enjoy life, a companion sounded like a good idea, so I agreed. As soon as I set up my profile, all these pictures of men came up. One in particular drew my attention, I thought, *Why not?* Therefore, I clicked on the picture and typed "Hi."

The message came back spontaneously. "Hi."

After exchanging a few emails for two weeks, I discovered it was a scam. The man wanted a hefty sum of money to be wired to him. He was in trouble, he said.

After five or six months, the boys were back with the subject. "Mom, one bad experience and you have given up," called Kabir.

While traveling for work, I saw an ad in an airline magazine for a professional match making company called, "It's a Date." I paid them a substantial amount of money to access professionals who had been rigorously vetted, including background checks.

They would introduce me to one guy each month, and we'd meet for lunch.

The first date was with a person who was highly accomplished as a business owner. He spoke only of his wealth, his personal aircraft, and summer and winter homes, which didn't impress me. Plus, there wasn't any chemistry. The second man, six foot four, was heavily into sports. Not for me. The third man and I had some chemistry, and he wanted to take me to his house on the very second date, and that was a "big no" for me.

I was done. I couldn't do this. I was not that person. I could not carry on the facade of sitting opposite a table a couple of times and deciding on my life partner without any chemistry, trust, or honesty.

If a relationship were to happen someday, then it would happen. If it didn't, it didn't. I couldn't design my own destiny. Let me leave this task to Him, my Father. I wasn't keen on the dating sites to start with, and I was in no hurry to jeopardize my freedom after it had taken me this long to get it back.

I was happy with my freedom. I was happy with myself.

Chapter 15

Companionship

2013–2015

My condo in Yorba Linda was in the Chino Hills, a quiet, serene location at the foot of the Santa Ana Mountains. Beautiful seasonal flowers, blooming in a riot of color, bordered the stone paths leading to each condo. These blossoms brought the complex to life, as did the profusion of pine trees. During the cooler months, the weather grew moody. Clouds gathered, bringing sudden bursts of rain, which ended as swiftly as it began, leaving the sky blue and the golden-brown hills a vibrant green.

As I walked along the stone pathways, I often spotted foot-long black lizards darting from one bush to another. At first, these lizards terrified me, but after observing them, I realized they were harmless and ran because they were timid and fearful of humans.

In the evenings, fog engulfed the higher elevations. The misty hills reminded me of the Shimla hills where the boys had studied, and Nina had attended school for one year. On warmer evenings, I'd sit on my patio or go for a walk, the cool breeze caressing my face as I listened to the murmuring of the trees and the whispering of leaves.

Although I certainly enjoyed the beauty surrounding me, I craved human contact, and conversation. The complex was quiet. I rarely ran into a human face. *Where are they?* Occasionally I'd see someone walked past on the way to the mailroom, and I'd hurry outside and wait on the patio for him or her to come back along the same path so I could say hello. Sometimes we'd exchange a few words, but people seemed content to keep to themselves. The stores in the area closed by 8:00 p.m. and, as if a curfew were in place, everything shut down afterward. *It was no Manhattan.*

Sometimes as I sat on the patio, I'd reminisce about growing up in the heart of Delhi on the Institute of Technology campus and the community living there—so many people everywhere, ready to talk, any time. Even for those who lived alone, there was no shortage of people around—people coming and going all day long. The morning started with the milkman, newspaper man, car cleaning man, cleaning lady, dishwashing woman, cook, washer man, gardener, vegetable seller, and driver. One would be busy opening the door, getting work done, engaging with the helpers, and asking about their families and their welfare, who was sick, who was getting married, and who was going to deliver a child. Our sweeper had delivered twelve children in fourteen years, of course that being an exception. Having been brought up in such an environment, I hungered for people and longed to connect and engage in conversations. I'm outgoing, and I love people. I need that interaction. *It's who I am.*

The boys sensed my loneliness from my low, flat voice on the phone, although I didn't share my feelings of sadness with them, since I knew they would worry unnecessarily.

They would ask what would make me happy and then suggest, "Ma, you have to look for your happiness within you."

I had become their guinea pig for practicing coaching and leadership, in business schools. They were better coaches then I was, more structured and more by the book. They'd urge me to go online to check out women's groups, wine tastings, knitting groups, or book clubs. To console me, each one would say separately, "Mom, things will be fine. Just wait a bit."

But my mom had a different opinion about feelings of loneliness.

"Internal loneliness proves a longing for God," she used to say. "The soul wants to connect to the higher power, which pulls you to merge with it."

The thought made me feel better. When I'd taken my vows, I thought I was blessed to feel such loneliness within me because it meant I would connect sooner. Now, I wasn't so sure.

I did connect with people at work, though. I'd made professional friends and would often go out for lunch with my colleagues. Also, being in HR, I liked to communicate with managers to take the pulse of their organization and their people.

The days were busy and productive. I was engaged in training and counseling shop floor workers and mentoring and coaching the office staff. I loved what I was doing. I was getting a lot of recognition and appreciation, which felt extremely satisfying.

Then one morning, Nina called. "Mom, guess what?" she said, sounding thrilled.

I had no idea. After my third incorrect guess, Nina told me Raj had put a ring on her finger. I jumped up and screamed at the top of my lungs. My little princess was engaged to her sweetheart of ten years!

Nina and Raj were officially engaged in 2012 in Boston. After having finished his MS from MIT, he'd expressed his desire to take advantage of the booming economy and rising GDP of India and start his new venture there. He had a plan in place. Soon, both families had decided on a date for their wedding in New Delhi. I wanted to go all out for my princess's wedding and make the occasion exactly as she wished it to be.

"I really want to make Nina happy," I told the boys. "This is a one-time memorable event in a girl's life."

She only had a poor representation of a father, but she shouldn't feel that absence on her wedding day. I was her mother and her father, so I would find a way to make it happen just the way my parents had done for me.

The boys made a substantial financial contribution to reduce my burden by digging into savings. I was reminded of what my dad had said to me, close to thirty years back when the twins were six months old.

"They are your gold mines."

It was so true. *They are my treasure.* I wished he could be here to see them. My mom, who was now disabled due to her age, couldn't attend the ceremony. I would miss them both dearly, we all would.

The two families decided on joint events, which is not the norm for Indian weddings, where everything is done as two separate families with two separate plans in two separate houses. Typically, one family is unaware of what the other is doing, and there are no discussions between the two parties.

However, since both families were modern, we discussed every step in detail. The wedding was going to be five days long. Having both families work together created a vastly unique experience from what I'd had. The joint wedding formed greater familiarity, congeniality, and respect for each family's values and wedding traditions, a kind of coming together of two religions: Hindu (Nina) and Sikh (Raj).

I debated about inviting Vijay. Although I felt he should see his own daughter get married, I didn't want him to get drunk and create drama. I talked with the boys, who said it was my decision to make.

I then broached the subject with Nina. "What if your father learns that you're getting married?"

She knew exactly where I was going. "No way," she said. "Don't even talk about it." She hadn't forgiven him for anything. She still carried the pain.

I arrived in India a week before the wedding. The boys came a day later with their American friends, also known to Nina. My close friend, Abhinav and his family, and Neel's family, who were also coming from the States, arrived two days earlier. Ravi, Leena, Jeej, and their family, all local, were present in full support with me. All of the cousins were close with each other and getting together after many years.

The wedding opened with bringing the Sikh holy book to Raj's house. The next morning, Neel did the Choora ceremony where the bride's maternal uncle presents the bride with red bangles to wear before the wedding day. Each day was filled with energy and vigor. We served copious amounts of top-shelf alcohol and delicious food and played lively fun music and loud Bollywood dance hits. The women dressed up in colorful, shimmering clothes with matching jewelry. Gold and diamonds glittered all around. The crowd from America enjoyed the wedding most of all, perhaps because they'd never seen such a colorful, elegant affair, lasting for five days of fun and frolic—a time to pamper the couple and ourselves. It was time for everyone to show off, which we did in abundance!

I just wanted to enjoy what I'd worked toward for so long, the first of my three children settling down. So, despite all the responsibility on my shoulders, I danced and was happy to my heart's content. During it all, the boys stood next to me, one on each side, like strong pillars, so I didn't once feel the lack of a man or partner by my side, nor was I treated like a divorced woman, available for the taking.

Finally, the time came for the *doli*, the ceremony where the bride is given away to the groom's family, who then take her to their home. This is always a sad moment for the bride's family. Kabir and Kuber joined me in the ritual of giving away Nina, with a heavy heart. Raj's family was much happier since they're taking the bride and groom back to their house to start a new life. As Nina was getting ready to leave, I felt hollow and empty for a few moments, starting to tear up until Nina stopped me.

"Mom," she said, "I'm happy to live the rest of my life with Raj, so be happy and don't cry."

She was right. Kabir and Kuber held their darling sister, then walked with her, one on each side, to the waiting limo. I was reminded again of my doli ceremony thirty-two years earlier. However, I quickly dismissed the thought when both Kabir and Kuber came up to me and we three held each other in a hug of comfort, missing our princess, Nina. We stood together while everyone gave their blessings, then waved as the car rolled slowly away.

The event came off flawlessly—no hiccups, no disruptions. The entire five days exceeded all my expectations. Departing guests complimented and patted my shoulder for a job well done.

To this day, my friends, both in India and the United States, remember the event as a benchmark wedding.

After Nina left, the boys went off with their American friends to the Delhi airport for an excursion to Goa, an old Portuguese colony on the west coast of India—silver sands, dark-blue waters, the sky mirroring the sea below, green paddy fields, coconut trees lining the coastal streets, and white churches. The boys had kept Goa in their itinerary, as well as the Taj Mahal and Jaipur, full of palaces from the time of kings of Mewat, to show to their visiting friends.

I finally relaxed on the sofa in the empty hall. I put my feet up and closed my eyes, reflecting on the past few days. I felt as if I floated, a great weight lifted from my shoulders. A daughter's wedding was a massive responsibility, and every ceremony each day had been performed seamlessly. Relieved, my taut nerves now loose, I unpinned my hair, raked my fingers through the strands, and sighed deeply.

For the past few days, I'd felt God's presence with me, His hands on my head blessing me, giving me the strength to successfully orchestrate this amazing event and provide beautiful memories, especially for Nina. Without His blessing, the ceremonies wouldn't have flowed so smoothly or been so perfectly executed, with no errors, no regrets, and, most importantly, no one feeling slighted, upset, or hurt. Tears of gratitude dampened my cheeks, ruining my mascara. I didn't care. I wasn't going to stop these tears of happiness and love for my Lord. Besides, everyone had gone. No one would see my smudged eyes.

I flew home to the States two days later, my heart heavy for having left Nina so far behind.

But Raj's words comforted me when he hugged me at the airport. "Don't worry, Mom, I'll take care of her."

The first thing I did when I arrived home was call Vijay to tell him his daughter was married. The boys had given me his number.

"What?" he shouted.

He started to get upset, so I told a lie, which would not harm anyone. "I was visiting India and Nina was also there, and Raj had just moved to India, so we said, 'Let's get her married.' And we held a small function."

He started to protest, raising his voice about not being invited.

I interrupted. "My job was to tell you because you're her father and I thought you should know. And now I'm hanging up the phone." And I did.

❋　　❋　　❋

I went back to my normal routine of going to work and coming home to an empty house, which felt even lonelier after the trip to India. To the extent that I almost considered dating again. Almost! In truth after my initial attempts, I'd never considered it. But the boys weren't going to allow me to stay alone for long. They had a strategy in mind. They were planning a cross-country trip from New York before starting business school—three thousand miles in five days, which would take them through Yellowstone and Zion National Park and end up at my condo, where they would stay with me for a month. I was thrilled!

Once they arrived, the condo was filled with humor, laughter, teasing, loud music, and cooking. I felt full of life.

The third day after they arrived, Kuber pulled me out to the patio and said, "Come sit down, Ma." When I did, he sat across from me. "You need a dog," he said.

"What? No, I'm not ready for a dog."

"It will be therapeutic for you, Mom."

I'd change the subject and he'd bring it up again. "Mom, you should get a dog. It will be your companion. It will bring joy to you."

"A dog is too much work," I said.

"Weren't we too much work?" Kuber argued. "But didn't we also bring you joy?"

Maybe Kuber had a point. Kabir came outside and sided with Kuber. The duo used their wit and craftiness to influence me.

"How about a rescue dog?" Kabir said.

"You're so humane," Kuber said. "You'll save a life."

A day later, as I came out of the morning shower, the boys, already showered and dressed up, came up to me.

Kuber said, "Mom, get in the car."

As we drove away, they told me their plan. I was surprised but not really. We were going to the nearby Petco in Irvine. At Petco, ten cages stood in a line, each holding a small breed dog. They all looked at us. I saw one on the upper deck to the left—Flower, according to the name on the cage. She looked at me timidly, her big round eyes hopeful. I felt an instant connection. I got a deep emotional feeling as though she were mine. We just clicked—we had chemistry. We all fell in love with her. She was a Maltese, Poodle, and terrier mix, docile and quiet.

"Mom," she pleaded with her eyes, "I need to go home with you." We completed all the required paperwork and brought Flower home. We renamed her Fifi, after my dad's dog in Iran.

I soon discovered she was so quiet because she was sick. She had to undergo surgery to remove her anal glands, but she recovered with no problems and became the love of my life. The house was no longer empty. I looked forward to coming home to cajole her and pet her. She understood my comforting and slowly started to ask for it. She loved having her belly rubbed.

And the boys were right: she required work, but she gave me back so much more than the effort I put in. We became inseparable. We went to the stores together, walked together, watched television together and even slept together. I no longer felt the sting of isolation. I'd found a companion—a companion who was faithful, who gave me unconditioned love, and who would never fail me.

Chapter 16

Roller Coaster

2017–2018

I was jolted out of my sleep when the phone rang early in the morning. It had to be a call from India at this hour.

Something was not right, my gut said. My hands turned cold before I reached for the phone.

"Hi, Mom." It was Raj on the other side, his voice hoarse. My heart pounded.

"Is everything all right?"

"I am calling from the hospital but nothing to panic about. Nina was quite unwell. She was under acute anxiety and had severe bouts of headaches, undiagnosed by a team of neurologists and physicians. Even alternative medicine didn't help."

I knew, from his morose tone, he was hiding something more acute. "Do you want me to fly to India to see her or, better, she could fly to the States and stay with me for some time, as well as seek medical help in the States?"

"That's a good idea. I think she's missing you. Let me go and tell Nina. She would feel better."

Since Nina did not talk over the phone, I intuitively knew she needed help desperately.

I kept the phone, took deep breaths to settle my pumping heart, gathered my thoughts, picked up my laptop, and pressed Google Chrome. I kind of knew what Nina was going through and what she needed. A mother's instinct! I had to take charge of the situation. She was my daughter in pain. She had already seen a lot and suffered more than she could take. She needed to live her life to its fullest. I would not let anything absurd happen to her.

I researched for a couple of days and, as God would have it, stumbled upon transcranial magnetic stimulation (TMS), a new therapy recently discovered, and FDA-approved as a solution for recovery from Nina's symptoms of depression. I YouTubed TMS and found several podcasts and interviews on this new discovery and its success rate. I made up my mind to convince Raj and Nina about this new treatment. They were ready.

Nina arrived a week later. She did not look good and was withdrawn.

I had found Dr. Stubbeman, who had optimized TMS protocol, and was in Los Angeles. The procedure was not invasive but external, delivering electromagnetic stimulation via pulses to the brain's frontal cortex, which activated brain cells, thereby improving mood. His office was far away, but that would not be a deterrent.

Dr. Stubbeman, a polite gentleman, extremely humble and soft-spoken, was in his late forties. He talked to Nina and said she was a perfect candidate for such a treatment. He was transparent, provided all the details, and answered all our questions patiently.

"Every individual's sensitivity levels are different, and some respond within ten, twenty, or forty sessions," he said. "The max you could go is up to seventy sessions of an hour and a half each. You will find, one morning, she will spring back to her original self all of a sudden, surprising you, as that's how the frontal lobes work with this treatment."

Raya, the charming administrative director in Dr. Stubbeman's front office, and Bijan, the tech who performed the procedure, were the most compassionate and involved human beings I had ever met in a doctor's office.

Since I was going to drive Nina to Los Angeles every second day in LA traffic, I had no option but to change my office hours from early morning at 5:00 a.m. to noon. And then we were off to LA. The sessions were long and painful for Nina. She felt weak after them. She would lie down on the back seat of the car while I drove back late night in bumper to bumper LA traffic. Not every patient reacted this way, but she was lucky to have Bijan on her side to take diligent care of her while she sat on that chair with the head gear. We reached home around 9:30 to 10:00 p.m. after every session.

Those were the most difficult days for Nina and me. I was physically and mentally fatigued due to continuous work and the drive to LA. Also, as a mother, I was hurting inside watching Nina endure pain at a youthful age when she should be out living life. I had seen a most happy, giggling, and chirpy girl turn into a person who had no interest in life, who slipped into a black hole and shut out from the rest of the world.

Dr. Stubbeman was easily accessible for reviewing the status. His discussions gave us hope. However, after forty sessions, there was no progress. Nina was getting tired and frustrated. She was ready to quit, but she understood that was not a solution.

And then, amazingly, the much-awaited day came, exactly on the seventieth day of treatment, the very day for which we were longing.

"Mom, can you stop the car on the shoulder?" Nina said as soon as we were on the highway from LA.

"Are you nauseated?" I asked

"Mom, quick, do it," she demanded like a little child.

I immediately pulled over on the shoulder and stopped the car. She got out of the car and came toward the driver side. "Go take the passenger seat."

"Are you sure, Nina?"

"*Mom*! Come on, do it please."

I trusted her instincts, so I quickly changed seats. Nina took the wheel, adjusted the mirrors, switched on the music system, and checked her playlist on the phone. She played Dan Martin and then Doris Day's, "Que Sera" and Elvis Presley's, "Can't Help Falling in Love" that we had listened to together many times.

"I know you love this song, Mom. This is for you. And here goes the volume, and this is for you, too."

We giggled and laughed, going wild, like maniacs, and sang the lyrics along in the same volume. It was a miracle never seen before. She took the exit and stopped on the way at Starbucks to have her favorite iced coffee and banana bread loaf and a lemon loaf for me. It was a surreal moment for both of us.

The next day, when I came home from work, she said, "Mom, I have checked the tickets to fly back to India. I would like to be with Raj. I have missed him."

She flew back, a week later, happier.

Nina's cheery and delightful voice over the phone from India brought solace and succor each time she called me after her visit.

❇   ❇   ❇

Kabir and Kuber came to visit me for one full week that time. The house was filled with energy and the sweet aroma of Indian spices and garlic from our Indian cooking. It was funny watching them run and quickly zip their suitcases. When I asked them what that was, they said the spices and garlic flavor get into the clothes, and they'd smell of Indian curry. And I laughed as that was true. My Systems colleague at work from Chennai actually smelled of curry when he passed by.

I cooked their favorite dishes each day while Kabir would help cut veggies. He was a great chef himself. Kuber, being an expert in creating cocktails, and would serve a new taste each evening.

One of the evenings when I was sitting on my patio, they both came back after a game of golf and sat next to me with a jug of Sangria.

"So, Mom, what are your future plans?" Kabir asked. "Are you happy at this juncture of your life?"

They had always made it a point to check in with me. I was truthful and forthright this time, instead of hiding from them. "I may be lacking the happy hormone, Pooja's health had taken a toll over me," I said, "but the big picture looks good. My job is going well, Nina is doing good, and you both have completed your MBAs, have jobs you love and ready to be married to the girls of your choice. What else do I need? God has been kind to us."

"But, Mom," Kuber said, "what about you?"

My eyes teared up. I had felt lonely and alone, especially during Nina's treatment. To add to the despair, my Business Unit Head (BUH) from the head office verbally reprimanded me for using flexible hours at work, showing no compassion for my situation despite me having permission from the divisional head. I had taken that provocation to heart as I felt that BUH's annoyance was unnecessary and inhumane, while my company was known to care for its people.

Both boys dragged their chairs close, each holding my hands.

"Mom," Kabir said, "we've lived apart for most of our lives. You've played the part of a father and a mother. Now it's our time to pay you back."

Kuber nodded. "We need to be together, close to each other, so we can take care of you."

I hadn't seen this coming. I never even once thought I would live close to them, especially since Kuber was now going to be married and settled in his life and Kabir would likely soon follow. This was the American way—an "individualistic society." I wanted to prove to my children that I had adapted and had changed myself based on Western culture and an entirely new environment. So, I believed I'd live the rest of my life in my home in Orange County. I also did not want my children to put their energy into looking after me in my old age as I had for my parents. I wanted to set them free.

That was what I wanted.

But was that what *they* wanted?

I became emotional, my throat choking, eyes tearing. The boys had tears in their eyes, too, as we continued to hold hands.

"Mom, it's high time we all live closer," Kabir said." It's essential to take care of each other."

I whole heartedly agreed with them and realized that deep down, I must have wanted this all along. But instead of agreeing to their plan, I said, "Now you're Americans. You may not want me living close to you."

They both reached out and hugged me.

Kuber said, "We want you close to us! It has nothing to do with being American."

We decided we all needed to live in the same state, at least, so flying time was no more than an hour. For the twins, we had to be near the financial hub of either New York, San Francisco, or Chicago. They'd lived fifteen long years in New York, so they were done with that. And since my company's headquarters were in Chicago, I might be able to ask for a transfer.

We would all live in the state of Illinois, as near as possible to Chicago. We raised our glasses to cheer for the plan we had firmed up. Who could sleep that night? We were awake until after midnight making our future plans.

By mid-June 2018, while visiting the corporate office for a conference, I expressed my desire to transfer to Chicago to the corporate office. Sure enough, beginning of July, a position opened up. I flew for the round of interviews, got the job offer, and before going back to California, firmed up a rental house with a plan to buy my own house soon after checking out the area.

Back home in California, I called the relocation company and put the condo on MLS for sale. The house was sold the very first Saturday of the listing. That night, my California condo in escrow, I thought of my Chicago rental house next to the marketplace, within walking distance of food places, Starbucks, an Indian restaurant, and a grocery store.

I desired all my family to be here in one country, one state, which meant Nina and Raj moving back to the States.

I put the secret into the Universe before closing my eyes that night.

Chapter 17

Coming Together

2018–2020

I had to pinch myself hard as I rested on the sofa after the movers left. *Is this real? Am I actually in Chicago?* I couldn't believe that, after so many years of living alone, I would now have my cubs so close. It felt as though everything in my life was finally coming together and making sense.

Fifi was having the time of her life, running at top speed up and down the stairs, right up to the third floor and back, and up and down again in a blur of paws and fur. I was watching her and laughing when both boys arrived home from work.

They gathered me in a warm hug, each planting a kiss on my cheek, one boy on my left, the other on my right. "Mom, you did it!" they said.

My colleagues and neighbors often asked me with surprise, "What made you leave California and move to this windy city?" My answer remained the same each time. The trade-off between weather and my children was worth it, and I was loving the new wardrobe, fashionable warm jackets, long boots, gloves, and hats.

Changing job locations meant getting used to a completely new environment, people, and politics, as well as adjusting to a new climate, traffic patterns, and navigating new streets. Then there was making new friends and finding a new hair salon, doctor, dentist, and veterinarian. However, the payoff was so huge, I refused to stress about it.

Even though it was the same company and both offices were in the same country, the work environments in the California and Chicago offices were different, which is often the case in the head office versus the off-site facilities. In California, I was part of the senior management team, whereas in Chicago, I was a small drop in the big ocean, in reverse gear as far as my professional career was concerned. The glass ceiling was not evident, but hidden discrimination existed. Still, I wasn't going to take the pressure of it, although it did affect me in some ways. I couldn't change the environment, and I wasn't there to do so. Instead, I would accept and acclimatize. And that's what I did. I lay low and focused on my daily tasks.

I planned on buying a house in a safe area, near a marketplace, midway between the boys and work. While driving home from work one day, I noticed a new housing development by the highway I had not seen before. I took the exit to stop and look. I was fascinated by the ranch-style family homes, built in stone and brick, with broad, well-paved lanes lined with trees and well-kept green grass. They made me nostalgic for my days growing up on the IT campus.

The salesperson took me to look at one of the houses. It felt spacious and well designed, with lots of windows and an open layout. The open kitchen had a granite island and granite countertops. The master bedroom had a huge walk-in closet, a laundry room, a pantry area, and wood flooring—everything I wanted in a house. It was a corner house with a wooden fence, safe for grandkids playing outside of Grandma's house someday. I chuckled.

The sprawling backyard was already planted with big pine trees, just like the front yard. This overlooked a large churchyard, flanked by a beautiful church, filled with huge, mature trees that appeared to be an extension of the yard I wished to make my own. I felt immense peace and serenity there. I fell in love with the house and its surroundings. I had made up my mind.

The next day, I came back to sign the paperwork. Moving to my own house gave me an opportunity to go through my boxes and organize things that I was not able to do when I moved from California.

I moved on November 1, 2018.

When I moved from California, I was enchanted with the fairly new fad of minimalism. Leaving California, I told myself, was the best opportunity. It would allow me to simplify my life and be a minimalist.

However, within a few weeks of moving, I found it difficult to tame my desire to decorate the house with artifacts, ethnic decorations, and lots of color. My idea of minimalism went out the window. But I did not discard it completely. I adopted it halfway by focusing on getting more organized and donating extra stuff I would not be using. I appreciated art, color, vibrancy, and harmony. I would not push myself to be someone I was not.

My first priority was to get the patio covered so that I could enjoy it in the cold and windy city of Chicago. I had always joked that my living room was my patio, as I would spend most of my time there.

My weekend routine was to sit with my morning ginger masala tea on the patio and read my book or listen to TED Talks or a podcast while watching the hummingbirds, house sparrows, and cardinals. The big squirrels would climb the trees, and Fifi would bark, desperate to run out and chase the squirrels, part Yorkee that she is. Some weekends, I would sit in Barnes & Noble and Starbucks, my favorite go-to places wherever I have lived in the States.

Most weekends we'd all spend together. I loved being in downtown Chicago, where both boys lived in their own apartments. I walked and watched people of all colors, ethnicities, and religions in the streets, every third person walking their dog, and everyone minding their own business and being cordial if their eyes met. Downtown had its own culture of live theater, musicals, ballet, live music shows, jazz shows, and artists from all over the world. I would pick a show and watch it. I wanted to see them all. It filled me with vigor and life. It made me feel like I was progressing in life.

The boys would take me to this pub within walking distance for a fun evening with Mom. It had a huge sitting space in the open on the corner of a street, crowded and noisy, filled with youngsters with their dates or friends. Everyone giggled and joked—the pub was full of energy and happy vibes. I would visit this happy place quite frequently, sipping my margarita on the rocks and enjoying the youngsters celebrating life. It was invigorating and riveting. And I always ended the evening with a special veggie burger and spicy fries, the only veggie item on the menu but to my taste.

My other captivating discovery was a small, cozy jazz bar run by Steve, the owner, on the small lake. It was an intimate setting of twenty to twenty-five people sitting around the podium where the orchestra played. I had a great time listening to the trumpet and clarinet, my favorite instruments, played by great artists invited from all over the country.

Art of any kind is close to my heart. It allows me to breathe and feel alive.

Since work was not fulfilling, it bothered me. I put some thought into doing something more gratifying and realized I could do something aligned with my desire to work with people of domestic violence. I went online to ask my friend Mr. Google and came across A Safe Place in Illinois supporting the victims. I enrolled for courses to become a professional advocate for supporting, counseling and coaching them. My degree in social work and my HR counseling experience was an added advantage. I then took a clinician certification to add more value to identifying any mental health issues they suffered from. I joined A Safe Place as a volunteer in the evenings after work. This filled my heart and soul. I understood and related to the victim's psyche and the emotional distress of their children.

Shortly after, Nina called from India. "Guess what? We are moving back to the States." I jumped at the news and screamed with joy.

My secret thought, left in the Universe, was coming together and so was my family. I was filled with delight and humility. I looked forward to hosting large family gatherings every Thanksgiving, Diwali, and Christmas with grandchildren!

"You need to come. I'm missing your hugs!" I would call Kabir and Kuber on weekends. We needed to make up for every missed embrace, and we were all huggers.

A good, warm hug went a long way toward solving all problems and pain, emotional or mental. It gave an assurance we're not alone. It said, "I'm here for you." I missed these hugs from a partner. However, I would have all the hugs I needed now . . . and more. No one could take them away from me. I truly began to enjoy my freedom.

Chapter 18

Rekindling My
Spiritual Journey

2021–Present

I was not lonely anymore. But there was a longing inside me. I began to feel the pangs, the ache, the restless yearning to do something greater, something that would fill my soul. The craving felt incredibly strong. *Is this what's called a "calling"?*

While driving to work, I stumbled upon Oprah's podcast, "Soulful Conversations." Oprah interviewed Gary Zukav, a spiritual leader and author of *The Seat of the Soul*. There was something compelling about the interview. The next day, she interviewed Brené Brown, the bestselling author of several books and expert on vulnerability, which was close to my heart. And the following day, Oprah interviewed Mia Farrow, who was once married to Woody Allen and Frank Sinatra. They discussed how meditation and spirituality had changed Mia as a person. I was hooked.

On the fourth day, I listened to Eckhart Tolle, wrapped in his interpretations of answers to Oprah's questions. He had a deep insight into the human mind and soul. The thoughts he expressed in the interview were in sync with my understanding of spirituality, though his, in general, were more scientific and accessible. I bought his books and read them cover to cover. His teachings had the same basis as those of my guru, which established a connection to me. I felt the same with Michael Singer's interpretations through his courses and books. A lot of clarity came to me.

I also listened to several other podcasts on spirituality by Indian gurus, and by Buddhist followers who had been talking about the path of spirituality, mindfulness, enlightenment, and nirvana, which originated several hundred years ago.

To grow as a spiritual being was now an intrinsic part of my mission. It was the part of my life that provided me with strength, peace, and courage. After feeling the longing to do more, I understood I was here to serve a higher purpose. I still did not know what would make me feel content, fulfilled, and whole.

I was like the Himalayan musk deer who ran after an optical illusion—a mirage. He carried the most expensive fragrance, known as kesar, in his body, but spent his entire life running from one place to another, wandering all his life to the source of the alluring scent, never realizing he was running after what was within himself.

My restlessness brought me to Leslie, my therapist. I'd seen two therapists previously, and though I received some valuable advice from them, I had never developed the necessary trust to go further. But I clicked with Leslie from the start; she was a good fit. We talked about my life, the turbulence, the escape, the survival and finding liberation. Talking to her, I began understanding how my relationship with Vijay had affected me. I thought I'd forgotten and moved past, but it still lurked deep inside me. Every time we talked about it, unburied it, and worked various aspects of it, I'd cry. Clearly, I had more healing to do, more insight to gain. But I didn't want to waste any more time on my past. It was over. I wanted to begin on a new path, a new journey.

I shared how much I'd achieved and how I had no regrets about anything or anyone. I had a good-paying job, was settled and happy with my children close by, and I had my companion, my Fifi. My life was great, but this was all to do with my worldly life. I told her about my innate desire to give back to my community and how I felt as though something more was required of me . . . the purpose in life, my journey, wouldn't be complete if I didn't do something more for humanity.

Leslie listened calmly and intently. Then she said, "Kanchan, I've heard your story, and it's so powerful that it needs to be heard by others. Why don't you collect all the pages you've written in past years and compile them? You need to share your story with those who live in a similar situation but don't know how to escape. Tell them how you came out as a survivor. Become an advocate for them. They need you. Make this your purpose."

I had goose bumps on my arms. My eyes swelled with tears, and I got up and hugged her. She took me into her embrace, and we stood there for a good thirty seconds.

I confessed I'd wanted to do so for many years. My children had been pushing me to write my story, but I hadn't given the idea any serious thought.

"Yes, this is my higher purpose," I said. "This is my calling. I can feel it. I need to write my story for those imprisoned as I was who are eager to be set free."

As I drove home from Leslie's office, I found myself with a new mindset. The thought had brushed past me several times, but I could not find the courage to unpeel and relive my past. The time was ripe now.

The book began to take shape in my mind. But I had never written before, except for essays in school. How could I become a writer overnight? My mind constantly fed my thoughts. But my resolution and conviction kept pushing those thoughts away.

I was determined to write my story and focus on the objective. I didn't want to waste one more day without my purpose in front of me, so I stood in the garage, looking for the box I had named, My Notes. I wasn't certain if it was a coincidence that, only a couple of months back, I had collected and kept all my notes together in a box, not knowing I was going to open the box and use those notes soon. Strangely, I had carried those notes with me all these years.

I carried the box over and moved my writing desk and chair onto my patio, where I could see the greenery outside. I opened the box, which had accommodated all my papers from 1981 onward, including small slips, Post-it notes, napkins, yellow legal papers, and spiral steno pads. I looked at the dates and chronologically assembled them in one pile. My heart was heavy reading those notes. However, nothing was going to stop me!

I conference-called my three children and told them, "I'm beginning to write a memoir, which you all desired."

Kabir said, "Mom, we are so proud of you. We wanted you to do this. This is the legacy you will leave for your grandkids. You need to be out there, talking to men and women," Kuber added. Nina was thrilled, "Mom, you can do it. You need to do it, not only for all of us but yourself and the victims who need help."

After all the initial spadework, I sat down in my chair, put my laptop on the desk, glanced at the church opposite me, thought about my guru, and started to create a framework of all the milestones, episodes, and events in my life. Then I divided the milestones into chapters and named the chapters. It was not tough. It came easy as it was right there in my head; I just had to retrieve the files. The difficult work started after this, when I had to visualize the horrid episodes and write all the details. I typed for hours, with all sincerity and concentration, almost every weekend and every evening until late at night during the work week.

The sadness came back. I would recall an episode or an emotion during the episode and get up in the middle of the night to note it. I developed insomnia and anxiety, perhaps PTSD, but my objective kept me as focused as blinders on a racehorse who wants to reach the finish line.

My Friday evening rituals remain my way of de-stressing and unwinding. Whatever the weather, inside me or outside, my evenings are spent on my covered patio or in my sunroom. It's a space of profound peace and good vibes, coming from the church opposite the house, where I sit for hours in the evening, enjoying the warm weather. The occasional cool breeze makes a whistling sound outside the patio window. I hear the sound of rustling leaves from the big, mature oak, maple, and hickory trees. The red-and-white flowers blossoming from the sassafras are mesmerizing, so I sit, enthralled by the beauty of nature, breathing in the here and now.

The winters bring even more pleasure, with trees engulfed in white snow, icicles hanging from them, and the church steeple pure and pious in a white blanket, as is my lawn.

If it's not snowing, I can see the bone structure of the big, dormant deciduous trees hibernating, holding the unclothed, bare branches with grace, not dwindling but standing there firm and strong, sleeping without their clothes under the dark, cold night. Inside them, they hold the optimism, the blossoms, the green leaves to be worn by the naked branches. The tree is awake as the morning sun rises and takes away the cold, snowy winter with it. I become a part of this stillness, surrendering to the divine nature created by the Almighty.

As night approaches, I light candles that fill the air with their subtle scent. In the background, I hear trickling water from the statue of Buddha and raindrops falling into the pond. It's soulful.

The modus operandi for this ritual has remained the same for years. This is my date with myself, a date filled with love, with the idea of self-preservation and self-compassion, with my body that has been with me through thick and thin, that has not weakened and given way.

The evening starts with a glass of wine accompanied by slow songs, mostly Bollywood songs from old movies, songs that are emotional, meaningful, and romantic. Or I mix it up with my favorite Andrea Bocelli or Dean Martin, maybe Frank Sinatra. It's followed by country music, Tim McGraw and Faith Hill being my favorites.

After midnight, it's time for sad songs of parting. It's Celine Dion, my favorite, plus Sufi songs and Urdu ghazals, which devour me with their lyrics. Their verses express their love for their beloved. The Urdu poets who write them have a dual meaning for the word "beloved"—a lover as a human face or God. They write lyrics on yearning for love, the pain of betrayal, the agony of separation, or the longingness to become one with the beloved. The top ghazal and Sufi classical maestros singing these lyrics take me to another world. Eyes closed, I'm enthralled, deep in stillness, focused, my soul completely wrapped in the music, getting closer to my Self.

I truly get into that state of pure joy and bliss, lost in the emotions of love around me. I sit late at night into early morning. My eyes close and remain closed for hours. I can't open them, even if I try. I walk on the stars and over the moon. I enter into a state of euphoria and do not want to come out of the pleasantness. I am in alignment with the Universe. I feel free and connected, free of any boundaries and shackles, enraptured in ecstasy. Tears of joy stream down my cheeks. I feel the romance in the air and love all around me. I am in meditation; my body numb and my mind still. It is empty, with no thoughts. I am not aware of myself or my surroundings, as if I am not present in this world. I am breathing but not alive. The exhilarating feeling is so soothing that I remain in bliss and harmony for hours. This is my identity, my being. This is who I am, in touch with my soul for these brief moments, in a pure state of surrender.

I don't want to come out of this ecstasy, this euphoria. This is my way of meditating, being in that moment. My soul is surrounded by love and grace showered on me by the Universe, the higher power. I feel free in body and soul. I still sing Dana Winner's empowering words as I continue racing destiny.

I feel happy to have deviated a little from the path of my guru so I can follow it on my terms, where there's no place for guilt or regret. I am still an ardent follower, and He remains my spiritual teacher and guide and always will be.

Although it's difficult to leave this blissful state, I'm always happiest when I wake up on Saturday morning. With a broad grin and a twinkle in my eyes, I feel energetic, jubilant, and determined to live this short life to the fullest.

Epilogue:

The Beginning of an End

This past Sunday, my three children, their better halves, and their pets got together at my house. The whole house reverberated with love and laughter. Even the dogs—all four of them—had fun chasing each other, creating a ruckus on the lawn. What a sight! My eyes welled, watching my children thrive!

Just before dinner, as we finished setting out the food on the table, Kabir and Kuber came up to me, each draping an arm over my shoulders.

"Mom, isn't this what you've longed for?" Kabir asked. Before I could answer, Kuber said, "You sure had a vision when you brought an eight-chair dining table into this new house, but today I realized, with all eight seats filled, where will the grand kids sit who are on their way soon?"

"Don't underestimate your ma," I said, smiling. "Perhaps you didn't notice that the dining table has two extra panels, which, when extended, allow for twelve. How could I forget about my grandkids, my interest on my principal investment, which will carry more value than my principal?" I laughed loudly and heartily, and everyone joined in.

We all cheered and clinked our glasses.

Nina stood up for a toast. "For all of us standing together as one solid family, a strong fist. *Ek muthi.*"

"Amen," we all said in unison.

All those years ago, I'd never imagined my future might hold a scene like this. Or that my children—my cubs—and I would be together with their partners, happy and safe under one roof. I clicked a virtual picture of all of us to memorize the moment and save it in my heart forever.

At this point, I'm recovered and healed. I'm at the beginning of a new life, which is driven by a higher purpose. My body and mind feel free, and now it's time to let go of my ego and free the soul, to surrender. People call it by different names: enlightenment, God-realization, or self-actualization. I like to call it nirvana. My spiritual journey has just begun, and I have miles to go. Thus, my story will continue, as will my journey.

On this journey, I see myself reaching out to the victims and survivors of domestic abuse. There are those who are held captive by their perpetrators and yearn to be free. There are also those who have set themselves physically free but still carry the emotional burden—their minds still in captivity—and need to let go. And then there are those who have escaped to their freedom and are not carrying the past but don't know what to do with their freedom. The trauma has a way of sticking to you, even when you think you've moved on.

I wish there was one formula for all of us, but there isn't. The formula that worked for me and liberated me was essentially powered by my three strong beliefs, my tools, and my mantras.

Belief in self. Belief in Universe. Belief in spirituality.

You may pick your own tools and form an equation of your own, depending on which state of life or which situation you are in. For me, it has evolved over the years.

Belief in self + belief in the Universe + belief in spirituality = freedom of body, mind, and soul.

These three beliefs are the fundamental tools, which I keep in my tool kit. I take out one or two at a time, depending on what works best in that time and space. These precision tools have given me focus, strength, and resilience. They're the reason I achieved my freedom and found my higher purpose. You can too!

To grow as a spiritual being is the part of my life that equips me with acceptance, compassion, and gratitude. It makes me complete. Writing this book is the beginning of a purpose-driven journey, and I'm far from my destination. My journey will end when I reach the finish line and cross over to the other side. Until then, I will keep marching ahead.

This is my new beginning to the end.

Acknowledgments

Although my children told me time and time again to bring my story in front of the world, it was Leslie Scofield, my therapist, who actually put the key in the ignition. Her encouraging words and belief got me to pick up the pen and start writing. Thank you, Leslie.

I am immensely grateful to all who helped me bring this book in front of my readers. My special thanks to Matthew Schnarr for handholding me throughout the process. Thank you, Matt, for your integrity and always being available.

Anna Rowser, my first editor, a talented, and kind person.

Kelly Malone and Susan Mary Malone for lending their keen and critical eyes editing the drafts.

Jennifer Thompson, my first website designer, a successful entrepreneur with a generous heart full of compassion, always ready to help. I will remain grateful to you for your valuable collaboration.

Rebecca Lowe, the cover designer. I salute you for your creative vision and responsiveness. I find it unique and a head-turner.

Brooke Warner of She Writes Press, my publisher, a connoisseur in the publishing world.

Fauzia Burke of FSB, my publicist, a woman of substance, dedicated to her profession, who treats each client special.

I am enormously indebted to all the angels and messengers, who appeared at various milestones and touched my life, mentioned throughout the pages.

Atul Srivastava for forwarding my resume, which landed me my first job, my first step toward freedom. Unfortunately, he succumbed to cancer.

John Gordon, a highly acclaimed chairman and CEO of a large global organization and a charismatic leader, who opened the door to me and my children to enable us to move to the States. You transformed our lives forever. I will always remain indebted to you.

My mentor and friend, Sumit Bose, managing director and my boss whose counsel and fervor built the foundation of my career and molded me from a shattered housewife into a successful professional. Sadly, he passed away from cancer in the early '90s.

My colleague and friend Abhinav Goswami, who has been in leadership positions in large global companies, whose continued support and presence have kept me afloat.

My friend Amrit, a towering personality, whose engagement and consolation became my support system. Her cheerful nature and sense of humor eased me into a smile and hope came with it. My heartfelt gratitude, Amrit.

My three children, Nina, Kabir, and Kuber, my heroes, who have been my rocks, who understand me. They are the pivots of this story. This story would not exist without you. You all make me so proud.

My parents, Om and Shashi, whose unconditional love and unwavering trust in me provided a solid foundation that I could, in turn, pass onto my children. Dad and Mom, you have been my lighthouse in this turbulent ocean.

I will not forget thanking my ex-husband, who brought me to the realization that if the offender is not willing to seek help to change, then one shouldn't empathize with them repeatedly and become their crutch, aiding them in their wrongdoing. Life is too short to be wasted on living in grief.

I am thankful to my idols, mentors, and friends, who may or may not even be aware of their existence in my life, enriching my journey in numerous ways.

My appreciation and humble acknowledgment to all the authors and speakers whom I have never met but whose awesome writings and talks have touched me, inspired me, changed my mental modules and beliefs, enriched my life, and shaped me into the person I am today. You are countless. I could only mention a handful in my book.

Last but not the least, my guru, who has shown me—and continues to show me—the path and keeps bringing me back again and yet again when I stray.

About the Author

Kanchan Bhaskar is a first-time writer, born and brought up in New Delhi, India. She is blessed with three loving children—a daughter and twin boys—who are well settled in their lives. Her compassion for and interest in people, coupled with her desire to work at the grassroots level and with mainframe people, prompted her to choose a related field of study. She earned a master's degree in social work from the prestigious Delhi University, after which she completed a postgraduate certificate in personnel management and industrial relations. While pursuing her studies, she worked closely with people in rural areas, slums, red-light districts, and resettlement colonies for their social and economic development. She also briefly worked in a psychiatric social work setting.

In 1987, Kanchan started her professional career in human resources at one of the global Fortune 500 companies. In 2000, she moved with her family to Syracuse, New York. She lived in Connecticut, New Jersey, New York, and Southern California before moving to Chicago, Illinois, where she continues to work in the corporate world.

During her thirty years of continuing career, earning business coach certification, and making a sincere attempt to earn an MBA degree from Syracuse University, which she was unable to finish due to her circumstances, she has trained hundreds of managers and blue-collar workers in competency development, leadership skills, team building, emotional intelligence, and related topics. For more than twenty years, she has mentored, counseled, and coached all levels of employees in the manufacturing and corporate environments.

Kanchan is now a certified advocate for domestic violence victims in the state of Illinois and is a volunteer speaker, mentor, and coach for victims and survivors.

Although she is a survivor of domestic violence, Kanchan prefers to call herself a fighter. She has no regrets in life and believes everything that happened was according to the blueprint He holds in His hands.

She strongly believes people have been given human form in order to serve a higher purpose and that it is their duty to discover that purpose and fulfill it in this life.

She lives in Chicago, overlooking a church with large green trees, which she believes bring good vibes to her house and her life.

Her Maltipoo, Fifi, is her companion and the love of her life.

Learn more at www.kanchanbhaskar.com.

Author photo © Bauwerks Photography

Selected Titles From She Writes Press

She Writes Press is an independent publishing company founded to serve women writers everywhere. Visit us at www.shewritespress.com.

Have You Seen These Children? A Memoir by Veronica Slaughter. $16.95, 978-1-63152-725-8. After being abducted from the Philippines and brought to the US by their alcoholic American father in 1959, four young children fight to survive for four long years. Hauled from state to state, hungry and afraid, they endure what they have to in hopes of getting back to their mother.

She Rode a Harley: A Memoir of Love and Motorcycles by Mary Jane Black. $16.95, 978-1-63152-620-6. After escaping an abusive marriage, Mary Jane finds love with Dwayne, who teaches her to ride a Harley; traveling together, they learn to be partners, both on and off the road, until Dwayne gets cancer. Without him, Mary Jane once again must learn to live on her own but she'll never be the same again.

Letting Go into Perfect Love: Discovering the Extraordinary After Abuse by Gwendolyn M. Plano. $16.95, 978-1-938314-74-2. After staying in an abusive marriage for twenty-five years, Gwen Plano finally broke free—and started down the long road toward healing.

Once You Go In: A Memoir of Radical Faith by Carly Gelsinger. $16.95, 978-1-63152-429-5. Carly Gelsinger is an awkward and lonely thirteen-year-old when she stumbles into Pine Canyon Assemblies of God, the cracked stucco church on the outskirts of her remote small town. Soon, she is *on fire for God*—speaking in tongues, slaying demons, and following her abusive pastor's every word—and it's not until her life is burnt to the ground that she finds the courage to leave.

Pieces of Me: Rescuing My Kidnapped Daughters by Lizbeth Meredith. $16.95, 978-1-63152-834-7. When her daughters are kidnapped and taken to Greece by their non-custodial father, single mom Lizbeth Meredith vows to bring them home—and give them a better childhood than her own.

Parent Deleted: A Mother's Fight for Her Right to Parent by Michelle Darné. $16.95, 978-1-63152-282-6. A gripping tale of one non-biological, lesbian mother's fight for shared custody of her children an intimate, infuriating, and infectious story of perseverance, sacrifice, and hope in the face of debilitating adversity.